THE PRO STYLE

THE PRO STYLE

BY TOM BENNETT

Designed by David Johnston

A National Football League Book
Distributed by Prentice-Hall, Inc. Englewood Cliffs, N.J.
1976

A National Football League Book

Prepared by National Football League Properties, Inc.,
Creative Services Division, Los Angeles, Calif.

Publisher: David Boss
Editor: John Wiebusch
Vice President-Marketing: Bob Bell
Vice President-Operations: Jack Wrobbel
Managing Editor: Tom Bennett
Associate Editors: Tom Patty, Rick Smith
Editorial Staff: Patricia Cross, Earlene Doran
Production Manager: Patrick McKee
Designer: David Johnston
Production Staff: Rob Meneilly, Jere Wright,
    Felice Mataré, Kathleen Oldenburg;
    diagram drawings by Jill Prestup
Administrative Assistant: Muriel Lorenz

Library of Congress Catalog Card Number: 76-4058

First Printing 1976
Printed in the United States of America

Contents

Preface

Historian John A. Garraty of Columbia University wrote that, "History is made up of facts, but also of opinions . . . Opinions are easily formed, but are as evanescent as ice in August . . . Those that retain their plausibility longest are those developed in minds steeped in knowledge of the past."

In attempting to construct a historical scenario for a peripheral subject, football, Professor Garraty's rule still applied. Perhaps even more so. In this very inexact science, there are now 28 professional teams and thus 28 "brain trusts," and the composition of each of them changes often. As each new coaching staff begins its work, it alters in some way the practices and jargon of the last. Starting with its own material, it picks up more along the way. No team keeps a secret long because of television and because of game films criss-crossing the country. When a team sees a new formation or play or defense it likes, it writes it into its own playbook. Inevitably, it is used a little differently than it was by its "inventor," and a new name is hung on it; one team's "slot" formation becomes another's "wing over" and another's "flip."

New strategies and language proliferate due to imitation, but there is a general unwillingness to admit imitation. Fashionable terms become unfashionable and new ones created or old ones revived with new meaning. As outsiders discover a combination, coaches move to change the locks.

A coach successful with a new formation is naturally asked by the press to explain it. However, he is not anxious to do so because he doesn't want to give away secrets. He also may be aware of the subtle ways in which earlier strategies of past coaches have crept into the formation for which he is presently being hailed as a genius. So he is further disinclined to talk about it for fear he will appear to be taking credit for what other men actually invented.

As the figures of the past enlarge year by year, there is a tendency for the events and strategies of their times to be built around them as new histories are written. Another problem in sorting out fact from fancy about strategy is that playbooks from the thirties and forties are rarities. Coaches duplicated only enough for themselves and their assistants—if they had any; it was not until the time of Paul Brown in the late forties that players also were required to keep and use playbooks. And photos from the early years are almost exclusively ground-level shots. Studying them is frustrating because there was no rhyme or reason to the scheme of jersey numbering; a player wearing number 43 could have been a halfback, an end, or a tackle.

In order to explore in detail the strategy played today in the National Football League and make it simple and easy to understand, it was necessary to wade through as much of the past 100 years of the game as possible, to find the starting points—the bedrock beginnings of each strategy. Underlying the research was a conviction that each time a formation or play or tactic was presented a phalanx of old grads would stand and sing in unison, "We had that in thirty-four!" It was interesting to learn that those old grads are probably right.

Three persons were especially helpful in this venture. The first was special assistant coach Jack Faulkner of the Los Angeles Rams. He drew on nearly three decades of experience in college and professional football and, in addition, contacted other coaches and former coaches and players to create a history of the game in diagrams. It is possible through this to see real links between the distant past and present. Faulkner also provided invaluable help with the manuscript.

The second person was Bob Oates, Jr., who may have the best understanding of the inner workings of pro football among all "civilians." Oates worked out the order of the chapter, Confrontation, and studied the photographs to identify them and ensure that they depict the strategy they purport to.

The third person especially helpful was librarian Jim Campbell of the Pro Football Hall of Fame in Canton, Ohio. He performed endless feats of research. The Hall is unchallenged as the most complete center anywhere for studying football. Nothing like it exists for college football although plans for a college hall of fame have been discussed since December, 1947.

Strategy is an area that writers often have found fraught with danger, but men such as Dave Brady of the *Washington Post,* Bob Oates of the *Los Angeles Times,* and Murray Olderman of *NEA* have fearlessly delved into the subject.

I am also grateful to collector Goodwin Goldfaden; to Jim Cheffers and Jim Lineberger of the Southern California Football Officials Association; David Nelson of the National Collegiate Athletic Association; the libraries of the University of Chicago, Notre Dame, and Yale; and to gracious and knowledgable pro football persons Tom Bass, David Boss, Joe Browne, Sid Gillman, George Halas, Ed Healey, Frank (Bucko) Kilroy, Chuck Knox, Tom Landry, Art McNally, Seymour Siwoff, and Jim Trimble.

A little-known Philadelphia man named John (Ox) DaGrosa, who had much influence in the world of football as a coach and administrator, once wrote that the five-man line, "had its inception in 1926, was used in colleges as an organized defense in 1930, appeared in high schools in 1932, in the National Football League in 1934, and was adopted by all sections of the United States in 1937."

I thought about that when considering the zone defense played by the San Diego Chargers in 1961. The Chargers set the all-time professional record of 49 interceptions that season with the same zone strategy that finally began to reach public understanding through books and magazine articles about 1972. I thought, perhaps all strategies take about 10 years from conception to their comprehension by the football fans who subsidize the whole thing by their purchase of tickets. I hope that the 10-year timetable can be beaten through the explanations of new strategies in this book.

Tom Bennett

THE PURSUIT

OF PERFECTION

The evolvement of the style of professional football, its
environment, and the influences at work on
it during the history of the National Football League.

In the tropical waters of the South Pacific, great coral reefs have risen from the sea bottom. Some of them are hundreds of feet high. They are the accumulated skeletons of tiny life forms that have died, forming layer after layer and fusing together by chemical processes that have taken millions of years.

The present generation of coral, vibrant and colorful, adorns the surface of the reef. It is one of nature's most beautiful sights. But eventually it too will die and form another layer in the endless cycle by which the reef grows. Evolution has been at work, of course, but the fundamental chemistry of the coral at the lower depths is the same as that nearer the surface. The reef, a scientist has said, "is a delicately balanced dynamic system, a self-fueled machine."

This also describes how football and the style in which it is played has grown in the National Football League. If you step into any era of the game, you will find skeletons. For example, spread formations, used today against zone defenses, were played in the 1870s.

Harvard ran trap plays in 1915.

The Decatur Staleys had formations like the shotgun in 1920.

Lehigh made crackback blocks in 1921.

The idea of "run to daylight" appeared in a 1930 *Athletic Journal* article. It noted that on a given play run by Colgate, "the man with the ball dodges either to the outside or inside as he sees fit."

A 1937 pamphlet written by a Philadelphian named John DaGrosa explained at least 10 fundamentals of defense as played in the NFL today, including man-to-man, combination, and zone pass defense; rota-tion of deep backs; under and over shifting of linemen; dropping linebackers back to help in pass coverage; the concept of "containment" of the ball carrier when he cuts back instead of going outside; cooperative line play; slants; and stunts.

Oklahoma played the three-four defense against Army in 1946.

Legal and physical limits restrict what can happen. They are the 53-yard width of the field and, latitudinally, as far as the fastest man can run before the passer is tackled and, in the other direction, as far as the passer can drop back and still reach the receiver with a pass. Those are the confines. Within them just about everything that can be done with 22 players on a football field has been done. So what the pro game has come down to is a cerebral guessing game best described by the term, "mind-messing."

Andy Russell, the Pittsburgh Steelers' linebacker, talks about the problems. "What I find difficult about Dallas," he said as the Steelers were getting ready for Super Bowl X, "is that they change formations as many as three or four times before snapping the ball. They may start out strong right and you have called a certain coverage. Now it's no good so you audible. Then they motion back to double left and you audible again. You've called three defenses and they haven't snapped the ball.

"You could end up with some guys playing one defense and some guys another. If you don't clearly define their strengths you could have both guys rotating to the outside and nothing up the middle."

Pittsburgh won the game 21–17 and it was supposed to have been the victory of a fundamental team over one that will try

An 1878 Harper's Weekly *engraving of "scrummage" in the new game, football.*

anything. But the Steelers' first touchdown, a seven-yard pass from Terry Bradshaw to Randy Grossman, was scored on a play in which *a tackle set up as an eligible pass receiver and then went in motion.*

What's behind all this, anyway?

THE CAVALRY AND OTHER INFLUENCES

There were seven important influences on the beginnings of the National Football League and the professional style of football that had little or nothing to do with the flying wedge, the buck lateral series, or the center-quarterback exchange. Further, they have never been properly recognized

before. They were:

(1) the Tenth United States Cavalry of 1867;

(2) the University of Illinois;

(3) the United States Navy;

(4) Robert and Louis Hupps of Detroit;

(5) the interests of a New York City man who had never seen a football game;

(6) a Spanish novelist named Vincent Blasco Ibáñez; and

(7) Katherine and Theodore Nesser of Columbus, Ohio.

Lieutenant Richard Henry Pratt, a former captain in the Union Army, reinlisted with the Tenth United States Cavalry in 1867. The seeds of social consciousness

The Fathers of Football

College football was their realm and they may seem out of place here. But these four men, more than any other, shaped this sport.

In a football game the ball does not pass back and forth at random but instead is held by one team for four downs. The team must make a given number of yards in those four downs or lose the ball. There are 11 men on a side. The center snaps the ball to the quarterback.

All these rules or innovations were the product of Walter Camp.

In the brutal era of the wedge formation, in the abundant years of the twenties, and in all the years between, Camp was the most eminent person in college football.

Princeton or Lehigh first used the wedge in the 1880s. Camp, coach of Yale, drew up the "shoving wedge." The players formed a V around the runner and pushed him ahead, the runner actually leaning back on the men behind him so he could climb over the opposing line, and to keep from being shoved over on his face.

Harvard invented the "flying wedge," with two groups of players charging from either side of the field to converge around the ball

carrier, all 11 of them then slamming into the opposition. And there were formations called "tackles back," "guards back," and "ends back," all of them lethal.

Football became overland assault. It became necessary, someone has written, to save football from those who loved it. Theodore Roosevelt, president of the United States, ordered the famous conference in New York City of college football luminaries such as Camp, Amos Alonzo Stagg, and others, and as a result rules changes in 1906, 1907, and 1909 made the game safer and led to the formation of the National Collegiate Athletic Association.

Camp was on the college football rules committee for 48 years. And he and he alone, in his annual article in *Collier's*, decided which players were "All-America."

Amos Alonzo Stagg was born in New Jersey during the Civil War. He died during the presidency of Lyndon B. Johnson. That was in 1965, when he was 102 years old.

After playing end at Yale, Stagg coached at Springfield, Massachusetts, College. He then moved to the University of Chicago, where he

coached for an incredible 41 years. Knute Rockne once said either that "All football comes from Stagg," or he said, "All football comes from Yale." It is not clear which because the quotation varies depending on what book you are reading. In any case, here is an alphabetical list of football inventions that have been credited to Stagg, drawn from the works of responsible historians: crossbucks, the direct pass from center, end-arounds, fake hand-offs, flankers, the hidden-ball play, huddles, laterals, man-in-motion, numbers on jerseys, onside kick-offs, pivots, placekicks, quick kicks, quarterback keepers, shifts, spiral passes, a standing not a squatting quarterback, unbalanced lines, and wind sprints.

Professional football never had a more virulent critic in its early years than Stagg. The NFL record manual recorded that the first time pro football ever got an eight-column newspaper headline was this one in Chicago in 1922: "Stagg Says Conference Will Break Professional Football Menace." This wasn't the most upbeat historical item the NFL could take note of, but a milestone *was* a milestone.

A former player for Stagg named Red Jackson joined the professional team in Hammond, Indiana. Jackson is supposed to have dyed his red hair and eyebrows black when Hammond went to Chicago to play the Cardinals, so he wouldn't be recognized there and word get back to Stagg that Jackson was playing pro football.

Glenn (Pop) Warner, the man who is second to Stagg in all-time college coaching victories, 313 to 314, probably was the second most innovative coach after Stagg. "Pop" was an appropriate name for him because he fathered the single wing and double wing formations, which

The feared wedge of the Yale University football team, 1893.

Walter Camp

Amos Alonzo Stagg

Glenn (Pop) Warner

Knute Rockne

made up the Warner "system," rival of the Knute Rockne system for the affection of football coaches everywhere.

Warner coached Jim Thorpe at the Carlisle Indian School and he coached Ernie Nevers at Stanford. These two players became two of the three most famous in pro football before 1930; the third was Red Grange.

As a young man playing guard for a professional team in Syracuse, New York, Warner took part in the first indoor pro football game in 1902 at Madison Square Garden in New York City. Syracuse defeated the Philadelphia Nationals 6-0. This game made Warner and all the other participants in it forerunners of the pro football players now competing indoors in Houston, New Orleans, Detroit, and Seattle.

Warner coached college football 43 years, at Georgia, Cornell (his alma mater), Carlisle, Cornell again, Carlisle again, Pittsburgh, Stanford, and Temple.

He wrote a book, *Football for Coaches and Players,* that used simple, forthright language and clear, dimensional drawings of plays, making it far more useful than some of the theory-ridden coaching books of today. He was one of the first coaches with a good passing attack. Two or more responsible historians credit him with the invention of the body block, the reverse play, and the sprinter's stance for backs. And a national youth football organization was named for him— "Pop Warner Football."

Warner's single and double wing, Rockne's Notre Dame box, and the popular shifts—these *were* football before 1940. There was the Minnesota shift, the Heisman shift, the Rockne shift, the Sucker shift (named not for a college or individual but for a maneuver designed to pull the other team offside), and the Sing Sing shift of Centre College and coach Charley Moran, former quarterback of the Canton Bulldogs. (Other shifts named here are diagrammed in the appendix but the details of the Sing Sing shift, sadly, have been lost to history.)

Virtually every strategy that Knute Rockne used at Notre Dame had been tried before. No matter. The coach of the Irish from 1918 to 1930 was a figure of such stature as to rival Babe Ruth or Charles Lindbergh or Bobby Jones in the glittering decade of the twenties.

An impressive number of former Rockne players influenced pro football. Stan Cofall of the Massillon, Ohio, Tigers was elected vice-president of the new league at its organizational meeting in 1920.

When the NFL decided to name a commissioner in the style of baseball's Kenesaw Mountain Landis in 1941, its choice was Notre Dame coach Elmer Layden, who was a former member of Rockne's famous "Four Horsemen" backfield. Layden, who did not prove to be either a Landis or a Rockne, served the NFL from 1941 to 1946.

Jim Crowley, another former member of the Four Horsemen, coached a guard at Fordham named Vince Lombardi. Later, Crowley was commissioner of the All-America Football Conference, late-forties rival of the NFL.

Curly Lambeau founded the Green Bay Packers. Heartley Anderson was George Halas's longtime assistant coach with the Bears. Joe Bach, Dutch Bergman, Clem Crowe, Jimmy Phelan, Buck Shaw, and Adam Walsh became NFL head coaches. All were Rockne graduates.

An article in the 1939 *Spalding's Official NFL Guide* declared that, "until the era when the great master, Rockne, proved to the football world that a great offensive team had color and drawing power, most coaches stressed defense." This tribute to a college coach was written by the president and coach of the Philadelphia Eagles. Later, he became commissioner. His name was Bert Bell.

A trolley is halted nearby, flags flutter from goal posts, and some patrons scale the fences to see Canton versus Massillon at

were all around him because the Tenth was a black regiment with white officers. They waged bloody war against the Indians of the plains. After these experiences, Pratt began to feel compassion for the Indians, and in 1879 he formally opened the Carlisle Indian Industrial School in Carlisle, Pennsylvania. It was destined to become a blueprint for failure in social experimentation, but not before it had fielded some very good football teams and had given the world Jim Thorpe, a man who may have been the greatest athlete of all time.

In 1915, Thorpe became a professional football player. The small Ohio towns of Akron, Canton, and Massillon had been hotbeds of pro football before 1906 and the scandal of Blondy Wallace, the manager of the Canton Bulldogs. Wallace was accused of having tried to get one of his players to throw the big game with Massillon, and was forced to leave town, according to Dr. Harry March's account, "on the first train, in his playing togs, his belongings following later, maybe." Wholesome support of pro football departed with him. But in 1915, interest was revived and a team was assembled again in Canton. With the signing of Thorpe, its future was assured.

Five years later, a league was formed with Thorpe as its centerpiece. His name was even used to adorn the league letterhead as president. The new creation was called the American Professional Football Association and in 1922 that was changed to National Football League.

George Halas grew up in the Bohemian section on the west side of Chicago. His parents were immigrants from Pilsen, Bohemia in what is now Czechoslovakia. In Chicago they operated first a tailoring shop, then a grocery, then an apartment building. As a boy, young George had experienced the sort of rigorous upbringing that promotes resourcefulness and ambition. He and his brothers found the spirited competition in which a young athlete can thrive among the boys of the Bohemian district.

From Crane Tech School, Halas went on to the University of Illinois in Champaign, where, in addition to being a successful student, he was an end for the football team, an outfielder for the baseball team, and a guard for the basketball team. He graduated in 1918, when World War I was on and he volunteered for service in the U.S. Navy immediately after his graduation. George Halas was sent to the same Great Lakes training station in Waukegan, Illinois as other midwestern college football players such as Jimmy Conzelman of Washington University in St. Louis and Paddy Driscoll of Northwestern.

Football was suspended in the colleges because of the war but the military bases

the state asylum grounds, 1906; grids on "gridiron" enforce the five-yard passing rule.

were allowed to field football teams because it was considered part of the training. With Halas at end, Conzelman at quarterback, and Driscoll at halfback, Great Lakes became the service champion of the East. It then defeated the western champion, Mare Island marine station in San Francisco Bay, in the Rose Bowl game before 27,000 persons.

(Twenty-eight years later, Halas and Conzelman and their families were residents in the same exclusive lakefront apartment building in Chicago. Halas was coach of the Chicago Bears, who won the NFL championship in 1946, and Conzelman was coach of the Chicago Cardinals, who won the championship of 1947. Driscoll also spent most of his lifetime in pro football.)

After the 1919 Rose Bowl, George Halas pursued a brief career in baseball. He played right field for the New York Yankees in 1919 but they farmed him out to St. Paul. An injury to his hip in spring training the next season ended his baseball career. He returned to Chicago, played pro football with a team in Hammond, Indiana that fall, and took a job with a corn products company in Decatur, Illinois operated by an avid sportsman named A. E. Staley.

The Staley company sponsored a baseball team and Halas was made its shortstop and captain. When Staley decided to form a football team as well, Halas was placed in charge of it. The 25-year-old manager, coach, and right end set off on a tour of colleges to sign players for the team, and began making contacts with professional teams around the Midwest. The Staley company later withdrew sponsorship and the team was handed over to Halas. He moved it to Chicago and renamed it the "Bears." But in the course of preparing for opening that first season of the Decatur Staleys in 1920, Halas made an historic off-hand remark. The date and place of this historic event aren't recorded, only the fact that he suggested to Ralph Hay of Canton, Ohio that it would be advantageous to all the pro teams of the area if they could get together and form a league.

Robert and Louis Hupp of Detroit, Michigan began building "Hupmobiles" in 1908. According to automobile historian Tad Burness, this car "was not noted for speedy performance, but it was fairly durable because of its simple construction. The most noticeable identifying characteristic of Hupmobiles was the unusually tall filler necks on the radiators. Another feature was the unique fan-shaped tail lamp. You could therefore 'spot 'em coming or going.'"

The Hupmobile dealer in Canton, Ohio, Ralph Hay, was also the manager of the pro football team, the Bulldogs. The organizational meeting of the league that became the NFL was held in his showroom in September, 1920. There were not enough chairs in the room and some of the persons present had to sit on the running boards and fenders of the automobiles.

Of this meeting, Arch Ward wrote in 1946 that, "Every hour a young grease monkey from the rear room was dispatched to a nearby restaurant for a flagon of lemonade."

By the time of the wave of pro football books in the sixties, this story had become: "A mechanic from the back shop went out for a pitcher of beer." In 1975, a new book on pro football reported, "On the fenders of one of the cars hung buckets of beer." The image of the league may not be able to stand it if by the 1980s football books have that tireless mechanic at Ralph Hay's garage going out for highballs.

The severe penalties awaiting anyone in

Ralph Hay and Jim Thorpe, Canton Bulldogs.

professional football caught gambling on games makes it hard to believe that the league was influenced in part by the betting booths of the race tracks in and around New York City. But it's a fact that success at this trade by Tim Mara made him wealthy enough to buy a franchise for New York in the National Football League in 1925. Until that year, the NFL was a small-time accessory to the otherwise Roaring Twenties. Mara had never seen a football game but when he was quoted a price of $2,500 for a New York franchise, he quickly agreed, saying that a franchise for *anything* in New York was worth $2,500. It was one of the most important decisions in the history of the NFL because it gave the league respectability.

In this same year, one of the most sensational runners ever to play college football was coming out of the University of Illinois. Normally, hiring someone from one's own university is considered an employer excess akin to nepotism. George Halas can be forgiven, however, for hiring Red Grange from his alma mater to play for the Chicago Bears.

The Bears and Grange, "the Galloping Ghost," went on a coast-to-coast tour. It put the dazzling All-America on display against a variety of teams in 18 cities in three months. The most significant game of all came in December, 1925, at the Polo Grounds in New York against Tim Mara's New York Giants. A crowd of 65,000 was attracted to the game; it exceeded by 5,000 the number that had viewed the Army-Navy game there a week before.

The tour of Red Grange and the Bears opened the news columns of the nation's press to pro football, proved its drawing

Red Grange, the Galloping Ghost.

power in New York and around the country, and turned a tidy profit that helped insure the solvency of George Halas. A year later, the NFL had swelled to 25 teams and a rival league—the first American Football League—had been formed. Built around Grange, it folded after one year and he rejoined the Bears. A knee injury turned Grange into an ordinary player but he had already made an immeasurable contribution to the future of the NFL.

If it seems unlikely that betting booths influenced the history of the NFL, consider too that the game and its color and drawing power were affected by a writer of romantic stories who was born in Spain. His name was Vicente Blasco Ibáñez and he was Spain's most famous novelist after Cervantes. A political dissident, he lived in France. Ibáñez felt a strong affinity for the allied cause in World War I and he wrote a novel personifying the German onslaught as the evils of war appearing to Saint John in Revelations 6. *The Four Horsemen of the Apocalypse* went through 200 printings around the world. Hollywood filmed it with Rudolph Valentino in his first starring role.

One of the vast number of theaters it played was the recreation hall on the University of Notre Dame campus in South Bend, Indiana. It was seen there by student sports publicity director George Strickler. The next Sunday, during halftime of the Notre Dame-Army game at Yankee Stadium in New York, Strickler was talking to a group of sportswriters in the press box and he commented that the Notre Dame backfield was playing "like the Four Horsemen." Only Grantland Rice picked it up. After the game he wrote the memorable sports lead in which four college football players became "famine, pestilence, destruction, and death." Grandiloquence and football were irreparably joined.

The same Blasco Ibáñez also wrote *Blood and Sand,* about a Spanish bullfighter. It, too, was filmed by Hollywood. It, too, starred Valentino. Again, there was a football spinoff.

Two college football players wanted to find assumed names so they could join a professional team in Minneapolis called the East 26th Street Liberties. On the way to the ball park, they passed a theater where Blood and Sand was playing. One of them said, "That's it; I'll be Blood and you be Sand."

John McNally became Johnny Blood. He was an exceptional player who already owned a reputation for the ribald. With this name, he was on his way to immortality. Johnny Blood is now in the professional Hall of Fame.

The most unnoticed and unsung contributers to the National Football League may have been Katherine and Theodore Nesser of Columbus, Ohio. Katherine and Theodore were German immigrants. *Six of their sons*—Al, Frank, Fred, John, Phil, and Ted—became professional football players in the NFL with the Columbus Panhandles.

No other family has ever even come close to equaling the contribution of Mr. and Mrs. Nesser to the league.

THE SIMPLE AND CHARMING TWENTIES

The Grange Tour of 1925 "took the NFL out of the small towns and into the big cities and the giant stadiums." But it was a temporary deliverance. Steve Owen, later the New York Giants' coach, recalled that two years after the Grange game at the Polo Grounds, "the Giants played in the same park in the rain to a handful of cash customers, and we won the championship."

Hagemeister Brewery Park in Green

Hagemeister Brewery Park, home of the Packers, Green Bay, Wisconsin.

The First Giant

The NFL is a league of football not basketball teams, but height is nevertheless one of the most important assets a player can have. Hampton Pool, director of the QUADRA scouting combine, once created a mythical team in which he listed the ideal size for each position. He made his defensive ends 6 feet 7 inches tall; his tackles and defensive tackles 6 feet 6; his tight ends, guards, center, and outside linebackers 6 feet 5; his defensive backs 6 feet 3; and his fullback 6 feet 2.

Cal Hubbard, a legendary figure from the twenties and thirties, was the NFL's first really big player.

"The greatest tackle I've ever seen, or been pulverized by, was Cal Hubbard," Red Grange said. "I've often wondered how many foot pounds of pressure he developed when traveling at full speed as he smashed into a halfback."

Cal Hubbard

Hubbard was 6 feet 5 and weighed 250 pounds. He played with the New York Giants on a great defensive team in 1927-28 and then moved to Green Bay to become part of three championship teams in a row. Other players who were wider than Hubbard may have equaled his weight, but none matched his height. He towered over everyone and he was so fast that he often played linebacker on defense.

Hubbard was a charter member of the Pro Football Hall of Fame and holds a unique position in American sports. He also was elected to the halls of fame for baseball and college football.

He became a baseball umpire and performed a similar duty as a football player in Green Bay. "In those days each club carried a 'policeman,' a strong man who was level-headed and even-tempered," said a Pro Football Hall of Fame press release. "It was his duty when an opponent was getting away with dirty playing to convince the culprit of the error of his ways. Hubbard was the Green Bay 'policeman.' He was so highly respected by both teams, by the fans, and the officials that when he took summary action it was recognized that the victim merited the punishment that befell him."

Bay, Wisconsin, was probably a typical NFL stadium in 1925. It was a ramshackle pile of plank nailed together by Marcel Lambeau, father of the founder of the Packers, Curly Lambeau. There was a roller rink next door.

But in college football this was the era of the construction of massive stadiums that are still in use today. The first had been Harvard Stadium in 1903. The Yale Bowl, then Princeton's stadium, followed. Soldier Field went up on the Chicago lakefront in the early 1920s, and a mighty crowd of 110,000 watched Army play Navy there in 1926.

Stadiums were going up everywhere at costs that seemed astronomical. The most expensive of all was the one built in a city that would remain a football capital years later. It was the new Ohio State stadium in Columbus, constructed at a cost of $1,400,000, the first million-dollar monument to football.

The disparities between the tiny playing grounds of the pro teams and the monster college stadiums could not have been lost on NFL president Joe Carr. How could they? His office was located right in that manic college football town of Columbus.

The Frankford Yellowjackets were the pride and joy of the section of Philadelphia in which they played. "It is worth the time of anyone to wander out to Frankford on a Saturday afternoon in the autumn," Bill Roper wrote in *Football Today and Tomorrow* in 1927. "A steady stream of men and women flow toward the football field. On the arms of girls are the colors of the Yellowjackets, in their hands, pennants. They cheer for the players because they know

The 1924 Chicago Bears. George Halas is fifth from right.

them, because it is their team. They have a clannishness that is refreshing, that would put most colleges to shame, and very few of them ever saw a college."

He added that, "every dollar taken in at the gate over expenses is expended toward the welfare of Frankford. Not a nickel is made by the promoters."

However this may have glorified idyllic Frankford, it seems to explain why after 1931 there was no more pro football in Frankford. (The franchise was later revived and became the Philadelphia Eagles.)

The Duluth, Minnesota Eskimos featuring running back Ernie Nevers were a road team that rarely played at home. The Eskimos would arrive in a town and parade around in woolen greatcoats to promote the upcoming game. Similarly, the Kansas City Cowboys appeared in western wear, boots, and 10-gallon hats.

The Oorang Indians played out of Marion, Ohio. They were an Indian team formed by Thorpe and other former Carlisle players. Their sponsor was the Oorang dog kennels (the Oorang is a strain of Airedale).

The Columbus Panhandles, rife with Nessers, took their nicknames from the fact that all the players were mechanics for the Panhandle Division of the Pennsylvania Railroad in Columbus. They saved on road trips.

A precious relic from pro football's past can be viewed at the Hall of Fame in Canton, Ohio. It is a motion picture of 1927 and 1928 games of the Providence, Rhode Island, Steamroller (singular, like the World Football League teams of a later era). The Steamroller, coached by Jimmy Conzelman, won the NFL championship in 1928. The film was made during home games at the Providence Cyclodrome, where bicycle races were held, and which seated 15,000 persons. The banked wooden oval of the bicycle track is visible in the film. The crowd was substantial in numbers.

In this movie, the Steamroller and its opponents run up the middle, off-tackle, and around end. They lob passes with a ball that is shaped more like a cantaloupe than a modern football. There is a long punt return, probably by a player named Curly Oden. There is a halftime show in which a small band dominated by a tuba of ominous size marches along the grandstand. And there is a man in an overcoat standing on the sideline announcing the down and distance with a megaphone.

In that simple and carefree scene at the Providence Cycledrome, one can get a glimpse of the charming world that was professional football in the twenties.

LIFE BEFORE HUTSON

Elsewhere, the pros were not accepted as readily. The existence of a professional league did not put off the public mind as much as it confounded it. What enrichment beyond their meager pay could these men, severed from their old school ties, hope to gain? "A pro game is motion," coach Bob Zuppke of Illinois said. "A college game is emotion."

The pay was low and the helmets absent or insubstantial. Therefore, head-on collisions and swarming pursuit by defenders were far from the norm. For $50 to $150 a game, why risk life and limb?

In the strategy they played, the pros were copycats. They used what the big college teams used—the Minnesota shift, the single and double wing of Glenn (Pop) Warner, the Notre Dame box of Knute Rockne, or short punt formation, which reflected the conservatism of the day in-

asmuch as a punting formation was frequently used as a team's basic attack.

These "direct snap" formations had replaced the T. It was considered a thing of the past. Now the center snapped the ball several feet to a tailback, fullback, or blocking back, instead of raising it into the hands of the T quarterback.

Warner's influence was considerable. Jim Thorpe played for him at Carlisle Indian School and is said to have brought the Warner system into pro football. It is virtually impossible to read the memoirs of a twenties player who does not have a story of how he tackled or was tackled by Thorpe, and it follows that a player who made such an impression would have been widely imitated.

George Halas alone clung to the T formation. It was one of the oldest formations in the game. During the 1870s, teams arrayed themselves across the field with arms interlocked for interference—a "spread formation." But this practice was outlawed and the tightly drawn T emerged, with a seven-man line and the two halfbacks and fullbacks behind the quarterback in the shape of the letter T.

Amos Alonzo Stagg played this formation at the turn of the century at the University of Chicago. Notre Dame was in the T in 1913 against Army when the tandem of Gus Dorais to Knute Rockne attracted national attention to a daring new tactic—throwing forward passes. And the T was the formation used by Bob Zuppke when he had an end on his Illinois team named George Halas.

Clark Shaughnessy later said, "The T was the only football Halas ever knew." Not so. A small notebook of Halas's 1920

Ralph Jones, Chicago Bears.

often. Each drew up a playing schedule for the 1926 season and the league had to choose between the two; Halas's won. Each owner also prescribed solutions for the team's plodding offense. Morale steadily grew worse. In 1929, after nine years without a losing season, the Bears were 4-9-2.

In situations such as this, a strong paternal influence helps. The feuding owners found one in their former Illinois backfield coach, Ralph Jones. He was now head coach at Lake Forest Academy outside Chicago. The Bears' fortunes were placed in his hands and he proceeded to dress the ancient T in new clothing and lay the foundation for a pro football revolution.

Jones told the feuding owners that if they kept out of his way he would win a championship in three years. He did just that. He moved the Bears' ends wide, spaced the halfbacks wider, and made one of the halfbacks a man-in-motion. This meant that the halfback moved laterally away from the formation, while the quarterback was calling the signals.

The acceptance of football playing by professionals, and the use of spread formations, have gone hand in hand. Wide-open football is possible in spread formations. Jones was the first pro coach to spread the game horizontally, with his split ends and man-in-motion, and he was the first to spread it up and down the field as well because once they were out wide the players could get downfield for passes.

Furthermore, sending a man in motion created a third end, in effect. He may have been called halfback but by the time he reached the periphery of the formation he really was an end. The Bears would wait another 10 years before they would find

plays, still in his possession, has in it not only the T but the single wing and what Halas called "Minnesota formation," "ends back," "guards back," and "backs left." He threw them all out at the end of the 1920 season except for the T and that is what he used in his next 39 years as a head coach.

He is a wealthy man today and has many helpers, but during the twenties Halas needed a partner to put more money into the team and to help run it. He decided on his friend, quarterback, and former Illinois teammate, Dutch Sternaman.

There are many partnerships in the business world that do not work and this was one of them. Halas and Sternaman feuded a quarterback who could exploit this advantage; consequently their attempts at it in 1931 were rather crude. But it was really Ralph Jones who devised the professional "three-end offense."

The man-in-motion could turn back in and crackback block the defensive end. Or he could get the defense moving in one direction for a quarter or so, then cross it up by going in motion the other way. He could lead a linebacker away, opening up running space, or he could lead a defensive halfback away, opening up passing space.

Jones's teams had another powerful weapon. At the same time he accepted the Bears' head coaching job Bronko Nagurski of the University of Minnesota joined the Chicago team as a rookie fullback. Never mind the T with man-in-motion; Nagurski alone was a new offense. What strategy Jones devised, Nagurski made it work.

By 1932, the Bears were champions. But this was in the depths of the depression. Jones's former position at Lake Forest Academy appeared more secure than the one he held with the Bears, and he departed. Halas secured a loan that allowed him to buy out Sternaman, and he restored

Chicago Stadium, Bears vs. Portsmouth Spartans, 1932.

himself as coach. The Bears won the championship again in 1933 and barely lost a third straight in 1934. All this paralleled a startling set of rules changes in the NFL. These new breakthroughs in the game would put on display a fleet-footed end for the Green Bay Packers, a man they would call "the Antelope," Don Hutson.

THE EMERGENCE OF A PRO STYLE

The way football is played has expanded in relation to our national view of it as composite of shared discipline, order, and manliness. A strict moral code has prevailed. At certain times the paying of men to play football has been termed heresy and the throwing of passes dismissed as the lazy man's way of making yardage. The pros have violated both these principles and more during half a century on the edge of the secularization of football.

When the NFL legalized passes from anywhere behind the line of scrimmage in 1933, it did so a full 12 years before the colleges passed the same rule. Previously, all passes had to be thrown from five yards behind the line of scrimmage. This is where most are thrown from anyway, but the rules change of 1933 removed strictures both real and imagined from the passing game. And the way was opened for rollout, sprint-out, and bootleg passes.

Two other moves also opened up pro football. The ball was slimmed a full two inches. And the NFL created inbounds lines, to which the ball had to be returned for the start of a new play whenever it was carried near the sideline. Football's first inbounds lines were 10 yards from each sideline.

The offense could now use more of the field and was not compelled, as it had been in the past when it was trapped at the sideline, to waste a down in order to move the football nearer the middle. The short side of the field could be attacked more often.

An impoverished NFL greeted the life-giving changes. This was the league of 1932: Chicago's two teams, the Bears and Cardinals; the New York Giants; the Brooklyn Dodgers; the Stapleton Stapes on Staten Island; the Boston Braves; the Green Bay Packers; and the Portsmouth, Ohio, Spartans.

The crowds for their games were modest; since the professional debut of Red Grange in 1925, there had not been a gathering of more than 25,000. Ralph Jones and the Bears' players were being paid with promissory notes by Halas. The league president, Joe Carr, also operated the minor league baseball team in Columbus, and the secretary-treasurer, Carl Storck, made ends meet by supervising the production of shock absorbers by General Motors in Dayton, Ohio. Clearly, the NFL of 1932 was not a sports colossus.

The league had not even advanced itself to the point of compiling and distributing regular statistics to the press. This practice began during the renaissance of 1933. Finally, the NFL adopted divisional play. From this came regular playoffs between the divisional winners for the championship—the embryo of the Super Bowl.

Pennsylvania's big cities joined the league, Bert Bell with the Philadelphia Eagles and Art Rooney with the Pittsburgh Pirates, who later became the "Steelers." Curly Lambeau of Green Bay followed Halas in having daily practice sessions.

The Lost Art of Mel Hein

Each time an ancient formation such as the shotgun is revived in professional football, attention is focused on the center and whether he can carry out the seemingly simple task of snapping the ball. Yet as quarterbacks grope at their feet for wayward snaps and plays crumble because the quarterback does not have the ball, it becomes increasingly apparent that the direct snap is a lost art.

Mel Hein centered for the New York Giants for 15 years and never made a bad snap. He threw the football backwards between his legs to any of three different players—the tailback, fullback, or blocking back —in different locations in the Giants' single wing and A formations. As players came and went at each position, all favored different types of center snaps—on the left knee, on the right, in the stomach, or higher up for passing. And in some of the Giants' plays the back took the football on the move.

He bent over for a long time. And on defense, as one of the tallest linebackers of his day—6 foot 2 inches and 225 pounds—he often was blocked low. Now living in retirement in California, he says, "My back's all right but my knees bother me."

Hein participated in three important strategic developments that Giants' coach Steve Owen worked out before World War II. They were the center-eligible play made especially for Hein, the five-three defense, and the A formation.

There is a yellowing clipping in a Hall of Fame scrapbook from the 1934 season. It was published in a Chicago newspaper the day the Bears took the train to New York to play the Giants for the '34 championship. The clipping is headed, "Some Giants' Plays."

It reads in part, "A favorite with

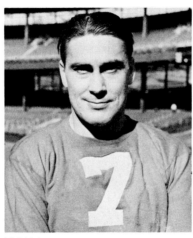

Mel Hein

the Giants is their so-called 'suicide play,' which they worked for fourteen yards deep in Bear territory, when they met the Bears at Wrigley Field early in the season.

"They call it the 'suicide play' because it's used once, and then is dead for the season."

New York actually tried it a second time against the Bears and, Hein recalls, "they almost killed me." He therefore has his own reasons for calling it the "suicide play."

In it the Giants went into a spread with only an end to Hein's left. Before the snap the end dropped back, making Hein an end eligible for a pass. He centered to his quarterback, who handed the football back to him.

Hein had disciplined himself to then walk casually downfield with the ball hidden in his arms, the defense distracted by the continuing backfield action behind him. The excitement of the moment was too much for Hein, however, and he broke into a run. Carl Brumbaugh of the Bears dragged him down.

New York adopted the five-three defense in 1934 to try to stop the Bears' man-in-motion and quick-opening plays. In this defense,

Hein, Nello Falaschi, and Johnny Dell Isola played linebacker in bruising fashion, ranging up to stop runs and dropping off on passes. This was a full quarter-century before some of the more famous line-backing trios in the four-three defense of the fifties and sixties.

The third strategic development was the A formation. An "A" was roughly the shape formed by the Giants' backfield, but its meaning went farther. The backfield was strong one way and the line strong to the other. There were splits of a yard or more between linemen, giving the Giants better blocking angles for their traps, sweeps, off-tackle runs, and crossbucks.

All these creations would have been impossible without a strong force in the middle. That was Hein. He came to the Giants as a wide-eyed All-America from Washington State. A friend there had convinced him to accept an offer from Providence for $125 a game. He did and placed the contract in the mail. He then ran into Ray Flaherty, a Giants' player, at an all-star basketball game in Spokane. Flaherty said the Giants were interested, too.

"I always wanted to play for the Giants," Hein told Flaherty. "What in the world will I do? I just mailed a signed contract to Providence today."

Hein sent a telegram to the Providence postmaster and the letter was returned. He signed with the Giants. He then married his college sweetheart and they drove a 1929 Ford coupe across the country to New York City. In a state of fright, they came through the Holland Tunnel, crossed on the 125th Street Ferry, and ended up going the wrong way on a one-way street. Mel Hein then joined the New York Football Giants and became an institution.

Tuffy Leemans running for New York Giants against Brooklyn, 1936.

Players came to view football as their living and established residence in the town or city in which they played.

The Bears ruled. The name "Monsters of the Midway" emerged in this era. Bronco Nagurski bulled through the middle, Red Grange went in motion and threw option passes, and in 1934 Beattie Feathers followed Nagurski's blocking to become the first thousand-yard rusher in NFL history. The Bears played an exhibition game in Los Angeles and humorist Will Rogers was among those in the audience. He wrote in his newspaper column, "I came away raving about it, especially the rules under which they play, where you can pass from anywhere, anytime. You college fellows

better open up your game for this pro game was just made for an audience. . . ."

That summer of 1934 the Bears played another game that probably was the moment in history when the National Football League at last made it as a sports organization. Arch Ward, sports editor of the *Chicago Tribune* and promoter nonpareil, pitted the champion Bears against the College All-Stars at Soldier Field. It ended in a scoreless tie but 74,000 saw it in person and millions more read its press accounts.

The 1934 season was a tumultuous one. It ended an era. "Until then football had been essentially a running game," Halas says. "Thorpe was a runner. So were Grange, Feathers, Nagurski, Nevers, and Clarke

The Draft

The first time National Football League teams met to conduct a draft of college football players was in February, 1936, at the Ritz-Carlton Hotel in Philadelphia. There were only nine pro football teams that year and they proceeded through only nine rounds of drafting. It was a simple beginning for what became a complex annual occurrence which had its own profound effect on the pro style.

Bert Bell, then owner of the Philadelphia Eagles and later NFL commissioner, had suggested the idea of a draft to his fellow owners, and it was Bell who made the first choice—Jay Berwanger of the University of Chicago, a halfback and winner of the Heisman trophy. Berwanger eventually declined to sign a contract with either Philadelphia or the Chicago Bears, who obtained the rights to him.

Included in the selections in that first draft, however, were Joe Stydahar of West Virginia and Dan Fortmann of Colgate, who went on to great careers with the Bears and eventual election to the Hall of Fame.

It was a simpler time in pro football. It was common for team executives to base their draft choices on college players who had been the subject of articles in fan magazines such as *Street & Smith*. Earle (Greasy) Neale and Harry Thayer of the Eagles were laughed at, therefore, when they arrived at the Stevens Hotel in Chicago in 1942 armed with 64 notebooks on college prospects they had assembled at a cost of $8,000. It took "two bellhops and a baggage truck" to get the Eagles to the draft that year. The amusement they gave others would subside in coming years as the Eagles became one of the strongest teams in the NFL. Their number-one draft choices included such

The NFL draft, Roosevelt Hotel, New York City, 1976.

men as Joe Muha, Steve Van Buren, Chuck Bednarik, and Bud Grant.

Dan Reeves of the Los Angeles Rams was the next club executive to commit his team to an elaborate scouting program. The Rams became the model for NFL scouting in the fifties. Los Angeles's draft skills were advanced by general manager Tex Schramm, who later moved to the Dallas Cowboys and helped that club become the first to use computerized scouting. The Cowboys pioneered in drafting players from other sports such as track star Bob Hayes and college basketball players Pete Gent and Cornell Green.

As the age of soccer-style kickers dawned, it became common for player personnel directors to make trips to Europe or Africa in search of such kickers.

Scouts trusted in the computers to spare them criticism for bad choices; to assimilate data they had earlier confused (Pettis Norman of Johnson C. Smith had been listed as "Johnson C. Smith of Pettis Norman College); and to save them from missing potentially great players.

Mistakes in the simple measurements of height, weight, and speed were corrected. Scouts descended on college spring practices armed with stopwatches, tape measures, skepticism, and resolution. The colleges submitted and set up "timing days" given over wholly to the pros.

George Allen of the Los Angeles Rams and Washington Redskins was one coach who disdained the draft and instead assembled his teams by trading with other clubs for experienced veterans. The Pittsburgh Steelers, however, were an outstanding example of building a team through the draft. From a 1-13 season in 1969, they drafted skillfully and won a Super Bowl five years later.

Competitors on the field but partners in scouting combines, teams sent representatives to group meetings that became lively with disagreement. As the number of teams increased, the careful selection of new talent became more vital. Teams maintained a "best player available" rationale, which simply meant that they watched the board and its list of the top ratings, and when their turn came, took the highest-rated survivor, whatever his position. Arrayed around them was more data on the college prospects at a single position than all the books Greasy Neale and Harry Thayer carried into the draft in 1942.

Footballs fill the arms of Don Hutson of the Green Bay Packers.

Hinkle. Now, Arnie Herber and Don Hutson were warming up at Green Bay. An exciting new era dominated by great passers and receivers was at hand."

The Packers, who matched the Bears as perennial powers, might never have ac- quired the services of Alabama's Don Hutson if there had been a draft. There was none, however, in 1935; the practice began a year later. Green Bay won a duel with the Brooklyn Dodgers for the affections of Hutson; Green Bay's triumph no doubt

The Fabulous Baugh

In the years ahead, quarterback Sammy Baugh would coolly pick apart the greatest defenses in pro football. He was filled with mortal fear, however, as he faced walking to the microphone to address a banquet before his rookie season in Washington in 1937.

The Redskins were the new team in town, having just been moved to the capitol from Boston, and All-America sensation Baugh was their biggest attraction. They were now being introduced to the populace. A glib toastmaster went on with an introduction that seemed an eternity, and at last he said, "And here's Sammy Baugh to say hello."

There was a thunderous applause and Baugh walked to the podium. "Hello," he said, and sat down.

Sammy Baugh literally was a man of few words. He let his actions do his talking for him.

Testimonies to how well he could pass make the quintessential Baugh story believable. His coach Ray Flaherty is supposed to have told him to hit a receiver "in the eye with the football."

"Which eye?" Baugh is supposed to have answered.

He quarterbacked Washington to the NFL championship in his rookie season and in the first half of the title game he threw a pass out of his own end zone for a 42-yard gain en route to a fabulous 335-yard passing performance. It was supposed to have been the first pass ever thrown out of an end zone in a National Football League game. Baugh's passing helped Washington win the championship again in 1942.

He was, however, the losing quarterback in a 73-0 game. The Redskins lost by that score to the Chicago Bears in the 1940 championship game.

Baugh was the greatest quick-kicker in history, setting unequalled punting records with that technique. He was still playing both ways in the late forties and was one of the finest safeties ever. When he retired in 1952, an entire page in the NFL Record Manual was set aside to display his achievements.

The Redskins had Baugh but little else after World War II. Speaking to a meeting of FBI agents, he said, "This is the most protection I've had in a long time."

He went out ingloriously in 1952. Sacked by massive Don Joyce of Baltimore, he delivered a solid right to Joyce's face. He and Joyce were ejected from the game. During a game at Washington later in the season, Baugh went in to hold for an extra point . . . and it was blocked. So ended Baugh's career.

When he had joined the Redskins for the first time, Baugh had been instructed by owner George Preston Marshall to arrive in Washington in western gear. He did, and complained, "My feet hurt." But he became a Texas cowboy made in the nation's capitol. His cowboy boots and 10-gallon hat were his trademark.

He used his football salary to buy a ranch in Rotan, Texas, near his hometown of Sweetwater. After his retirement he had less-than-successful terms as coach of Hardin-Simmons College; the 1960-61 New York Titans, who later became the Jets; and the Houston Oilers. Baugh retreated to his ranch and became a virtual hermit who rarely left the ranch for public appearances. He finally was lured to Los Angeles in 1975 to tape a segment of "The Way it Was" about the 1940 championship. He sat there looking old and out of place and anxious to get back to Texas. He did not remove his hat.

Sammy Baugh passes for the Washington Redskins in the mid-1940s.

contributed to the eventual disappearance of the Brooklyn Dodgers.

The Bears were the opponent when Hutson played his first league game for Green Bay in 1935. On the first play of the game, Hutson escaped Bears' safety Beattie Feathers, caught an over-the-shoulder pass from Herber, and completed an 80-yard touchdown play.

Hutson was 6 feet 1 inch, 180 pounds; he could run 100 yards in 9.8 seconds. The Packers played the Notre Dame box but spread Hutson and the other end, Johnny Blood, wide, the same way the Bears spread their ends. Hutson lined up in a variety of locations in order to get an advantage on the defensive halfback or safetyman (something all split ends do today), and to escape the pounding given him at the line of scrimmage—the first signs of the bump-and-run technique of the sixties.

His speed—exceptional for that day—made Hutson a better man than any of those who tried to cover him. He compounded the edge he had with an array of fakes and changes in direction and speed. An arching Herber pass usually came down into Hutson's arms just as the end broke free from his coverage.

During 11 seasons in the NFL, Hutson was the leading pass-catcher eight times. He once caught four touchdown passes and kicked five extra points against Detroit—in one quarter! His coach, Lambeau, said Hutson was, "the most valuable player to a team in the history of the game."

The new wide-open pro football had its model receiver. In 1937, it got its model passer. The teams of the Southwest Conference, notably SMU under Ray Morrison and TCU under Dutch Meyer, were advo-cates of the forward pass. Sammy Baugh of TCU was the best passer that conference—or any in college football—had ever seen. He came into the NFL in 1937 as the first draft choice of the Washington Redskins, who had just moved to Washington after four seasons as the Boston Braves. The NFL draft had begun a year earlier.

Baugh passed the Redskins to the 1937 championship game against the Bears. In that game, Baugh made more yards passing, 335, than whole teams had gained by any means during an entire season in the twenties. Washington won 28–21.

"Slingin' Sammy" threw baseball-style sidearm passes and could reach any receiver with a bullet pass. He made the primitive three-deep defenses of the day easy pickings. If the middle safety committed himself in one direction, Baugh threw in the other. When coverage grew more complicated, he looked to his backs. "He would cock the ball," Steve Owen wrote, "bring it down to drift off as if about to run, cock again, make a mock throw to one side, and shoot a touchdown to the other. . . He was never committed until he was flat on the ground and the ball with him. I have seen him make bullet-like throws with his tremendous wrist action as he was nailed by a hard tackle and falling."

The Redskins played the double wing formation that had been invented by Pop Warner, probably before 1910. The formation was very much like the T double wing of NFL teams, and the shotgun formation of the San Francisco 49ers in the early sixties and the present Dallas Cowboys. The biggest difference is that Baugh was without the fifth receiver passers have today—the tight end.

Baugh influenced professional football with his short passing game. His wingbacks flared to the sideline and he threw the ball in to them hard. Washington became the first team to nibble its way down the field making first downs by passing instead of running.

The forward pass became irreversibly identified with pro football. Every championship team from 1936 on had a good passer—Herber of Green Bay in 1936 and 1939, Baugh in 1937, and Ed Danowski of New York in 1938. Then Davey O'Brien, a diminutive All-America who like Baugh was from TCU, carried it to extreme. Playing for the Philadelphia Eagles in 1940, he tried 60 passes against the Redskins and completed 33. For the purists to whom rampant passing was abhorrent, things were getting out of control.

THE IMPROVED T WITH MOTION

Every pro team today is a small science laboratory. The Chicago Bears of the late thirties were the prototype for this phenomenon. Since the primitive—by comparison—era of Ralph Jones, the accumulated knowledge of the varied possibilities of the T formation with man-in-motion had built up year by year. The way it was played had evolved as defenses took measures to stop it. But in 1939 a quarterback was found who could operate it, a smart quarterback who could absorb it, call the plays assertively, and make the ball-handling feints. The quarterback was Sid Luckman of Columbia University. Luckman was broken

Clark Shaughnessy and his University of Chicago team, about 1935.

in slowly during his rookie year, playing left halfback and learning while Bernie Masterson finished an admirable career at quarterback.

The Bears' brain trust of coaches was served by a consultant, Clark D. Shaughnessy, the coach of a condemned football team at the University of Chicago. The new Chicago president was in the process of cancelling big-time football.

Shaughnessy did not even use the T formation at the university. But, as a regular visitor to Bears' practices, his appetite for football and his enormous imagination expanded as he saw what could be done with the T. He began making the daily trek from the university on the south side of Chicago to the Bears' camp on the north, bearing a suitcase full of newly drawn T plays.

It cannot be said that Halas's assistants welcomed the interloper warmly. But the head coach did and he took what he liked from Shaughnessy's suitcase and made them Bears' plays. A new offensive system was emerging. Luckman spun from under the center and faked, handed off, or pitched. Linemen moved out fast and did not engage their opponent for what seemed an eternity but instead "brush-blocked" and continued downfield to throw a block at someone else. Ends developed precisely-timed pass routes—ins, outs, hooks. All this obsessed Shaughnessy.

And so did language. As the seemingly infinite T plays mounted, what should they be called? What was to be the jargon of the T formation with man-in-motion?

The body of language that Shaughnessy placed atop the Bears' existing method of play-calling made the Bears' players feel

that they were superior and exclusive, that what they were doing was wholly original. It would not have been possible without the Columbia-educated Luckman. He and Shaughnessy studied late night after night. At last, Luckman was ready. He was equipped to go into a huddle and order up the Bears' formation, play, type of man-in-motion action, and line blocking. A typical call was, "spread left O scissors 39-46." It meant that the left end was spread wide, the guard away from the play ("O" for "off") would pull and lead it, the center and other guard would work a "scissors" block, the number three back would carry the ball through the nine hole in the line,

and the number four back would go in motion and turn upfield on the six count. Such was the language of pro football's prototype science laboratory.

Shaughnessy left Chicago in 1940 and became head coach at Stanford University. The Bears lost only three games in 1940, the last 7–3 to Washington in a disputed game in which the Bears demanded a pass interference call on a late play but were denied. George Preston Marshall, owner of the Redskins, savored his victory and called the Bears "crybabies."

The two teams met again for the championship. That Chicago won 73–0, that it was a hallmark of pro football history,

and that it riveted national attention on the Bears and their T with motion, has been written many times. Four elements of strategy propelled the Bears.

First, Shaughnessy briefly returned from Stanford, where he had become the toast of college football by winning 10 straight games. Through exhaustive study of the film of the 7–3 game he learned the Redskins were playing a very predictable defense in which they shifted linebackers toward the man-in-motion, and concluded they were likely to stay in this defense. Second, the Bears devised counter plays, old as football itself but especially useful against a defense such as the Redskins were using. Third, Chicago decided on ball control, to keep it away from Baugh, the master passer. Finally, Shaughnessy made the Bears' blocking attack more efficient through newer language he had recently invented at Stanford.

Those who view the 73–0 game as a methodical display of careful strategy view it wrongly. On the second play of the game, Bears' fullback Bill Osmanski ran 68 yards for a touchdown; it wasn't a counter play away from the man-in-motion, but instead it was to the same side. And Osmanski ran in the wrong hole in the line. He corrected himself and cut to the outside, however, and sprinted down the sideline to a point where end George Wilson mowed down two Redskins and put Osmanski in the clear. After that, the Bears' offense continued flawlessly and their defense picked off interception after interception thrown by a parade of Redskins' tailbacks replacing Baugh, who left the game early.

An expansive Boston sportswriter covering the game wrote, "The Bears had the timing for their quick-opening plays down to the hundredth of a second." Well, not quite that precise. But the sentence reflected the admiration everywhere for this new formation. During the next 10 years it gradually replaced the single and double wing and Notre Dame box as the principal formation used by football teams at all levels. All who hailed the new T said it freed the game from the stereotyped patterns of the old systems. Yet this was exactly what had been said of the old formations when they had replaced the T during, roughly, the administration of William Howard Taft. The T with motion succeeded other systems in the forties mostly because it was something new.

Shaughnessy's 1940 Stanford team made a perfect 11–0 record by defeating Nebraska in the Rose Bowl. The next appearance of the T was in 1941 at Missouri, where coach Don Faurot devised the spectacular split-T. While coaching the team of the Navy pre-flight school at the University of Iowa in 1943, Faurot taught this system to his assistant coaches, Jim Tatum and Bud Wilkinson. They arrived later at Oklahoma as head coach and assistant, with Tatum subsequently moving to Maryland to be succeeded at Oklahoma by Wilkinson. Each won national championships with the split-T.

Out of that came the belly series, which means the quarterback rides the ball into the belly of one back and then may leave it there or take it out and hand it off, pitch it to someone else, or keep it himself. This spawned the triple option, wishbone, and veer offenses that have been prominent in college football ever since. In each the quarterback performs techniques that are

43

Quarterback Rivals in a Golden Age

Otto Graham, the cog in the machine.

They were two pro quarterbacks who led two teams in what was called the golden age of the sport, the fifties. Year after year, they met in some of the most titanic struggles ever. Each won his share of those games and left an indelible mark on pro football. And perhaps the most interesting fact of all about Otto Graham of Cleveland and Bobby Layne of Detroit was that they were as different from each other as night and day.

Harry Gilmer was a quarterback and defensive back for Washington and Detroit in 1948–1956, almost exactly paralleling the period when Graham and Layne were the premier players in pro football. In addition, Gilmer was on two Pro Bowl teams with them and was Layne's teammate on the Lions for a time. He has some revealing observations about the two men.

"They were entirely different in their personalities and in the way they quarterbacked," Gilmer says. "The only similarity between them was that they were both competitors, two of the greatest who ever played.

"If you were trying to find someone to compare Otto to, a good choice would be Bart Starr of Green Bay. There was a slot for Otto in the Cleveland Browns' machine of Paul Brown, so to speak, and he fit it and fit it well. The same could have been said about Starr in the system of Vince Lombardi at Green Bay.

"Layne was more of an individual. He dominated the Lions to such a degree that he had control of all of them. If you put him in an all-star game, for example, he would just capture everyone. Graham or Starr, on the other hand, would not be the best quarterback to take to a Pro Bowl, unless their coach was there, too.

"Graham was an excellent passer. Layne was, too, don't get me wrong. It was just that Layne was not a picture passer, but the ball came down at the right place when he threw it.

"Where Layne was great was in the clutch. In my opinion, he was the greatest two-minute quarterback the game has ever had."

Their coaches mirrored the differences in the two quarterbacks. Brown was methodical and controlled every play used by Graham through messenger guards. Buddy Parker, Layne's coach in Detroit, left play selection up to his quarterback.

"Both coaches were very, very sound and predictable," Gilmer says. "There was nothing razzle-dazzle about either team. The difference was that Brown dominated Cleveland's offensive thinking while Layne dominated Detroit's.

"The way Parker and Layne worked it, Parker did for Layne what I thought was the finest job I have ever seen of schooling his quarterback. The two of them had a very close relationship and they thought exactly alike.

"If you put Parker and Layne in a room and gave both of them the same problem to solve, they would probably both arrive at the same answer for it."

"Graham was "Automatic Otto," or as *Sports Illustrated* wrote, "Charlie McCarthy to Paul Brown's Edgar Bergen." But Layne was the heart and soul of the Lions. He led them on the field and off, convening unofficial team meetings at the Stadium Bar across the street from Briggs Stadium, where the Lions sat for hours playing absurd word games, the losers being compelled to chug-a-lug a pitcher of beer while the others roared with convivial laughter.

Norm Van Brocklin of the Los Angeles Rams was much the same kind of character. Like Layne, he led through the medium of the backslap and in shared good times. But neither man took subordination of any sort in the huddle and both were quick to remind players in colorful language that the quarterback was boss.

A different style evolved through Graham, whom Brown first spotted at Northwestern University. Graham was then a single wing tailback. "I was coach at Ohio State," Brown said. "The only Big Ten game we lost was to Northwestern in 1941, fourteen to seven, and we lost it on a play where Graham ran left from the single wing then threw back to his right to a man going lickety-split away from him, right on target, for the winning touchdown. I asked myself, 'What kind of player is this?' He was the first man I picked for the Cleveland team."

Service in World War II intervened for them, and each came in contact with men who were products of the Chicago Bears' new T formation with man-in-motion. Brown succeeded Tony Hinkle, a former Bears' player, as coach at Great Lakes Naval Training Center. Hinkle had installed the Bears'

Bobby Layne, the individualist.

offense there. Graham was in naval flight training with Ray Bray, a former Chicago guard. The Bears' system would be advanced as never before when Brown and Graham got together at Cleveland.

The Browns won every championship in the four-year history of the All-America Football Conference, then won the NFL title the first year they competed for it in 1950. Graham completed his first year in the NFL by being named player of the game in the revived Pro Bowl game in Los Angeles.

Graham retired after the 1955 season. He had passed for 23,584 yards and 174 touchdowns. Those figures were exceeded by other men but through a complicated system in use today in which passers are assigned rating points on various categories, Graham ranks as the leading passer in NFL history.

The biggest disappointments in Graham's career were brought about by Layne and the Lions. Their teams were the kingpins of the American and National, later Eastern and Western Conferences, of the NFL. Detroit upended Cleveland 17-7 for the 1952 championship and they met for the title again in 1953. Detroit won 17-16 when Layne and converted defensive end Jim Doran combined on a 33-yard touchdown that tied the score and halfback Doak Walker kicked the winning extra point.

But the next year, Cleveland gained revenge by swamping the Lions 56-10. Graham played perhaps the greatest game of his career, passing for three touchdowns and running for three others.

Graham played one more season, won another championship for the Browns, and retired. Brown coached in Cleveland another eight seasons without finding another quarterback in the mold of Graham.

foreign to those of his pro counterparts, which frustrates professional scouts.

The I formation of Tom Nugent at VMI and the power-I of John McKay at USC were other college formations that grew out of the T. Another novel formation was that of Ossie Solem of Syracuse, in which the center lined up with his rear to the defense and performed the functions of both centering and quarterbacking. This may have earned plaudits for economy of manpower but it was the greatest of affronts to middle guards. It is now illegal.

In 1941 the Philadelphia Eagles became the first pro team to copy the Bears' T. The Washington Redskins, victim of the 73–0 massacre, hired Shaughnessy to teach it to them in 1944. All other pro teams followed, the last of them the Pittsburgh Steelers in 1952. "Slot-T" followed. The "flanker," offspring of the man-in-motion, was set up in a "slot" inside one of the spread ends. At the end of the decade, the first "tight ends" emerged. They played in tight as an extra blocker, leaving the other end and the flanker spread wide. Thus the T with motion had at last evolved into the modern "three-end offense."

A number of formations having facets of both the T and the old direct snap formations emerged in the sixties. The best-known was San Francisco's shotgun offense, with Bill Kilmer, John Brodie, and Bobby Waters at tailback. But there were also the Baltimore Colts' "pistol;" the Detroit Lions "zephyr;" the Philadelphia Eagles' "stacked deck;" the Los Angeles Rams' "outpost and settlement;" the Dallas Cowboys' "tail-gunner;" and the revival of double wing but with a T quarterback, by St. Louis and Cleveland. (See appendix.)

Clearly, what the Bears made popular in 1940 is not what the pros play now. It is but a framework. The lasting contribution of the Bears of 1939–1940 has been the position of quarterback. All who have played it since owe a debt to Sid Luckman.

THE REVOLUTION ON DEFENSE

The history of defense is the step-by-step decline in the number of players on the line. In the early days there was a nine-man line. Then came a seven, a six, and a five—used in the NFL for the first time in 1934. The five-man line carried the pros into the age of the promiscuous pass. Greasy Neale of the Philadelphia Eagles refined it when he moved the linebackers up close to belt pass receivers, and by adding a fourth man to the secondary. This last innovation was advanced further by Steve Owen of the New York Giants. From the "Eagle" and the "umbrella" defenses of Neale and Owen, there emerged a four-man line, which became the ultimate defense. But as passes increased, coaches were pressed to drop more men back to cover them. On downs when they were sure the offense would throw a pass, they reduced their line to three men in a "prevent" defense. The 1972 Miami Dolphins made this their daily diet. Other teams have followed in doing so. We are now on the verge of the universal adoption of the three-man line. History, and the widespread assurances it will never happen, argue that it will.

Pro football detonated in all directions during the 10 years after World War II. The last strictures were gone from the passing game and virtually every contending team had a hot combination—Sid

47

Frank (Bucko) Kilroy (76), key man in the Eagle defense.

Luckman to Jim Keane and Ken Kavanaugh, Sammy Baugh to Hugh (Bones) Taylor, Bob Waterfield of Los Angeles to Jim Benton, and Paul Christman of the Chicago Cardinals to Bill Dewell and Mal Kutner.

The Eagles had their own gifted receivers for one-eyed passer Tommy Thompson. Mostly, though, the Eagles were punishers. Their idea of the correct T formation play was to hand the ball to left halfback Steve Van Buren and send him powering off-tackle, bulling through opponents until enough of them could get him down. The Eagles' defense, meanwhile, resembled Saturday night longshoremen. Middle guard Frank (Bucko) Kilroy and linebackers Joe Muha and Alex Wojciechowicz were its leaders. The defense was a departure from the historic declination of the front line because with the linebackers up close it amounted to a seven-man line. The four deep backs brazenly played no more than five yards off the line. They were able to do this because of the immense pressure the line put on the passer. Neale paid $10 for every sack of the quarterback. Going for that $10, the Eagles worked combinations in which seven players might rampage in on a given play and at other times some would rush and others drop off. With this defense, Philadelphia won the NFL championship in 1948 and 1949.

The Eagle defense was effective against the NFL's great passing combinations. But there was another good one playing in a rival league. The Cleveland Browns were the center ring attraction of the All-America Football Conference of 1946-49 and, having won it every year it existed, were one of the reasons it folded its tents.

The brilliant Paul Brown coached Cleveland. He had developed what was perhaps the most devastating pass attack ever around quarterback Otto Graham, ends

Paul Brown, who grounded the Eagle.

An example of the passes from Otto Graham (60) that Eagle couldn't stop.

Dante Lavelli and Mac Speedie, and halfback Dub Jones. It was augmented by the powerful draw play and trap runs of fullback Marion Motley.

The Browns' passing game was a combination of the precise timing of Don Hutson and the equally precise pass routes developed in the Bears' laboratory of 1939-1940. Lavelli and Speedie ran turns, outs, and comeback patterns with surgical precision. They worked out careful timing with their quarterback, Graham. He released his pass so it arrived just as the end had covered a measured number of yards and had made his turn to look for the ball.

Cleveland and two other former AAFC teams, San Francisco and Baltimore, were taken into the NFL for 1950. Commissioner Bert Bell matched Cleveland against NFL champion Philadelphia on the Saturday night before the first Sunday of the season.

Philadelphia was expected to win easily even without Van Buren, who had an injured foot. Hadn't the Browns won all those championships because of inferior competition? But Philadelphia was overcome by a team intent on proving it was the equal of the NFL. In the first half, Graham hit 41- and 26-yard touchdown passes to Jones and Lavelli. Graham decided the issue with a touchdown pass to Speedie and the Browns went on to win 35-10.

"We had never seen such a spot passing

"Umbrella" defense stalwarts Al DeRogatis (78), Arnie Weinmeister (73), and Ray Krouse (70).

program as they had," Philadelphia defensive halfback Russ Craft said later. "We would be on top of the receivers, but they caught the ball anyway because the pass was so well-timed."

Paul Brown had been the only coach to kill a league. The AAFC lay dead by his all-winning hand. Now he had, in his first league game in the NFL, crushed its champion. Would he *ever* lose? Viewed in this light, one can understand why longtime defensive specialist Steve Owen of the New York Giants carried the hopes of the NFL coaching fraternity into his two 1950 games against the Browns.

The "umbrella" defense Owen created for these games had four deep backs. It had a variety of deployment of front linemen. And it had, when its ends dropped off, three linebackers. Every one of these elements had been played previously in the five-man line defense or the Eagle— only not as well. Giants' ends Ray Poole and Jim Duncan and middle linebacker John Cannady were exceptional players and so were the four members of the umbrella secondary—Tom Landry, Harmon Rowe, Otto Schnellbacher, and Emlen Tunnell. When all seven were back in pass coverage, the pass rush of only four men was substantial enough because it was buttressed by tackles Arnie Weinmeister and Al DeRogatis.

The press coined the defense's name. They referred to middle man Cannady as its "stem" and Owen called him the "bumbershoot." Cannady's presence was the major difference between the Eagle and the umbrella. The Eagle did not have a middle linebacker.

The General

In all the years of pro football, there has never been a situation more strange or a defense more daring than that of the Chicago Bears when Clark Shaughnessy was defensive coach and Bill George was shaping the position that came to be the most glamorous one in the four-three, middle linebacker.

The Bears' defense played by the oddest code of language ever devised, and operated as a secret society independent of the other half of the team, the offense.

In 1962, offensive tackle Stan Jones had to move to the defense because of an injury there.

"The offense held its meetings in the clubhouse at Wrigley Field and the defense met in the usher's dressing room," says Jones. "I went down there to report for their meeting and they immediately broke it up, said the meeting was over.

"We were going into a game against Minnesota. I was supposed to start at defensive tackle and I knew nothing about the defenses. All that 'Minny Purple Blast Shuffle Left' they used was Greek to me.

"George Allen [Shaughnessy's defensive assistant] saved me. He said, 'Sit by me on the plane.' And on the flight to Minnesota he slipped me a three-by-five card with all the defenses on it. Also, during the game, Bill George kept telling me, 'Move to your left a little,' or 'You go on this play.'

"I think Shaughnessy was afraid Halas would learn what he was doing and fire him. Shaughnessy carried everything with him. He lived in a hotel on the north side that could be called a flophouse and each day he rode the 'elevated' to Wrigley Field. You could see him coming down the street carrying his projector and his big suitcase of plays.

"During the defensive meetings, no one was allowed to take notes except Bill George. He was the only man other than Shaughnessy who completely understood what was going on. At practice Bill would go through one of those long audibles like 'Minny Purple Blast' and we would all stop what we were doing and give him a standing ovation.

"Shaughnessy had a whole chain of command for the defense. It started with George; he was the General. Richie Petitbon, the safety, was the Colonel. It went all the way down to buck privates.

"Halas was very frustrated with Shaughnessy. He told him one time, 'I'm paying these men; how can I know whether or not they've done their job if you don't tell me what they're supposed to do?'"

Shaughnessy's separation from the team occurred in 1962. The Bears won the 1963 NFL championship with Allen as defensive coach.

Bill George was the defensive captain for nearly a decade, the man who played 14 years, longer than any other Chicago Bear in history. He was a big Syrian, 6 foot 2 inches and 230 pounds, from a college in South Carolina, Wake Forest. He began as a middle guard and became one of the first middle linebackers in the four-three.

Jones says, "George was extremely quick. He had a knack for anticipating the cadence count and getting a jump. He had all the ingredients for the position you look for today. George probably had more physical gifts than the other middle linebackers you hear the most about— Joe Schmidt of Detroit, Les Richter of Los Angeles, and Sam Huff of the New York Giants. George seemed taller than they were and he had unusually long arms. And he had the head for Shaughnessy's defense. He was a very sharp football player."

The pioneer middle linebackers in the four-three era retired the middle guards of the older Eagle defense such as Les Bingaman of Detroit and Stan West of Los Angeles. A new era was dawning. The Eagle's nose men departed the way Hollywood stars with poor speech were out of a job when talking pictures arrived.

Bill George.

Big Daddy

Eugene (Big Daddy) Lipscomb was a giant, but he played "soft." Despite his size, he ran down smaller ball carriers, and then he helped them up. At practice, he lifted little children and set them on his shoulders, a lofty perch because this was a man who stood 6 feet 6 inches and weighed 290 pounds. He said of his kindnesses, "I don't want people or kids to think Big Daddy is a cruel man."

"For sheer strength, I have not seen any defensive lineman to compare with Big Daddy," fullback Jim Brown of Cleveland said. "He was the one man in the National Football League I tried to psyche. I won't say I was afraid of him, but I will say I was conscious of the damage Daddy was capable of performing."

The first time Lipscomb and the Baltimore Colts met Brown and the Cleveland Browns was in 1959. Lipscomb was blocked expertly that day by Cleveland guard Jim Ray Smith and Brown scored five touchdowns.

Smith varied the way he took Lipscomb on each play and Brown cut to the left or right before the

Eugene (Big Daddy) Lipscomb.

big lineman could grab him. Lipscomb was incensed and took his anger out on the other Cleveland running back, Bobby Mitchell, when he managed to run him down on end sweeps. Brown was thankful he had escaped unhurt and said, "I made up my mind I would never again let him get mad at me. In future games, I psyched him. I'd say after he knocked me down, 'Daddy, you're really looking good out here today.'"

Lipscomb was a forerunner of the defensive linemen today. He used the technique of "spying," laying back to read the action instead of charging all-out.

Quarterback Norm Van Brocklin of the Philadelphia Eagles compared the styles of Lipscomb and another leading defensive tackle, Ernie Stautner of Pittsburgh:

"Stautner charges like a bull that has just had the toreador's cape waved in its face," Van Brocklin said. "He does this on every play, charging as hard at the end of the game as he did at the start.

"Big Daddy, on the other hand, is the 'soft' type of tackle . . . he is what we call a 'piano player.' He puts his huge paws on the guard's shoulders, takes a look, then pursues."

Lipscomb had been an easy target for trap plays when he first signed with the Los Angeles Rams in 1953. Buddy Parker of Pittsburgh said, "We used to kill him. He was so easy to trap. Later we handled him by running right at him. That is how you handle all great tackles. What you do not want is Big Daddy chasing you. When you run away from him, he makes tackles all over the field."

Esquire wrote of Lipscomb's upbringing in Detroit, "He was not born great and nothing was ever thrust upon him. He never knew his father. When he was eleven, living in a rooming house in Detroit, a man came to the door and told him his mother was dead. She had been stabbed forty-seven times by a man she knew while waiting for a bus."

Lipscomb took odd jobs after school, and later joined the Marines. He was playing for the football team at Camp Pendleton in Southern California when the Rams discovered him. His playing skills were raw because he had had no high school or college experience, but he became a starter.

Probably the best-remembered moment of his Rams' career came in a 1955 game when he held defensive back Don Burroughs, who was himself 6 feet 4 inches, on his shoulders trying to block a field goal attempt by George Blanda of the Chicago Bears. It didn't work because Blanda's kick was successful, but, as a result of the play, such action by the defense was declared illegal.

The Rams put Lipscomb on waivers in 1956 and he went to Baltimore, there to be part of two NFL championship teams in 1958 and 1959. He was traded to Pittsburgh for three players in 1961. There he was paired with Stautner and the Steelers reached the highest pinnacle they knew until the later teams of coach Chuck Noll.

In May, 1963, Lipscomb died. Heroin was blamed. *Esquire* wrote, "No one who knew him can believe he was addicted, and there is no evidence that he was."

As a memorial to him, artist Daniel Schwartz created the portrait of Lipscomb now hanging in the National Art Museum of Sport at Madison Square Garden. And the late Randall Jarrell wrote a moving poem titled, "Say Goodbye to Big Daddy."

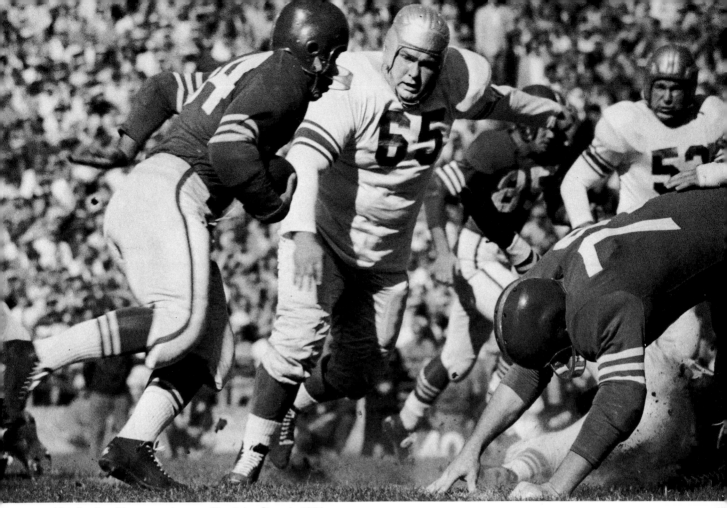

Massive Les Bingaman sizes up 49ers' Joe Perry in 1954.

The Giants shut out the Browns 6-0 with this defense and, three weeks later, beat them again, 17-13. However, Cleveland won a third game against New York when they met in a playoff, and the Browns went on to beat Los Angeles 30-28 for the NFL championship. But the umbrella had made its mark.

Football teams do not react in patterns as quickly as some histories claim. There was no overnight rush to the four-man line. The Browns stayed in a five-three; their arch-rival, the Detroit Lions, played the Eagle. Middle guard Les Bingaman, who weighed more than 300 pounds, was the key performer for Detroit.

The four-three defense emerged with Bingaman's replacement, Joe Schmidt, and other outstanding players who filled the position in ensuing years. Bill George

of the Chicago Bears, Les Richter of the Los Angeles Rams, and Sam Huff of the New York Giants were developing the position at the same time as Schmidt. Who the first middle linebacker was seems a less important argument now that the four-three has competition as the definitive pro defense.

The three-four is so old that it probably influenced its supposed predecessor and semantic opposite, the four-three. Oklahoma coach Bud Wilkinson developed the three-four in 1947. It was identified throughout college football as the "Oklahoma." Bum Phillips, coach of the Houston Oilers, learned the Oklahoma or three-four defense while attending a Wilkinson clinic in the fifties. Bill Arnsparger of the New York Giants, who as a Miami assistant guided the Dolphins' three-four, learned

53

it while a college assistant at Kentucky.

The three-four is a defense that has been in virtually every pro playbook for years just waiting for someone to use it full-time. Buddy Parker used it as coach of the Detroit Lions in the fifties. The Los Angeles Rams had it as early as 1958. The Houston Oilers, one of its exponents now, had it in 1964. Pittsburgh, coached by Bill Austin, used it against the Dallas Cowboys in 1966 and lost 56-7. That game is probably still fresh in the mind of Dallas coach Tom Landry, since he remains the foremost advocate of the four-three.

THE DROPPING OF THE BOMBS

Quarterback John Brodie of the San Francisco 49ers looked over the Dallas defense as he began to call signals during a 1971 divisional playoff game. To his left he saw all-pro Dallas cornerback Mel Renfro. To his right he saw Herb Adderley, a former all-pro cornerback. Brodie's decision was to forego Mel Renfro and throw everything at Herb Adderley. Brodie actually smiled wryly at Adderley and nodded his head. "I knew what he was telling me," Adderley said later. "They were coming my way."

NFL cornerbacks have seen them come their way for a long time now. They play the most dangerous position in football; on one play, they can lose a game. The greatest of them have succeeded in covering the fast spread ends alone, but the rest have not. The evolution of pass defense is the gradual process of getting more help for cornerbacks who come under attack.

Don Hutson caught "bombs"—long

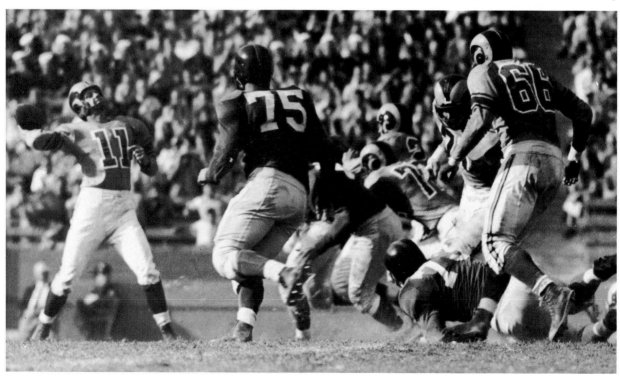

The Rams' Norm Van Brocklin about to release a bomb.

Experiments in Speed

Before a vast throng of people in a giant arena in Tokyo, Bob Hayes of Florida A&M and the United States crossed the finish line in a blur, leaving the second- and third-place finishers far behind to win the 100 meters in the 1964 Olympics and tie the world record of 10 seconds flat. Later, he put on an incredible sprint to bring the American team from behind to win the 400-meter relay.

Within two years the same man became the most feared offensive threat in professional football. Joining the Dallas Cowboys as a wide receiver in 1965, he began a 10-year career in which he caught 71 touchdown passes. For his adopted sport of pro football, Hayes's day in the sun in Tokyo was one that football has not gotten over since, and probably never will.

Attempts to find men who can outrun everyone else on the field actually have been going on since the dawn of the National Football League. The star, playing coach of Canton, and first president of the league was Jim Thorpe, hero of the 1912 Olympics.

In recent times a steady flow of sprinters, hurdlers, and long jumpers have tried their hands and feet at pro football. Some have failed, some have been successful, and one became both Olympic champion and pro football superstar.

"Bob Hayes was the first man who could sprint who also had football ability," says Dick Bank of Los Angeles, one of the leading experts in the world on track and field. "He ended up the greatest sprinter of all time and he was a quality football player, too."

Henry Carr of Arizona State, on the same U.S. Olympic track squad as Hayes and 200-meter champion at Tokyo in 1964, was one of many sprinters who couldn't equal Hayes's

Ollie Matson, Chicago Cardinals, 1958.

Bob Hayes.

success in professional football. Carr spent two seasons as a defensive back for the New York Giants. Frank Budd, John Carlos, Jim Hines, and Tommie Smith were other sprint sensations in the sixties who tried and failed to become regulars in the NFL.

Glenn Davis of Ohio State, two-time Olympic champion in the 400-meter hurdles, was an earlier failure. He joined the Detroit Lions in 1960 and they created a special formation, the "Zephyr," that set Davis out wide where he could get downfield fast. But in two seasons with the Lions, Davis caught only 10 passes.

There have been many success stories, however. Men of speed who made names for themselves in pro football included Don Hutson, George McAfee, Buddy Young, Jack Christiansen, Ollie Matson, Del Shofner, Lance Alworth, Billy Cannon, Homer Jones, Warren McVea, Bobby Mitchell, Travis Williams, Mercury Morris, O. J. Simpson, and four burners who became the new deep threats in the age of zones—Cliff Branch of Oakland, Isaac Curtis of Cincinnati, Mel Gray of St. Louis, and Harold Jackson of Los Angeles.

Clyde Scott, Hugh McElhenny, Boyd Dowler, Bernie Casey, and Earl McCullough were among the hurdlers who starred in pro football. And the long jumpers included the legendary Thorpe, Elroy Hirsch, Jon Arnett, Gale Sayers, Jimmy Johnson, Mel Renfro, Paul Warfield, and Lynn Swann.

Speed is really the mark of every man in pro football. The unit of measure is the 40, not the 100-yard dash, and each player wears his speed for that distance like a birthmark. It follows him from the day he is first scouted in college until he retires.

Baltimore's Unlikely Superstars

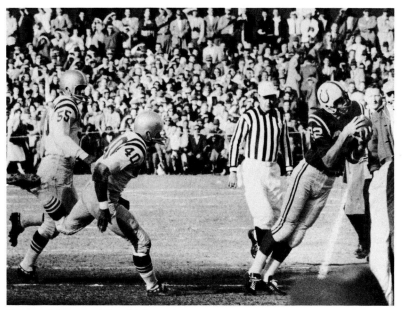

Raymond Berry and the sideline catch.

John Unitas and Raymond Berry may have been history's best passing combination, but they were far from its most glamorous. Quarterback Unitas was stoop-shouldered, pale-skinned, and crewcut, and played football wearing the last descendants of Gay Nineties high-buttoned shoes on his feet. End Berry was skinny and slow and had poor eyesight; away from the field, he might have been mistaken for the club's accountant.

Unitas was a sandlot quarterback earning $6 a game when Baltimore found him and claimed him from Pittsburgh's waiver list in 1956; the Steelers had cut Unitas the year before in favor of quarterbacks Jim Finks, Ted Marchibroda, and Vic Eaton. Berry joined the Colts from SMU in 1955, surprising everyone when he made the team as a twentieth draft choice. From those beginnings, Unitas went on to become the man voted the greatest quarterback in the first 50 years of pro football and Berry set professional

football's career pass-catching record with 631 receptions, a record since broken by Don Maynard and Charley Taylor.

The Colts' sudden death overtime victory over the New York Giants in 1958 was the game that established Unitas as the sport's master quarterback. His play selection and field leadership was flawless as he marched the Colts down the field at Yankee Stadium. Berry, his favorite passing target, caught 12 passes that day for 178 yards; those figures are still records.

Baltimore repeated as champions in 1959 and Unitas completed a record 32 touchdown passes for the season. In 1960 he set an NFL record with 3,099 yards passing. Disappointments followed for the Colts in the 1964 championship game against Cleveland, and against the New York Jets in Super Bowl III, and Unitas often was nagged by injury, but he kept piling up completions and yardage. He was a Colt for 17 seasons, from 1956 through

1972, and played one more season in San Diego before retiring.

There is no receiver today who does not have a little Raymond Berry in him. All receivers attempt to copy his infinite variety of moves —his precise timing on cuts and his technique of screeching to a halt at the sideline and hanging there on tiptoes to catch a Unitas pass just before tumbling out of bounds.

Berry defined all the moves that could be made against man-for-man coverage and thus hastened the coming of zones. Those blankets of coverage might be even more ominous today if not for Berry, whose receiving science taught receivers skills on which to fall back; receivers learned to use the Berry moves and work intricately under the zones.

Perhaps no one ever appeared less suited for professional football. Berry was not a starter in high school until his senior year—and his father was coach. He scored one touchdown in high school and three in college. Inexplicably, he made the Colts. "What saved Raymond," defensive end Gino Marchetti once said, "was the fact we didn't have any good offensive ends. Berry didn't look like any seven-alarm fire himself but at least he hustled all the time."

"I came into football with a lot of limitations," Berry said. "I'm not fast, nor strong, nor big [he was 6 foot 2 inches, 186 pounds]. I knew I had to concentrate more, practice harder, give more of myself than most."

He overcame his limitations with hard work and an outrageous array of gadgets. He arrived at practice with a clipboard and pencil to chart his work. He built a net out of old batting cage netting and placed it behind him while he caught passes in practice. The net stopped errant

John Unitas, master quarterback.

throws and allowed him to retrieve the ball faster. He squeezed putty in his hands constantly while standing idle to strengthen his hands and forearms. He wore contact lens while playing, and experimented with various shades of lens depending on the sort of day it was. For games in Los Angeles, Berry acquired sun goggles, which prompted Jim Murray of the *Los Angeles Times* to write that Berry "looked out of place without a biplane and white scarf."

While other Colts took Mondays off, Berry practiced. He ran fakes and patterns even while jogging around the field to warm up. His coach, Weeb Ewbank, said, "In all my time in coaching, I never saw a more serious athlete. I had to drive him to the shower room after practice or he would have stayed out until it got dark."

Berry said he had 88 moves and had to practice all of them every day. He enlisted coaches, groundskeepers, ball boys, sportswriters, even his wife Sally, to throw footballs to him after practice in front of the ever-present net. He said he preferred other throwers to Unitas during drills. "John throws too accurately for me to get any good out of my special catching practice," he explained. "I like the passer to be wild because sometime in a game I might have to catch a ball in a bad position."

He studied films of opponents incessantly. While Sally operated the projector, Berry ran the movies back and forth late into the night. Alex Hawkins, then "Captain Who" of the Colts' special teams and a Baltimore nocturnal figure of repute, recalled cruising past Berry's house in the darkness and seeing the light of a film projector still flickering upstairs in the Berry bedroom.

Elroy Hirsch, Los Angeles Rams.

Billy Howton, Green Bay Packers.

scoring passes—long ago, but the term was invented to describe the aerial bombardment of the fabulous Los Angeles Rams' team of 1951. Two quarterbacks and two wide receivers from that team are in the Hall of Fame. They are Bob Waterfield, Norm Van Brocklin, Tom Fears, and Elroy Hirsch. Van Brocklin once had more than 500 yards passing in one game, Fears 18 catches in a game, and Hirsch caught 17 touchdown passes in a season. A 73-yard bomb from Van Brocklin to Fears won the 1951 championship game as Los Angeles defeated Cleveland 24-17, proving the Browns human and ending their five-year domination of football leagues.

In primeval man-for-man coverages, cornerbacks dug in and gamely tried to stay with the likes of Hirsch, Lavelli of Cleveland, Harlon Hill of Chicago, and Billy Wilson of San Francisco. And the defense took the first steps to get them some help.

The zone defenses played by college teams arrived in force, and there were combination coverages that allowed three men to cover two, depending on where they went, or ones that were a zone in one part of the coverage and a man-for-man in another.

Mighty pass rushes were sent against the quarterback. The glamorous "front fours" appeared—New York's with Roosevelt Grier, Jim Katcavage, Dick Modzelewski, and Andy Robustelli; the Baltimore rush led by Gino Marchetti; and later, the Fearsome Foursomes in Los Angeles.

The era of the blitz dawned. Waves of

Billy Wilson, San Francisco 49ers.

Harlon Hill, Chicago Bears.

linemen and linebackers poured it on the passer. St. Louis invented the safety blitz with Larry Wilson. Everything was moving *toward* the quarterback, not *away* from him as in today's age of zones. The blitzers gambled that they could get the quarterback down before he could find someone to pass to. When they blitzed, these defenders forced the deep backs left behind them to cover man-for-man. This was the accepted theory—to rush madly and hold on for dear life in the secondary.

The quarterbacks in the new American Football League of the sixties loaded their bomb bays as no one had before. Passing combinations such as John Hadl to Lance Alworth in San Diego, George Blanda to Charlie Hennigan in Houston, and Jack Kemp to Elbert Dubenion in Buffalo ter-

rorized the inexperienced cornerbacks of the new league.

There is a page in the 1963 Denver Broncos' playbook that may appear at first glance to be an American Kennel Club record of breeds in Boston. It is not. It is a scouting report on what was the maddest blitzing team in the early AFL. It is headed, "Boston Dogs." The Patriots were often successful with their blitzes, or red dogs, but often they were not, as when San Diego crushed them 51-10 in the 1963 championship game.

The unrestrained application of zone defense was still years away. To throw a big rush at the quarterback was better than dropping eight men back in the way of his receivers. The NFL was populated by passers who were experienced, crafty, and accurate, such as Brodie, Bart Starr of Green Bay, John Unitas of Baltimore, and Bill Nelsen of Cleveland. They could not pick apart a coverage, the defense reasoned, if they were being rushed relentlessly by a Deacon Jones of Los Angeles or a Bob Lilly of Dallas. And they had fewer receivers available if they had to keep their backs in to block the blitzing linebackers.

But there was a more subtle reason why zone was delayed in its arrival. The code of manhood that has governed the game has in the past required that a man play his position for 60 minutes without a substitute, that a quarterback call his plays without aid from the sideline, and that a defender take on one man and beat him. Such a code still prevailed when the cornerbacks of the American Football League made the technique of bump-and-run popular. They confronted a pass receiver on the line of scrimmage and they ran off together, the cornerback battering the receiver with open hand or forearm until the pass was in the air. Then they both went racing for it. Bump-and-run was a dangerous technique that has all but vanished today; it is played only by high draft choices who come into the league filled with the bravado of youth. At its zenith, it represented the professional cornerback's most admirable attempt to prove he could cover alone for four quarters without aid.

COORDINATION AND RUNNING TO DAYLIGHT

The great running backs—Jim Brown of Cleveland, Gale Sayers of Chicago, and O. J. Simpson of Buffalo—have not influenced the game as much as awed it. They have not been copied by others, because who could copy them?

The one running system that has shaped pro football the most, that of Vince Lombardi of the Green Bay Packers, led to a technique of blocking that benefited Brown before he retired and became the common-sense principle for Simpson and all runners today.

The feared plays of Lombardi's system were the sweep and the weakside slant. In these plays we see the best example yet that football strategies of the present day are rooted in the deep past, that what we see at the surface was given life long ago.

The ancient wedge of the nineteenth century propelled itself at one spot on the defense and kept hammering away at it. So did the "tackles back" formation that followed. These were outlawed but their fun-

Bump-and-run: Willie Brown, Oakland vs. the Chargers' Alworth.

damentals remained in the off-tackle sweep of the single wing and box formations, in which a mass of blocking humanity assaulted the defense's weakened flank.

Curly Lambeau of Green Bay went to Notre Dame in 1918 to play the box formation of Knute Rockne. Lambeau was followed at Notre Dame by another son of Green Bay, Jim Crowley, who became quarterback of the famed Four Horsemen. Frank Leahy also came to Notre Dame to play for Rockne.

Later, Crowley became head coach at Fordham University in New York City; Leahy was his line coach. They tutored a guard from Brooklyn, Vince Lombardi.

They taught him the pulling action of guards in the sweep. He would coach it well at Green Bay.

"If we block well here," Lombardi wrote in *Run to Daylight,* "it began with Crowley and Leahy . . . They drilled Nat Pierce and me on that guard-pulling action until we could do it without thinking . . ." Leahy went on to become a successful coach at Notre Dame. After he retired, he followed Lombardi's great years. "There were times when Vince was doing so well with the Packers and Frank knew he'd never coach again because he was getting too old and too sick that he kind of thought he was the keeper of some sacred flame," the Rev.

Vince Lombardi and quarterback Bart Starr.

A Coach, Two Men, Two Plays

In the Green Bay Packers' playbook, the plays were 49 Sweep and 36 Slant. Vince Lombardi was the coach and the author of the playbook. Paul Hornung and Jim Taylor were the archetypical performers of the two plays, both of which are fundamentals of modern pro football.

Left halfback Hornung ran the option sweep to the right side and fullback Taylor ran the slant to the weakside. When the Packers' matchless guards, Jerry Kramer and Fred (Fuzzy) Thurston pulled out of their positions and started to the right, the sweep was coming. And virtually anytime the Packers needed short yardage and lined up in the brown formation, as it was called in their simple language, everyone who was watching knew the slant was coming. Each was thoroughly predictable and yet these men ground out yard after yard in the days of the Packers' dynasty.

Hornung was the "Golden Boy," the Heisman trophy winner and two-time All-America quarterback from Notre Dame who was a player without a position before Lombardi arrived in Green Bay in 1959. It was then that the coach, noting Hornung's multiple talents on the football field, told him, "You're not playing quarterback anymore. You're my left halfback. You're either going to play left halfback, or you're not going to play at all."

Hornung was taught the sweep and option pass skills that Lombardi had developed in Frank Gifford of the Giants while Lombardi was an assistant coach in New York. Hornung became one of the best option passers in history. He also kicked field goals and extra points, setting an NFL scoring record with 176 points in 1960 as the Packers reached the championship game

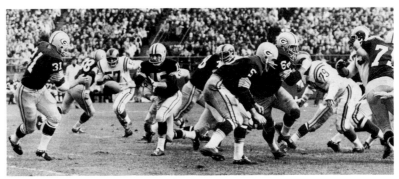
Paul Hornung (5) blocks as Starr laterals to Jim Taylor.

for the first time under Lombardi but lost to the Philadelphia Eagles.

The following year, Hornung scored 33 points by running and kicking in one game against Baltimore and 19 in a 37-0 rout of the Giants as Green Bay won its first title under Lombardi. In 1965, he had five touchdowns in the fog at Baltimore in a key victory of another championship year. Hornung once kicked 96 consecutive extra points for the Packers.

Overweight and slow after absence for Army duty during the Berlin crisis of 1961, Hornung was ridden hard by Lombardi. And he brought sadness to the coach's heart with his 1963 suspension for gambling. But he was Lombardi's favorite. "In the middle of the field Hornung may be only slightly better than an average ballplayer," Lombardi said once, "but inside that twenty-yard line he is one of the greatest I've ever seen."

Taylor never held the niche in Lombardi's heart that Hornung had but no player embodied the spirit of Lombardi power football better than Taylor. He was only 6 feet 2 inches and 212 pounds but, as Lombardi said, "When you bump into him it's like bumping into a cast-iron statue."

For a record five straight seasons, 1960 through 1964, Taylor gained

1,000 or more yards. In 1961, when the Packers played Cleveland in the first meeting ever between a Lombardi team and a Paul Brown-Jim Brown team, Taylor ran for four touchdowns and the Packers won 49-17. Taylor's greatest season came a year later when he gained 1,474 yards, beat his arch-rival Jim Brown of Cleveland for all-league fullback and most valuable player honors, and played an epic game in the championship against New York. He and the Giants' linebacker, Sam Huff, dueled for four quarters on a bitter cold day at Yankee Stadium. Taylor had 84 of the hardest yards of his life and the Packers won another championship.

Hornung was injured, but Taylor was still a powerhouse when the Packers won Super Bowl I over the Kansas City Chiefs in January, 1967. Before another season, Taylor had failed to agree on a contract with Lombardi and joined the new team in New Orleans, the Saints. The same team also got Hornung. Filled with sadness, Lombardi had placed the ailing Hornung's name on the expansion list and the Saints claimed him. Physical infirmities prevented Hornung from ever playing for New Orleans, however. Taylor retired from football after only one season with the Saints.

Frank Cavanaugh said in a biography of Leahy, *Shake Down the Thunder* by Wells Twombly. "Old Rockne had patted him on the head and told him to go out and beat everybody he could and, somehow, he convinced himself he'd passed the power on to Lombardi during those years he coached him at Fordham."

So there was a lot of history bound up in Lombardi's famous power sweep. It was true, too, of the weakside slant. As offensive coach of the New York Giants in the fifties, Lombardi had an off-tackle play to take advantage of the many talents of halfback Frank Gifford. But it didn't work as planned.

"The play was designed to go inside the left end and our right guard, Bill Austin, was to pull and take the left end out," Lombardi wrote later. "But that end would pinch so hard you couldn't get him out, so Gifford, as that end would close, would dip outside of him. This was the first time I realized in pro ball it is to your advantage not to run into a specific hole but to run to daylight. We started to coach it and that was the beginning of that."

Packers' fullback Jim Taylor applied this thesis best and his favorite play was the weakside slant. "He is a natural at that running to daylight," Lombardi wrote. "When Jimmy doesn't predetermine where he is going, he is as good as they come at running inside or outside that block."

"Running to daylight" and "option running" mean the same thing. And they give birth to "option blocking." During a scouting trip to the University of Kentucky, when he was a Giants' assistant, Lombardi planted the idea in the mind of Blanton Collier. This erudite and kindly coach had previously served Paul Brown as a Cleveland Browns' assistant. Collier developed option blocking, and it underlies most offensive thinking in pro football today. In it, the blocker puts the blockee "on an island," takes him where he wants to go, and sees that whatever decision he makes is the wrong one. The ball carrier cuts in the other direction after the defender makes his move.

When Paul Brown left Cleveland in 1962, Collier replaced him as head coach. Fullback Jim Brown had been used by Brown in every possible type of attack—draws, traps, sweeps, and slants. Now Collier added option running and blocking and Brown thrived on it for the final three seasons of his productive career. Thereafter, the popularity of option blocking spread throughout pro football.

Brown once gained over 1,800 yards in a single season. It seemed no one would ever equal that achievement. But in 1973, Simpson of Buffalo reached it and passed it, completing the season with 2,003 yards. It was an incredible achievement.

John Kennedy once said in addressing a dinner and reception for Nobel Prize winners at the White House, "I think this is the most extraordinary collection of talent, of human knowledge, that has ever gathered together at the White House, with the possible exception of when Thomas Jefferson dined alone."

Similarly, there may never have been as much football knowledge on one staff as when Lombardi and Tom Landry were together as New York Giants' assistant coaches from 1956 through 1958.

It was the greatest of ironies that Landry, having been a father of the four-three de-

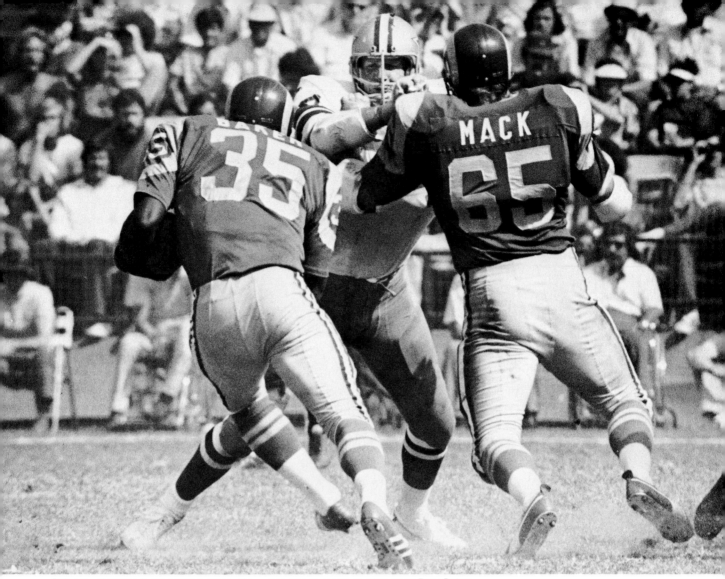

Bob Lilly of Dallas fights off Tom Mack of Los Angeles to reach running back Tony Baker.

fense in New York, was forced to find ways to stop it while building an expansion offense in Dallas. Further, when after six hard years he at last had built the Cowboys into the best team in the Eastern Conference, he was denied the NFL championship by the Western Conference champions coached by Lombardi. The preparation made by these two men for each other led to today's principle of coordinated defense.

The Green Bay sweep actually lived a very short life. It was a successful play during 1959 and 1960, but its productivity slipped when defenses "read" it and brought their strong safety up to meet the sweep or confused the blocking at the point

of attack by exchanging the positions of defensive end and linebacker. But stopping runs to daylight wouldn't be that easy.

For all intents and purposes, use of the four-three defense by any NFL team for four quarters of a game is already dead. All who play it also employ other defenses periodically and more often than not while in the four-three use an "odd" line.

Instead of lining up "evenly," tackles on offensive guards and ends on offensive tackles, one tackle shifts over head-on the center. That is a "four-three odd" defense.

The defenses have also "stacked," or hidden, linebackers behind linemen. They have slanted and stunted—programmed

Jim Brown . . . and Then All the Others

Jim Brown of the Browns.

Jim Brown was in the Syracuse University locker room changing into lacrosse gear to play against Army. He had just left a track meet where he had won the shot put and discus for Syracuse against Colgate. A student manager from the track team rushed into the locker room out of breath. "The meet is close and the coach wants you to come back and throw the javelin," the manager said.

Brown returned to the track meet, threw the javelin 162 feet virtually without practice and won second place, giving the meet to Syracuse.

He was all-state in several sports in high school on Long Island. He once scored 55 points in a basketball game. At Syracuse, he made All-America in football and lacrosse and lettered in basketball. From there he went on to a pro football career with the Cleveland Browns. In nine seasons in the NFL Brown gained a fantastic total of 12,312 yards rushing.

"He had this God-given body,"

recalls Browns' trainer Leo Murphy. "He weighed two twenty-eight and he had a thirty-one inch waist. He could have been heavyweight boxing champion of the world."

Jim Brown holds more records than anyone: most rushing attempts, 2,359; most yards; most seasons, 1,000 or more yards, 7; most games with 100 or more yards, an unbelievable 58; highest average gain, 5.22 yards; and most touchdowns rushing, 106, making him the only man with more than 100.

Attempting to describe Brown's running style, a Los Angeles Rams' tackle named Glenn Holtzman said, "The only way I've found to stop him is to hit him right at the ankles with my shoulder. Otherwise, it's like tackling a locomotive."

Defensive end Gino Marchetti of Baltimore said, "If you tackle him and don't get a good hold, he's liable to tear your fingers right out of your sockets."

John Unitas claimed Brown could be "read"; one hand down in his

stance meant he was going to run one way, the other hand down meant he was going the opposite way. Yet Brown still went unstopped. He was the most durable ball carrier ever. He played most of his rookie year with a broken toe but gained 942 yards. In nine years, he made the Pro Bowl every year, and led the NFL in rushing eight years.

Resenting the trade that sent halfback Bobby Mitchell to the Washington Redskins in 1962, Brown led a revolt against coach Paul Brown. Under a new coach, Blanton Collier, Jim Brown had his greatest season ever in 1963 with 1,863 yards. He continued to be a devastating force for two more years as the Browns won one NFL championship and just missed another. He retired at his peak, when he was 30 years old, and became an actor. He made a series of motion pictures that did not approach the awe-inspiring majesty of Jim Brown running with a football.

charges between linemen and linebackers exchanging lanes of attack.

All this is useless unless it is coordinated. That is the theme of present-day defense. "Each of the eleven defensive players has a specific assignment on every play, and every assignment is coordinated with others," Jack Youngblood of the Rams told the *Los Angeles Times*. "There are two objectives. The first is to stop the probable play, whether run or pass. The second is to make sure that when we overload, we still have guys in position to stop unexpected plays.

"We coordinate between each man in the line and also with the linebackers, whose other job is to coordinate with the deep backs. On a given play, a linebacker might be playing what amounts to a defensive lineman's position or a safetyman's."

Any stunt by a lineman is supposed to be covered by a linebacker, who moves into the vacated area to protect it. A blitz by a linebacker weakens an area that a lineman must protect. And on every running play one of the cornerbacks or safeties comes up to force the play while others have the responsibility of containment—stopping the runner when he has been turned to the inside by the force man.

The most talked-about system of coordination has been the one Landry devised to stop Green Bay's runs to daylight. Reasoning that it would be impossible to predict where the runner will be, he arranged to fill every possible space in the line with a Cowboy and wait for him. That is "gapping," a Landry contribution to pro football.

The Dallas linemen do not charge across the line or chase quickly after the play; instead, they sit in an evenly spaced line strung across the line of scrimmage and wait for the luckless runner to decide which tackler he wants to challenge.

During the era of his "Doomsday Defense," Landry had the massive figure of tackle Bob Lilly in the middle of the Dallas line. Lilly hugged the line so closely he was almost offside. At the snap, he penetrated immediately, fouling blocking patterns and drawing as many as three of the blockers to himself. If that worked on first down, the defense was now facing second-and-long, and that was "Doomsday."

The "Flex" was the next product of the Landry defensive laboratory. This is the system in which two of the four Cowboys' linemen are well off the lines. They read the combinations of blocks they see, while the other linemen attack and clog up the blocking patterns. It is easy to identify because the "flexed" end is always in an old-fashioned four-point stance. Therefore, to study this newest of defensive line techniques, watch for the player in the most primitive of stances.

THE ZONE AGE

Coordination was needed in the secondary, too. And with the new pragmatism born of "run to daylight," the man-for-man machismo of the old order was discarded. Zone defense was not only acceptable but rational.

But again, the zone was nothing new. Paul Brown played it in the forties. The Eagle and umbrella had varieties of zone. "Chris's Crew," the superb secondary of the Detroit Lions in the fifties led by Jack Christiansen, played near-flawless zone.

Gale Sayers of Chicago against the San Francisco 49ers.

The San Diego Chargers of 1961, with Chuck Noll as defensive secondary coach, set a pro football record that may never be equalled when they made 49 interceptions. Later, the Baltimore Colts, whom Noll had joined in the same coaching capacity, and the Minnesota Vikings were zone specialists in the late sixties.

Its fundamental principle appeared during the Hoover administration. It is "rotation" of the secondary. The Green Bay Packers of Lambeau and the Detroit Lions of Gus Dorais rotated their defenses toward the Chicago Bears' man-in-motion in the thirties.

In the simplest zone, one cornerback

The Celebrity

The two representatives of the St. Louis Cardinals walked through the carpeted elegance of Paul (Bear) Bryant Hall on the campus of the University of Alabama. Presently, they located quarterback Joe Namath, their team's number one draft choice for 1965. They made opening contract offers. The quarterback, who was following the advice of the dormitory's namesake, responded, "I want two hundred thousand dollars."

The men from St. Louis returned to Missouri. They had played small roles in a drama that would irrevocably change the sport of football. Namath later signed a contract with the other team that had drafted him number one, the New York Jets of the American Football League, for a $225,000 bonus, an annual salary of $25,000 for three seasons; a $7,000 Jet-green Lincoln Continental; no-cut and no-trade clauses; and deferred payments of his bonus.

It can be argued that the fiscal preoccupations of not only pro football but all sport dates to Namath's contract with Sonny Werblin, the millionaire talent agent who had rescued a team called the New York Titans from bankruptcy, changed their name to "Jets," and signed Namath because he saw charisma and star quality in him.

It also happened that the young man from Beaver Falls, Pennsylvania, who had gone to Alabama to play football under Bear Bryant, also was an unusually good quarterback. With his leadership abilities and his virtually unequaled passing arm, Namath would become one of the greatest of all. And his personal lifestyle would influence other players and make him as much a celebrity as a quarterback.

He first tore cartilage and ligaments in his right knee while he was a college senior. He had forgotten before that game to go through the regular ritual of wrapping white tape around his football shoes. Later, the Jets ordered white shoes for him. They became his trademark, but 10 years later football shoes of all colors, white included, were the rule in the pro game.

He was "Broadway Joe." He quarterbacked the Jets to the AFL championship and then guaranteed they would beat the NFL Baltimore Colts in Super Bowl III. He made good on the promise. He made movies, had his own syndi-

A man with style – Joe Namath.

cated television show, and hosted the Tonight Show.

He was, however, a virtual cripple. His first knee operation followed his first signing of a Jets' contract. There were three more operations later. Other injuries beset him. He suffered a broken wrist in 1970 and a shoulder separation in 1973. He came back from each injury and played with an unnatural protrusion under his socks —the steel and rubber braces supporting his erector-set knees. It seemed he had made an almost Faustian arrangement in which he would risk permanent injury in exchange for the chance to keep playing, to keep quarterbacking the Jets, to keep being Joe Namath.

As one of the premier passers of all time, he carried the Jets to their Super Bowl III triumph in 1969 on his strong right arm. He did not complete a touchdown pass in the game, however, winning it instead by carefully reading what he considered a very basic Colts' defense and expertly selecting the right play every time.

Jim Finks of the Chicago Bears called Namath "the supreme artist at quarterback. When he is hot, you literally accept the fact he will score points. He knows his position better than anyone in the game. He has it all—the quick release of the ball, the quick setup, and he will stay in the pocket."

Closing in on a phenomenal 4,000 yards passing in 1967, Namath was hit by Oakland's Ike Lassiter and Ben Davidson and suffered a broken cheekbone. He went into the season's final game wearing a protective mask, but that did not keep him from throwing touchdown passes to George Sauer (one) and Don Maynard (three) to complete the season with 4,007 yards, the all-time record.

Miami's Zone Masters

In the age of the zone defense, two of its most skilled performers were safetymen Dick Anderson and Jake Scott of Miami. For five years, 1970 through 1974, they played together without injury at the inside positions of a Dolphins' secondary that was a swirling web of deception and precise coverage. It demonstrated just how blanketing zones could be.

The Dolphins played the traditional four-three rollup or rotation or revolve (the terminology is different from team to team; Tom Landry called it "pure zone"). Miami also had varieties of coverage —the safety zone and the linebacker zone. But Don Shula, the brilliant coach who had developed the NFL's best zones in the sixties, also crafted more four-three coverages in which cornerbacks and linebackers set up in five short zones, with only the two safeties deep. Additionally, there were combinations, defenses that were part zones and part man-for-man. And then the "53" arrived giving Miami eight men deep and even more varieties. In addition, it was difficult to predict which defense Miami would play.

In explaining how the Dolphins disguised their coverages, Anderson sounded the words that symbolized a period in pro football in which players were facing cerebral challenges unlike any they had ever faced.

"We're out to confuse that quarterback, mess up his mind, get him to where he's not sure what he's facing and he's not sure what to do," Anderson said.

As the Dolphins miraculously made the playoffs in Shula's first year as Miami coach in 1970, were AFC champions one year later, and Super Bowl champions in each of the next two years, many quarterbacks came away with their minds thoroughly messed.

Teams with two of the best passers in history met the Dolphins twice each season. Injuries were slowing down John Unitas of Baltimore and Joe Namath of the New York Jets, however, and there were precious few confrontations between them and the Dolphins.

One week after winning a memorable Christmas day six-quarter playoff at Kansas City, Miami met Unitas and Baltimore for the AFC championship. Miami led 7-0 in the third quarter and was threatening to keep the ball away from the Colts indefinitely with ball control. Unitas decided to go for broke. Anderson picked off his pass and raced 68 yards for a touchdown in which Scott and five other Dolphins cut down Colts in his path.

Namath possessed the one weapon to which the Dolphins were susceptible—a tall, fast tight end. Rich Caster raced free inside Miami's two-deep in 1974 for an 89-yard touchdown on Monday night television. But in other forays against Anderson and Scott, Namath did not do well; he completed only 17 of 40 in one 1970 game.

Anderson was a veteran of the Dolphins' desolate years before Shula. Scott, however, joined the team in the turnaround season of 1970. He had played one year for Vancouver in the Canadian League, caught 42 passes, been traded to Montreal, and placed on waivers. It made little sense, and the expert way he played safety as a rookie for Miami was equally hard to understand. "He played like he had been back there all his life," Shula said.

In 1972, the Dolphins climaxed the only 17-0 season any team ever had by winning Super Bowl VII. Scott intercepted two of the Washington Redskins' passes and was named most valuable player.

They were two distinctly different types off the field. Anderson was a hard-working sort with an insurance business, while Scott was the blithe spirit away skiing in Colorado, shoving off on his skis with two broken wrists he had fractured playing football.

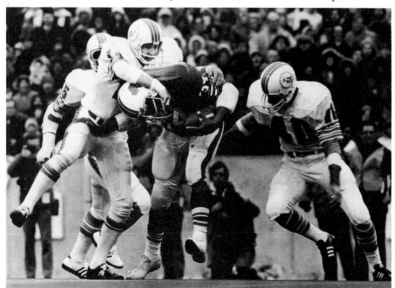

Superb safeties Jake Scott and Dick Anderson (40).

comes up tight and the nearby safety takes the deep zone behind him. The remaining safety and far cornerback play the other deep zones and the four short zones underneath them are guarded by the rolled-up cornerback and the three linebackers. There can be rotation to the strongside or to the weak. That is the type of zone played by the Chargers in their record season 15 years ago.

It has become considerably more sophisticated. That short zone the cornerback occupies may also be taken by a safety or a linebacker. All three move around swapping defensive zones from play to play. Keys to the type of zone being played are lost. Noll, now head coach of the Pittsburgh Steelers, and Don Shula, his former boss at Baltimore and now head coach of the Miami Dolphins, are two of the coaches who favor the new five-short and two-deep zone defenses. But it is only one of the many varieties at work in the NFL today.

The offense has had a battle plan against zones for 20 years—"flood" a zone with many receivers; throw into the uncovered areas between zones; "stretch" them deep with a fast receiver, if you have one, and horizontally with sideline patterns; pass to the tight end, covered often by a linebacker instead of a faster deep back; and run, run, run. With linebackers dropping off into zones, a back can make yardage before linebackers can recover and come up for the tackle.

The NFL's Competition Committee that influences the playing rules moved against zones when it brought the inbounds lines on the field closer to the middle in 1972. This widened the "short side" on which zones thrived. The committee also stan-

Zone defense by the Washington Redskins.

dardized placement of the painted yard line numbers on all fields. Coaches had been locating them where they pleased as reference points for their pass defense.

But the zones are still in charge. With them, the game has been extended to its topographic limits. "We've run out of room," Tom Fears complained in 1970 when he was coach of the New Orleans Saints. "The quick defensive backs and linebackers have filled up the field. There's not much space out there any more."

Dropping into their zones, the defenses merely thumb their noses at the artistic jukes and glides receivers have been practicing since the days of Hutson. Coaches who were oriented in man-for-man fail in the zone age; others who *are* zone-minded

The Return of Running

In the age of zones, the greatest characteristic of offenses was the decision to hand off, not pass, the football.

When passes were thrown, they were usually short ones underneath the zones. The short passes were designed to keep ball control, maintain steady marches down the field, and avoid the all-or-nothing gamble of long bombs. "You take the bus instead of the jet," said Hank Stram, then Kansas City coach.

This style of offense proved a disappointment for all who found long passes more exciting. They could gain renewed hope, however, in the fact that the shift to running attacks may have peaked in 1972. During that season, there were 10 1,000-yard rushers, an all-time high. The number has not been equaled since. Furthermore, the development of such young quarterbacks as Ken Anderson of Cincinnati, Bert Jones of Baltimore, and Steve Bartkowski of Atlanta, and the continued presence of such passers as Roger Staubach of Dallas, Jim Hart of St. Louis, and Ken Stabler of Oakland showed that pro football may have once more found the arms and the inclination to meet and master the zone defenses.

At least nine factors influenced the return of the running game in the first half of the seventies:

(1) dropping to their zones, defenders were leaving big spaces open underneath them;

(2) the weakside of rotated zone defenses, the most common among all the varieties, really was weakened and made an inviting target for running plays;

(3) general surrender to zones occurred, and ball control replaced big-play strategy;

(4) defensive lines shrank with the adoption of the three-four defense by some teams;

(5) emphasis in linebacking shifted to smaller, faster men who could cover passes instead of big men who could stop the run;

(6) O. J. Simpson of Buffalo flowered into full maturity, gained an amazing 2,003 yards in 1973, and expanded the frontiers of possibility in running;

(7) run-oriented college teams produced runners and blockers in that mold;

(8) hashmarks on the playing field moved nearer the middle in 1972, robbing the defense of its partner the sideline; and

(9) five quarterbacks who had the wisdom and the chutzpah to attack zones—John Brodie of San Francisco, Len Dawson of Kansas City, Sonny Jurgensen of Washington, Bart Starr of Green Bay, and John Unitas of Baltimore—grew old and weak-armed and retired.

---

dominate. And a new crop of quarterbacks is slowly being weaned. "The old heads at quarterback have retired," safetyman Neal Craig of Buffalo said, "and the younger ones can't read yet. So the zones have been killing them."

PRO FOOTBALL LANGUAGE

The mysteries of football language came early to Elmer C. (Gus) Henderson. The coach of the 1939 Detroit Lions described how it had happened in the very first football game of his life.

It was in Berlin Heights, Ohio, he said, and on the first play of the game he was on the defense. The rival quarterback yelled, "COW OVER THE BARN!" With that, the fullback came charging over the middle of the line right through Gus Henderson for a 10-yard gain.

On the next play, the quarterback signaled, "BLACKBIRD DROP THE EGG IN THE ROBIN'S NEST!" Whereupon the wingback circled behind the tailback, took a handoff, and ran for a touchdown.

Right there, Gus Henderson had gotten a lesson in the importance of language to football. No team, in fact, can operate without it. It is all the strategy the team uses and the code it employs to scout others. With it, communication becomes instinctive among members of the team, as in the sound track of the Super Bowl IV movie when Kansas City coach Hank Stram says to quarterback Len Dawson, "Fifty-nine-eight-GO Reverse . . . You know."

Language is drafted by bright coaches, written down in playbooks, and spread from team to team through the natural social interaction of coaches, and through player and coach transfers.

Most of it came about as a result of that distinctive pro contribution, the three-end offense. Its creation made new terminology essential.

Two backs were left behind the quarterback. It did not take the equivalent of an Einstein in ripple-soled shoes to see that their positions need not remain static, nor did those of the three ends. They could be moved left and right, on the line of scrimmage and off it, in a variety of locations all of which remained legal so long as the rule requiring seven men on the line at the snap was met.

You could spread the left end and have a flanker on the right. Or spread the right end with a flanker on the left. Or spread both ends to one side.

The backs could be split behind the quarterback, or they could favor one side or the other. For example, one could set up behind the left tackle and the other directly behind the quarterback. That would be favoring the left side. Or they could set up just the opposite of that.

The concept of "strongside" and "weakside" emerged from this strategy. The third end was now consigned to a less glamorous station inside and was called the "tight end." He remained a pass-catcher but did less of it and more blocking. The name given his position and the evolution of his role into its present characteristics are the exclusive inventions of professional football.

The pros had backed into an unbalanced line, another device as old as football. Unbalanced line meant that there were more blockers on one side than the other. To one

side was a guard, tackle, and tight end. To the other there was only a guard and tackle. The side with the tight end became the "strong" side, the other the "weak." And this provided a foundation for language.

The first and most primitive solution for naming a three-end offense was to number the backs one through four and call, for example, "two right." It meant the number two back, the left halfback, flanked to the left.

Clark Shaughnessy offered another terminology solution when he was coach of the Los Angeles Rams in 1948-49. He named formations based on the commands given by farmers while plowing with their mules. If the left halfback flanked to the right, that was "gee." If the right halfback flanked left, that was "haw." But that was

Tom Landry, a maker of language.

73

Bill Kilmer of Washington hands off to Moses Denson against Los Angeles.

just the beginning. If the left end spread out wide it was "east" and if the right end spread out wide that was "west." So the combinations of the alignments of the flankers and ends, and the formations called by the 1948-49 Rams, were "east gee" and "west haw." For all his brilliance, Shaughnessy gave football many things it later forgot and these formation names were among them.

It remained for coaches Sid Gillman, Paul Brown, and Tom Landry to mold a language that was sensible. Gillman and Brown adopted literal terms to name three-end formations and Landry adopted colors.

If the backs were split behind the quarterback and one of them, the fullback, was on the same side as the tight end, Gillman called that "full," Brown called it "split right," and Landry called it "red."

If the backs were split behind the quar-

terback and the halfback was on the same side as the tight end, Gillman called that "half," Brown called it "split left," and Landry called it "green."

If the backs were not split but the full-back was behind the quarterback and the halfback was opposite the tight end, Gill-man called that "far," Brown called it "opposite," and Landry called it "brown."

And if the fullback was in the same place but the halfback was on the same side as the tight end, Gillman called that "near," Brown called it "wing," and Landry called it "blue."

When a coach today talks about his "system," he is talking essentially about how he names his formations, and the system he uses probably grew out of one of those devised by Gillman, Brown, or Landry.

It was ironic that a defensive coach worked out the scheme of colors for formations. At the time, Landry was defensive coach of the Giants. But a defense needs language to identify what it sees.

Lombardi picked it up for the Giants' offense. He subsequently took it to Green Bay with him, and Landry took it to Dallas. During their classic meetings in the sixties they were using the same terminology.

It is a further irony that the New York Giants no longer use "the New York Giants' system." Instead, present coach Bill Arnsparger is from the school of Paul Brown through Don Shula, and the Giants now speak that language.

As an adjunct to formation names, it is common for teams to name their three ends "x, y, and z." Hamp Pool, coach of the 1952-54 Rams, probably invented this terminology and it has become more or less standard in the NFL. But Lou Saban of the Buffalo Bills says, "We just call the flanker 'the flanker.'" That may slow down play-calling but is an achievement in clarity that rookies can appreciate on their first day in training camp.

Changes in *public* language were necessitated by the arrival of the three-end offense, too. There are no more "ends" in pro football. There are no more "fullbacks" and there are no more "halfbacks." Rather, there are "wide receivers" and "running backs." They were placed in so many positions that the AFL and NFL adopted general terms for what they are, and it became league policy with realignment in 1970.

The fundamental method for calling a play remains the same, to assign numbers to holes in the line and to each position in the backfield, then combine the two numbers to get the play. Thus, play 34 is the 3 back in the 4 hole.

What has been added are blocking "rules," the inexorable growth of which can be traced to Shaughnessy and the Bears in the thirties. In the years since, the responsibility of calling every block in the huddle has been removed from the quarterback. Now the center calls "Odd!" or "Even!" when he looks over the defensive front, and "rules" governing every situation are applied by each lineman. But the Shaughnessy influence of long ago persists.

The most colorful language he gave the Bears had to do with pulling blocks. The scheme at which he arrived for them was to begin the name of a block with the same first letter as the name of the position about to make the block. Secondly, blocks on linebackers got masculine names and blocks on defensive halfbacks (now cornerbacks) got feminine names. These were the blocks:

A guard on a linebacker—George
A tackle on a linebacker—Tom
An end on a linebacker—Ed
A guard on a halfback—Grace
A tackle on a halfback—Tess
An end on a halfback—Eve

The complicated pattern also involved assigning a letter of the alphabet to each position. A tackle was "A," a guard "G" if on the side of the play and "O" if on the "off" side.

Linemen still make George and Ed blocks today, and the "GO" call for pulling guards became part of the Green Bay Packers' language for their famous power sweep.

The Los Angeles Rams have always been a source of new language. Sid Gillman arrived as its professor in 1955. He added a new body of blocking jargon by naming blocks for playing cards in a deck. He reasoned that since his players spent all their

Small Miracle: Rule Blocking

The Los Angeles Rams came out of the huddle and arrived at the line of scrimmage during a game in the fifties. Quarterback Norm Van Brocklin began calling signals. At the same time, a Rams' tackle spotted a change in the defense and decided to call a blocking adjustment.

"Trey!" called the tackle.

Van Brocklin, who could wilt the strongest player on the field with a look of disgust, stopped his cadence and turned to the tackle. "It's 'Duce,' you dumb bastard!" he said.

The tackle's incorrect choice of terms resulted from a poor reading of the defense. The man requiring a double-team block, based on the way he lined up, was the second not the third man from the center. "Duce" not "Trey" was the correct call.

This helps explain the value of "rule blocking" and the Rams' system of "call blocking" worked out by then coach Sid Gillman and used on that play.

The offensive line has a critical need for good language. A blocker finds a body of considerable size directly ahead and a collision with him imminent. The simple blocking plan for the play may not work if the defender is in an unexpected location. Out of this comes the small miracle of rule blocking.

Gillman very likely brought it into pro football.

"I was rule-oriented when I came into the NFL from the University of Cincinnati in 1955," Gillman recalls. "I had used rule blocking in college. We had thought of every sort of line spacing we might face and then made rules such as, for a tackle, 'Inside.' That's all, just one word. It meant he blocked any man that he saw to the inside of him unless the man was beyond the offensive guard.

"But in the pros, the four-three was the thing. The rules lost their usefulness because the fronts were not as difficult and did not vary as much as they had in college. So we again sat down and took every defensive design possible and came up with our call blocking using the name of playing cards. That's how it evolved.

"Today you need a combination of rule and call blocking. You could use rule blocking completely, but you don't want to. It is not the most efficient way to block. You don't want to block a certain play against a four-three defense the same way for sixty minutes. Rule blocking would force you to do that. You must block a given play many ways to beat the good player. You don't worry about the ordinary player; it's the good one you must defeat. This is the way you build your game plan."

spare time at cards this might be one way to get them to remember the team's blocking terminology. So the Rams made "jack" blocks and "queen" blocks and came up with an especially novel system for double-teaming. An "ace" was a combination worked on the first man to the left or right of the center. A "duce" was on the second man, a "trey" on the third. It proved a popular system and since that time plagiarists have borrowed the card terminology for naming formations, too, making double wing "duce" and triple wing "trey."

To understand the contributions Clark Shaughnessy made to defensive language, look at the example of another coach and his attempts to do the same thing.

Bo McMillin of the 1948 Detroit Lions was conducting practice one day when he announced that a certain defensive maneuver in which a tackle charged to the left would henceforth be called, "Nebraska." However, if the tackle charged in the other direction, that would be named, "Kansas City."

An assistant coach protested. "But coach," he said, "One's a state and the other's a city."

"You trying to tell me how to coach?!" bellowed McMillin.

Shaughnessy's terms had "memory hooks." They were hybrid words whose components could be broken down to yield —however baroque it might be—the meaning of the term. "Wig Hal," for example, meant the weak inside tackle was supposed to hit and look. Hearing that call in the defensive huddle, Wig got ready to Hal.

Shaughnessy demonstrated further

once in an interview. Here is a typical exchange:

Shaughnessy: "Stash. That means the crash from the strongside."

Interviewer: "Strong crash?"

Shaughnessy: "Strong crash. Now you cook one up for the weakside. Go ahead. You can't miss. Stash is a strongside, so what's the weakside? Wash. See, you never forget those. You can learn them that quick."

When he was defensive coach of the Chicago Bears from 1956 until 1962, Shaughnessy kept inventing such terms. I Men or defensive tackles (who played inside) were SI on the strongside, WI on the weak. O men could be SO and WO. The left O man was Lon, the right Roy. Corner linebackers were Cobs, or Stub and Buck, or in inside positions, Link, the left, and Rip, the right. The Deks, or deep backs, were Lou, Rose, Stock, Wot, Les, Rus, Sam, or Jill, depending on the call.

The blitz consumed Shaughnessy because it facilitated his language-making and he played it constantly. But the man-for-man coverage it forced allowed opponents to bomb the Bears easily. By 1962 Shaughnessy was bombed into retirement.

The pass rushes and blitzes his middle linebacker called had names such as "Brown Stash Mut Purple Jack Shuffle Right Wheel Left." Or "Green Shuffle Slant Strong Crush." Or "Green Squeel." Or "Green Storm," "Green Lightning," "Green Tornado," or "Green Castro Tight."

The practice—however inexplicable it seems—of assigning female names to linebacker positions must be rooted in Shaughnessy's earlier blocking terminology. The New York Giants began it with "Sara, Meg, and Wanda" in the fifties. It is the greatest of football ironies that the living metaphors for strength, speed, courage, and manliness may take the field as "Sara, Meg, and Wanda."

MATTER AND MACHINES

Four machines in particular dramatically changed pro football. They were the 16 millimeter film projector, the computer, the copying machine, and, outranking all others in influence, the television camera.

NFL teams today are permanently entangled in film. This condition can be traced to three developments of the forties and fifties and to two coaches, Sid Gillman and Paul Brown.

These were the developments: first, 16 millimeter was adopted by all football coaches because of the relative economy of the materials and the compactness of the camera; second, projectors (the Bell & Howell Time & Study model and the Eastman Kodak Analyst) were made that ran film backward and forward; and third, the

Good equipment is vital to pro football.

77

NFL wrote strict rules governing exchange of films by teams, bringing order and making it fair for all.

Sid Gillman has been the Darryl F. Zanuck of football. For his honeymoon in 1935, he took his bride to the Chicago All-Star Game. He then spent $15 of the $25 they had between them on a used 35 mm. De-Vray projector he saw in the window of a pawn shop.

After the football game, without a lot of wild spending, the Gillmans proceeded to Denison College in Ohio, where he was to begin work as an assistant coach. He knew projectors and film because as a boy growing up in Minneapolis he had worked for his father, who operated a chain of movie theaters. Now Gillman arranged for his father's employees to save newsreel clips of the big college football games of the day. (They had been destroying them immediately after use.)

That film held the tactical secrets of all

Sid Gillman, film-making genius.

the great coaches of the thirties. Hour after hour, Gillman ran it through his DeVray. Film was quite flammable in those days and it was not uncommon for Gillman, who favored a pipe, to tap ashes on the floor where film lay and accidentally set it afire. When that happened, the coaching staff of Denison or, later, Miami of Ohio or Ohio State would rush out of the room for a bucket of water to douse the flames.

Paul Brown and his original Cleveland Browns assistants, Blanton Collier and Weeb Ewbank, used a crude, hand-cranked moviola (a film-study machine common in the movie industry) to revolutionize pro football in the forties. They became the first professional staff to study film year-round.

Before Brown, *Football Yearbook* wrote in 1952, "Football coaches spent the off-season going through the motions of answering mail, idly picking their teeth until lunch, after which they wound up a tough day with an excursion to the nearest golf course."

Brown, Collier, and Ewbank screened every Browns' play, recorded its success or failure, and determined what or who went wrong if the play had failed. The film and notes were filed away for future practices and classroom lectures. "We're making football a science," Brown said, and he was right.

The Rams once decided to film in Cinemascope. This all but outraged other coaching staffs who, on receiving a Rams' film, had to stop what they were doing and change to an anamorphic lens, or else the images were elongated and fuzzy. This led to the occasion when Vince Lombardi appeared at a coaching clinic in the Catskills

A Fount of Coaches

There is a college in Ohio that is nowhere near the white beaches of Florida yet is named Miami of Ohio in the usual sports page abbreviation and without which the NFL would be poorer.

Its graduates have included Bill Arnsparger, Paul Brown, Weeb Ewbank, and Jack Faulkner, all of whom became NFL coaches of note. Sid Gillman coached at Miami, joining its exclusive fraternity.

Some of Miami's famous graduates did not aspire to pro football but became well-known college coaches. They influenced the pros, however, because the top college coaches always influence the pros. They were Earl (Red) Blaik, Paul Dietzel, Woody Hayes, Ara Parseghian, and Bo Schembechler.

Sid Gillman's four years as head coach at Miami were probably its most productive. But there had already been three famous graduates

—Blaik, Brown, and Ewbank.

Blaik went on to become a West Point cadet and then Army's most successful head coach ever, winning the national championship in 1944, 1945, and 1946.

Brown originally enrolled at Ohio State but when he was told that at 5 feet 7 inches he was too small to be its quarterback, he transferred to Miami and became a regular. Later he became the most successful football coach in history.

Ewbank became the only pro coach to win a championship with teams in two different leagues, the Baltimore Colts and New York Jets.

Gillman's Miami teams won 31 games, lost 6, and tied 1, and his teams included linebackers-backs Faulkner and Parseghian and linemen Arnsparger, Schembechler, and Dietzel.

Faulkner later was a "coach of the

year" with Denver in the American Football League. Parseghian coached national championship teams at Notre Dame, and Dietzel won the same honor at LSU. Arnsparger eventually became the assistant coach who masterminded the Miami Dolphins' "53" defense. He later became head coach of the New York Giants.

Schembechler, as coach of Michigan, became the annual rival of Ohio State's Hayes for the championship of the Big Ten Conference. Hayes, like Gillman, did not graduate from Miami but had been its head coach.

Why has Miami produced so many coaches? "First, it is a beautiful school, a gorgeous place that attracts students in all fields, and secondly, it has always had a tremendous physical education program," Gillman says. "There are coaches all over who went there."

---

and burst into the room carrying some Rams' film. "Who's in charge here?!" he demanded. "I gotta have an anamorphic lens right now!"

During their off-season the pros also become small publishing companies. Here another machine plays its part—the modern copiers made by Xerox and others. They make it possible for a staff of eight to ten men (the fewer the better, for security's sake) to duplicate thousands of pages needed for the 100 or more playbooks that must be ready for training camp. It is done quickly, efficiently, and without the ink mess of stencil machines.

Computers also are everywhere. They help teams scout draft choices and opponents; they program the giant message boards in some new stadiums; they help ticket managers allocate seats and keep

records; they make analyses of statistics; and the Atlanta Falcons, San Francisco 49ers, and New Orleans Saints have computer terminals in their press boxes to help compile game day statistics speedily.

No teams own computers; they're too expensive. The Dallas Cowboys, however, are the majority owner of the computer operated by the Quadra scouting combine in Palo Alto, California. The Cowboys computerized drafting of players from the start. Tex Schramm, their general manager, held the same position with the Rams in the fifties and the Los Angeles scouting system was the most advanced in the league at the time. Schramm then joined CBS Sports and coordinated, among other things, the coverage of the 1956 Winter Olympics, where computers were used to total scores and statistics. Schramm combined these experiences in Dallas.

An expert named Salaam Querishi made a secret computer analysis for the Cowboys of the measurable skills of a football player. This study formed the basis for the Cowboys' computer scouting plan. But it proved expensive. Dallas invited the Rams and 49ers to join, forming a scouting combine called TROIKA, because it had three members. San Diego became a fourth and the name was changed to QUADRA. The never-ending spiral of name changes has apparently been checked for now, because there has been no change to accommodate the recent addition of the Seattle Seahawks to the combine.

The other scouting combines are CEPO, BLESTO-VIII, and Galaxy. Any one of them may receive as many as 30,000-40,000 reports from scouts each year. Computers assimilate the data and give it back at draft time. But, beginning with the "full disclosure" principle of CEPO and falling off from there, philosophies vary markedly from combine to combine on how much information that is gotten by the scout for one team should be shared with all the others. Cincinnati, Kansas City, Oakland, and Tampa Bay do not belong to combines or put much stock in the worth of computers in drafting. It appears there is a considerable amount of revisionist thinking going on about using machines in this area.

Humans scout, humans err. Until computers are given Air Travel cards, five days' clean clothes, eyes to see, legs to walk with, arms to time and weigh and measure players, an understanding of how players move and react, and quotients to measure courage and desire, the same verdict will keep coming in on them: "If you put in garbage, you will get garbage."

It might be said that neither Bill McPeak nor Ed Hughes cut wide swathes through the NFL as head coaches. But these men pioneered computerized play analysis in pro football. McPeak was the head coach of the Redskins and Hughes his assistant when a computer whiz named Bill Witzel approached them about 1965. He offered the services of himself and his company's computer to help the Redskins get the goods on their opponents. Hughes, especially, embraced the idea from the start.

He and Witzel would sit together in the press box during games, Witzel with a printout before him. It contained data identifying the strategies used by the opponent in previous games. If the rival quarterback called a play he had not called in the same field situation in a recent game, Witzel would say to Hughes, "New Business." Hughes would call down to the field to tell the bench to make an adjustment. But if the rival quarterback called the predicted play, Witzel would say, "Old Business."

At least nine teams moved immediately to copy this system. The daring duo of the press boxes had set off curiosity everywhere. As others copied the Redskins, no team got a better rundown than Dallas. It had an assistant coach, Dick Nolan, who was a brother-in-law of Ed Hughes. At first, the Cowboys might have been behind the Redskins in this area of computerization, but they caught up fast.

Already a world capital of red tape, Washington continued to be a center for NFL computer technology. When Vince Lombardi went there as head coach and general manager of the Redskins in 1969, he made a trade with Cleveland for quar-

The view from the assistant coaches' booth, Busch Memorial Stadium.

terback Frank Ryan specifically so mathematics wizard Ryan could set up the team's new computer operation. Ryan later formed his own company, with Lombardi as executive consultant. The coach's only pay was to be the exclusive use of Ryan's services among NFL teams. Ryan is now director of computer systems for the U.S. House of Representatives.

The titan of play analysis today is a Southern Californian who is part owner of APEX Data Processing, Inc., which feeds data to as many as 20 of the NFL teams. He is Joe Guardino, and in 1967 he paid his way to a USC game at Northwestern to take down data on the game and later computerize it for coach John McKay of USC. McKay was ecstatic about the material and recommended Guardino to other coaches. Guardino's clientele spread throughout college

and pro football.

Guardino's teams may receive any of hundreds of varieties of printouts of their choice in their own terminology and with an absolute guarantee of privacy. They send data to APEX by Xerox telecopier or computer terminal and receive the assimilated printout by the same method in reverse. Three game films of an opponent painstakingly "broken down" play by play become a single sheet of data indicating the opponent blitzes 7 out of 10 times on third down and eight.

Another Southern Californian named Bud Goode performs a different type of computer service. It has been used by the Rams, St. Louis Cardinals, and Redskins. Goode carries out factor and multiple regression analysis of the regular weekly NFL statistics to determine, simply, what are the major criterions for winning games? Should a team run more, or pass more? How much should it expect to gain per pass in order to win? And so on.

Goode once advised John Guedel-Art Linkletter Productions of such things as how the ratings might be expected to dip in Bemidji, Minnesota if the daily Linkletter program had a guest on who would discuss extra-marital relationships. Goode also began syndicated newspaper columns in which he predicted the winners of college and pro grames and the voting pattern of members of the U.S. Supreme Court.

Not even the computer approaches the television camera for having made an enormous impact on pro football. The pro style of playing the game is expanded with each telecast as youngsters watch the techniques of the Ken Andersons and the Chuck Foremans so they can imitate them in every detail.

THE SWEEPING CHANGES IN EQUIPMENT

Teams of the twenties took to the road with each player carrying an unsightly package identified as a football uniform. The pants had built-in thigh and knee pads. This made them virtually impossible to clean thoroughly; an occasional scraping with a wire brush sufficed. And for traveling purposes, these soiled pants-pads were stuffed with the jersey down one leg and the shoes down the other. A team arriving with 20 of these must have added an aromatic charm to a hotel lobby.

In contrast, the Buffalo Bills travel today attended by two equipment managers who oversee 11 trunks of gear. The equipment is trucked directly from the airport to the stadium, while the players proceed unencumbered to their hotel by bus. This is standard practice for all teams.

The Bills' travel gear includes sparkling clean uniforms, pants, pads, jerseys, shoes, socks, medical equipment, and even capes for all players and members of the staff. According to the *Buffalo Courier-Journal,* the Bills must spend $9,000 a year on athletic tape alone and dispense up to 2,900 shoelaces in a season.

A myth of the NFL's early years was that Jim Thorpe wore shoulder pads lined with sheet metal. It wasn't so, and if he played today he wouldn't consider it. Players want protection from their pads but they also want them to be lightweight. For example, new nylon-mesh jerseys have become so popular that the Green Bay Packers, who play in the league's coldest climate, went through the entire 1975 season in the mesh jerseys, even though they also own a set of wool ones. On the coldest days, they fortified themselves with thermal underwear.

Improvisation is rampant, especially among the speed-conscious wide receivers and defensive backs. They may be seen trimming slices from their foam rubber thigh and knee pads in order to make them as light as possible. Or they may shun manufacturers' girdle hip pads in favor of homemade models fashioned by taping pieces of foam to their supporter strap. Washington Redskins' cornerback Pat Fischer wears disposable diapers for knee pads.

To look up into the crown of a helmet of the seventies is to view a marvel of space-age technology. Foam rubber and vinyl air cushions are packed into every available corner. They snap in or out, have valves

The Little Men

Buddy Young, Baltimore Colts.

Eddie LeBaron, Dallas Cowboys.

They make nice inspirational stories for *Boys' Life,* but inside they are driven men.

"All I heard through my career was that I was too small," 5-foot 10-inch running back Greg Pruitt of the Cleveland Browns says. "I despised it. I developed a complex about my size and have been trying to live it down ever since."

The little men live in a world in which they are so undersized they may be mistaken for office boys; that actually happened to 5-foot 8½-inch wide receiver Randy Vataha while he was waiting to negotiate his contract with the New England Patriots.

"The worst discrimination in the world isn't color, it's size," says Buddy Young, a black man who at 5 foot 5 inches was one of the smallest players in NFL history.

"When I came into the league I

was five-five and weighed one sixty-five. The [New York] Yankees acted like I was some kind of sideshow, like I was supposed to go out with the band at halftime."

Instead he took the field with the other players for the opening kickoff, and went on to an exciting nine-year career as a running back for the Yanks, Dallas Texans, and Baltimore Colts.

Two men of Young's 5-5 stature entered the league in recent years, Mack Herron with the New England Patriots and Howard Stevens with the New Orleans Saints. They left those clubs eventually but they were part of a seventies revival of the little man.

It seemed nearly every team had a man 5-foot-10 and 190 or less— Buffalo's Tony Greene, a safety and cornerback who became all-pro; 1,000-yard rusher Pruitt of Cleveland; Denver's Floyd Little and his running back successor, Otis Armstrong, who gained a stunning 1,407 yards one season; Houston's exciting kick runner Billy Johnson; Miami's Mercury Morris; Oakland's Clarence Davis, who scored a miraculous last-seconds touchdown to win a playoff game for the Raiders over Miami; Pittsburgh's Lynn Swann; Los Angeles's Harold Jackson; St. Louis's Mel Gray and Terry Metcalf; and many more.

How can the presence of these comparative midgets, in such numbers, be explained in a league in which the average size in 1975 was 6 foot 2 inches and 222½ pounds.

"One big reason is situation substitution," says Al LoCasale, himself a 5-foot 4-inch front office executive for the Raiders. "A small man today can be a defensive back who goes in in five- or six-back defenses. Or he can be a running back who is used the way Miami

used Morris and Jim Kiick when it had both of them. Morris might be in the game on first down to run the sweep and then Kiick would go in the game on third down to come out of the backfield for a pass. That's the kind of situation substitution that is helping give the smaller players a chance."

Size, LoCasale said, is relative. "When we drafted Jack Tatum first [in 1971 from Ohio State], some thought that at five-ten he was too short. But the man who had been playing free safety for us before Tatum arrived was Dave Grayson, who is five-eight. Compared to him, Tatum was a giant."

Professional football has always had its little men. Doak Walker, all-round great for the Detroit Lions teams coached by Buddy Parker, was 5 foot 10 inches and 172. Tommy McDonald, 5 foot 9 and 175, was virtually written off as too small by College All-Star coaches in 1957 but went on to become a wide receiver for five teams during a 12-year career, catching 495 passes.

And then there was Eddie Le-Baron. At 5 feet 7 inches, he played 11 years at quarterback in the NFL for Washington and Dallas. He succeeded the legendary Sammy Baugh as the Redskins' quarterback and in 1960 he was the expansion Cowboys' first quarterback. LeBaron led the NFL in passing one year, 1958, and played in the Pro Bowl four times.

Writer Mickey Herskowitz said LeBaron "looked like Johnny of Philip Morris," and Dallas end Billy Howton described what it was like catching LeBaron's passes. "You run your deep pattern and look back and nobody's there," Howton said. "You can't see him. And, suddenly, it looks like the ball is coming out of a silo."

for inflation, and are connected by tubes that carry the air in them away uniformly on impact.

A more visible aspect of the helmet is the characteristic team emblem on the outside. The first of these was the Los Angeles horn design, painted on the team's helmets by a halfback named Fred Gehrke in 1948. Since then the idea has been copied by every team in the league except the Cleveland Browns. These emblems have been central to the process by which pro football teams have gained identity with the American sports public.

The major contributions of the helmet face masks, or double bars, triple bars, or "birdcages," have been that players now usually go into retirement with something close to the full complement of teeth and with noses that do not resemble pancakes. On the other hand, face masks have contributed to the dehumanization of the sport, for where once a face and some hint of personality were visible, all that can be

Ernie McMillan doing lat pulldowns in the St. Louis locker room.

seen now are a helmet, a cage, and earholes.

It was an historic moment when, in 1934, the New York Giants changed into tennis shoes for the second half of the NFL championship game against the Chicago Bears. The tennis shoes helped give the Giants more traction on the frozen field and they posted a great upset 30-13.

Under the same conditions today, players for both teams would have two or three different models of shoes for the playing surface involved, would test one or more before the game, and probably change from one style to another during the game until at last arriving at the pair that worked best.

The apparatus on playing fields and in locker rooms further emphasize the influences machines have had on pro football. Outside, an array of sleds, dummies, "shiver boards," running ropes, and other training devices await each practice. They may also include weightlifting machines such as the Universal and Nautilius, which defy quick description except to say that one sits on them, lays on them, or hangs from them pulling or pushing weight and growing strong.

Within the locker room, trainers use many machines, always with the advice and counsel of the team physicians, and with many years of experience themselves in physical conditioning. Their helpers include diathermy, ultrasound, hydrocollator, and knee rehabilitation machines; bicycles; saunas; ice machines; and that old favorite, the whirlpool bath.

One of the most talked-about changes in football materiel has been artificial turf. NFL teams now play on AstroTurf at Buffalo, Chicago, Cincinnati, Detroit, Houston, New Orleans, Philadelphia, St. Louis, Seattle, and San Francisco; on Tartan Turf at Dallas, Kansas City, and Pittsburgh; and on Poly-Turf at New England.

Artificial surfaces drain better and dry faster, and during rainy games players' jerseys and the yard markers on the field are not obliterated by mud. The multiplicity of events in many stadiums make artificial turf seem a necessity. But those who argue against it say it causes more injuries, a claim not supported by surveys. In addition, the high costs of making and maintaining it has driven Tartan Turf and Poly-Turf off the market, leaving it virtually open to Astro-Turf. And a grass system called Prescription Athletic Turf has been installed at Denver, Washington, and Miami.

THE OTHER LEAGUES

It would be a serious mistake to assume that, because they have passed from the scene, the other pro leagues that have come and gone did so without leaving any lasting impression on the sport. They most certainly did.

There have been five of them—the American Football League of 1926, the American Football League of 1936-37, the American Football League of 1940-41, the All-America Football Conference of 1946-49, and the World Football League of 1974 and part of 1975.

The AFL of 1960-69 is omitted from that list because it is not dead. It is roughly half the NFL today as 10 of the 13 teams in the American Football Conference.

The All-America Football Conference folded in 1950, but three of its teams came into the NFL intact—the Cleveland

The Incredible AFC Success Story

The American Football League began as a struggling stepchild that Oakland's Wayne Valley, one of the first franchise-holders, named "The Foolish Club." The AFL grew, developing new stars, gaining television exposure, and eventually playing the NFL in Super Bowl I. Parity was reached in Super Bowl III with the victory of Joe Namath and the New York Jets. Since that Sunday in Miami, the scales have tipped farther and farther as the renamed American Football Conference has posted an incredible list of successes in its competition with the rival NFC.

The American Conference has had more celebrated players, made more news, developed more young quarterbacks, and won seven of the first 10 Super Bowls and three of the first six AFC-NFC Pro Bowls.

The sensational Miami Dolphins, winners of 17 games without a defeat in 1972, and their successors as Super Bowl champions, the Pittsburgh Steelers, were American Conference teams. The most talked-about division became the AFC Central of Pittsburgh, Cincinnati, Houston, and Cleveland; it replaced the NFC Central as "The Black-and-Blue Division."

A willingness to experiment with new areas of strategy marked the 10-year history of the American Football League, and that flexibility continued in the AFC. Miami gave pro football its version of the three-four defense, its "53," and the defense was adopted by other teams such as Buffalo, Houston, and New England. At the same time, no NFC team adopted the three-four as its primary defense. NFC teams stayed instead with the traditional four-three.

It should be pointed out, however, that the remarkable success enjoyed by the AFC in the Super Bowl was helped by the presence of two former NFC teams, Baltimore and Pittsburgh. These teams were transferred to their new conference as part of realignment in 1970 and Baltimore went on to win Super Bowl V while Pittsburgh was the champion in games IX and X.

Furthermore, the NFC held a lead entering the 1976 season in interconference games both in the regular season, 122 to 112 with six ties, and in preseason, 167 to 164 with 11 ties, since 1970. And the NFC, frustrated by the domination of the other conference in Super Bowls, started one of its own by winning back to back Pro Bowls in 1975 at Miami and in 1976 at New Orleans.

But the AFC had the game's most glamorous names. Namath predicted the Jets' victory over Baltimore in Super Bowl III, then made it happen.

It seemed as if AFC players always were making headlines. In 1970, George Blanda, an aging quarterback and kicker who was then 42 years old, saved five games in five weeks either by kicking or passing the Raiders to a win or tie. He threw two touchdown passes to lead Oakland past Pittsburgh. He kicked a 48-yard field goal to tie Kansas City with three seconds remaining and move Oakland into first place in the Western Division on percentage points. He kicked another last-second field goal, this one from 52 yards away, to beat Cleveland. He replaced Daryle Lamonica late in the game against Denver and threw a touchdown pass to Fred Biletnikoff to win it. And he finished his amazing five-week run when he kicked a 16-yard field goal with four seconds left to defeat San Diego.

Larry Csonka and O. J. Simpson were the next AFC players to dom-inate interest. Csonka, then with Miami, was the key ingredient in the Dolphins' powerful offense while Simpson was setting all-time rushing records for Buffalo at the same time. Csonka reached the 1,000-yard level for Miami in 1971, 1972, and 1973. Simpson reached 1,251 in 1972; the unbelievable figure of 2,003 in 1973; 1,125 in 1974; and was back in the stratosphere in '75 with a mercurial figure of 1,817 yards.

At least nine fresh faces appeared at quarterback on AFC teams. Pittsburgh rebuilt around Terry Bradshaw, whom it made the first choice of the league in the 1970 draft. Left-handed Ken Stabler surfaced as the number one quarterback in Oakland. Ken Anderson of Cincinnati won two passing championships. Bob Griese was the calm, steady leader of Miami's Super Bowl-winning teams (with the help of old pro Earl Morrall). Other young faces at quarterback were Bert Jones of Baltimore, Joe Ferguson of Buffalo, Dan Pastorini of Houston, and Jim Plunkett, traded by New England to the San Francisco 49ers.

In its infant years, the AFL also had pioneered in placing the names of players on the backs of its football jerseys. But not everything the AFL tried was successful. The two-point conversion after touchdowns, modeled after the same rule in college football, was used successfully only nine times in all the years of its existence in the rule book of the original AFL. In the beginning, the AFL dressed its game officals in unusual attire that could easily have doubled as softball uniforms. Later, the customary stripes were added, but in red not black. With the merger, orthodoxy came to the outfits worn by the officials of the AFC.

Browns, San Francisco 49ers, and Baltimore Colts. Cleveland won the NFL championship in its first year in the league. San Francisco had a stylish offense guided by T quarterback wizard Frankie Albert, trained at Stanford by Clark Shaughnessy. Baltimore had a sharp young quarterback in Y. A. Tittle in 1950 but little else; when another franchise came about in 1953 under new owners led by Carroll Rosenbloom, the Colts began upward mobility that would culminate when they won the championship in 1958 and 1959.

The AAFC also gave pro football Tom Landry. He was in a group of players who moved from the defunct franchise at Yankee Stadium across the Harlem River to the New York Giants at the Polo Grounds. The umbrella defense probably would never have emerged without that group because it also included Harmon Rowe and Otto Schnellbacher.

The World Football League has been so recent in our past that to call it up in detail would only cause more of the anguish that was rampant for every day of its 18 months of misguided existence. The WFL operated from March 31, 1974, when the Toronto Northmen, a team that never played a game by that name, gave the league believability for a time by signing players Larry Csonka, Paul Warfield, and Jim Kiick, until September 22, 1975. On the latter date, it announced termination of all its operations.

RULES—WHERE THE PROS DIFFER MOST

More than anything else, rules set apart the professional style of football from that played by colleges and high schools. The pros have legislated against the field goal, a play often regarded (except by the 28 NFL kickers) as dull. They kickoff from farther back to prevent the ball from being downed in the end zone. They start every play virtually in the middle of the field now that they have moved their inbounds lines farther in. They play every game to sudden death, except that it is limited to one 15-minute quarter in preseason and regular season. They protect pass receivers with limits on how much they can be bumped around. And they allow pass rushers to head slap, and pass protectors to block without their fists nailed to their chests.

But the colleges laid the foundation. They had all the hallmark rules—the size of the field, four downs to make 10 yards, a neutral zone between the lines, seven offensive men on the line at the snap—long before the NFL was formed. The pros did not make a major rules change, in fact, until the momentous league meetings of 1933. It was then that the professionals allowed passing anywhere behind the line, invented inbounds lines, and—in a change they would undo in the seventies—moved the goal posts to the goal line to help field goal kickers and increase scoring.

Rules are born of specific moments, plays, games, events. For example, the Super Bowl is always played under warm-weather conditions but its equivalent in 1932, the NFL playoff between the Bears and the Portsmouth Spartans, was scheduled for Chicago in December. And a blizzard was in progress. The game was moved indoors into the cramped Chicago Stadium. There the field came right up to the walls, so rules were made allowing for in-

The Professor

Referee Norm Schachter has retired. He leaves to become an observer of game officials after 22 years, an eventful time in which he watched—and helped shape—many changes in the way pro football is played and supervised.

If it were possible to study a time-lapse photograph of Schachter at work all those years, we would probably see the grass under his feet turn to artificial turf—although more than half the fields remained real grass. We would see the goal posts change from the rickety wood structures of the fifties into the sleek single standard metal models, painted bright yellow and reaching to a new height of 30 feet above the crossbar—the result of an important disputed game that Schachter worked.

We would see the NFL's 41-year experiment with goal posts on the goal line come to an end, as they moved back to the end line. Elaborate and often confusing decorations in the end zone would be forbidden, and the end zone would be ringed with safer foam rubber pylons instead of flags. The field would take on a broad six-foot-wide white border to protect photographers from sideline collisions. And further change would come when inbounds lines were moved all the way in to a point even with the goal post uprights.

As the time-lapse photo of Schachter's career continued, players would begin to wear their names on their backs, and what once had been called simply the chain crew would become the box-man, rodmen, drive start, and forward stake indicator. The ancient stadium clocks with their ponderous minute and second hands would give way to massive electronic scoreboards 30 feet high using thousands of tiny lights and circuits operated by a computer. And timing boxes would be installed nearer the field for ticking down the seconds used by the offense to start its play.

The referee's "crew" would increase to six men with the addition of a "line judge." These men would be forbidden to work any football game except at the professional level, a move Schachter called "the greatest thing that ever happened to NFL officiating." Now they would be obliged to arrive in the scheduled city a day ahead and carry out extensive film study of their past performance and carefully plan the next day's game.

The number of NFL teams would more than double and the season would extend in length until Schachter would begin flying on airplanes 120,000 miles a year.

Television would affect changes. It would fall to the referee—while technicians by the dozens in trucks and studios waited anxiously—to meet the three-and-four rule for commercials (three in the first and third quarters and four in the second and fourth, or vice versa, but never when the ball was inside the 20-yard line).

Referees would be drawn further into the world of electronics with the introduction of microphones worn under their striped shirts and operated by on and off switches on units at their waists. Now they would announce penalty violations as well as signal them.

Their habitual pattern of stepping off yardage, spotting the ball, signaling "ready for play," and going to their position, had already been altered by the new "preliminary signals." Now they reached to to switch on the mike. They had to form a new pattern of habit.

Sudden death, kickoffs from the 35 not the 40, missed field goals returning to the line of scrimmage, and only the two outside men going down on kicks . . . these would come in to change the game and the way officials worked it.

And there was a Super Bowl. More than anyone else, Schachter became the referee of the game of games. He worked the first, the fifth, and the tenth.

Schachter also called the 1965 playoff between Baltimore and Green Bay in which an argued field goal resulted in the extension of the goal post uprights. And he was the referee of the famous Ice Game at Green Bay in 1967 when, under arctic conditions, the Packers won the NFL title on Bart Starr's last-minute quarterback sneak. In that game, Joe Connell, the umpire of Schachter's crew, reached to take a whistle out of his mouth and drew away a part of his lips as well.

Schachter also was an official with a large sense of humor who ran his crew with firmness. Once he spotted his back judge staring aimlessly at the crowd during a break. At that moment, the public-address system blared, "Today's attendance is seventy-five thousand four hundred seventy-three, a new Cotton Bowl record." Schachter held up the game and called the back judge to his side. "That the same count you got?" he asked. The back judge got the message.

Schachter once endured the ignominy of being suspended from the league, along with his entire crew, for the remainder of a season after a head linesman—the crew member most responsible for knowing the down—lost count and took a down away from the Los Angeles Rams in a critical late-season game against the Chicago Bears.

Schachter returned to start the next season with no harm done to his reputation. Indeed, his competence, neutrality, and integrity

Referee Norm Schachter.

were regarded so highly that he could kid about his work without incurring prejudice. He once ruled intentional grounding of a pass against Philadelphia quarterback Roman Gabriel in a game against Dallas, and the Eagles put up a strong protest. On the next play, Schachter called roughing the passer against Dallas.

"Norm!" middle linebacker Lee Roy Jordan of Dallas anguished. "Are you making up for that last call with this one?"

"No, Lee Roy," Schachter deadpanned, "I usually wait two or three plays before I even it up."

No other person had a more encyclopedic knowledge of the rules. Schachter literally "wrote the rule book." He transferred his natural inclinations as a professional educator to his part-time work as NFL referee. Holder of a Ph.D. in education, he became principal of Los Angeles High School and then one of the 12 superintendents of the Los Angeles City Schools, drawing a tough area with big problems—south central Los Angeles. He was, in effect, the school superintendent of Watts.

His textbooks in English grammar sold over a million copies. The same high standards he applied to the learning of English, he applied to the 17 rules or chapters of the NFL rule book. He annually wrote the 200 questions submitted to officials for their off-season rules review, and the quizzes given them at an annual four-day clinic. In this manner, Dr. Schachter became professor and dean to 80 pro football officials.

The culmination of the merger of two leagues in 1970 accentuated the need for a revision of the professional rule book. It was then crammed into a pocket book and the latest changes, exceptions, and approved rulings filled every available space on inside covers and front pages. In supervising the revision, Schachter—while carefully staying within the limits of good judgment and altering in no way the essence of the content—made it clearer than it had ever been, tossed out much dead wood, and coded the rules to make them more responsive to all users of the book. It appeared for the first time in its new form in 1974 and won rousing approval.

Schachter had occupied a position of the highest eminence in his field when he was named to referee Super Bowl I. The honor was again his in game V. Then, in 1975, trouble was brewing in pro football.

A St. Louis receiver, Mel Gray, crossed into the end zone and a pass came into his arms, then caromed away. St. Louis was awarded a touchdown and, later in overtime, won the game. The losing Washington Redskins argued strongly against the decision. Other decisions in other games went under the microscope of public opinion, and a current of anti-official feelings ran strong. In Minnesota an official was struck by a flying bottle.

The integrity of all officials was in question and clearly they and the league could not afford to send anyone but the best-qualified to work the biggest, most widely watched game of all—Super Bowl X.

The choice, of course, was Schachter. He quietly arrived in Miami, assembled his crew, and grilled them constantly with the sort of quizzes the professor saves for graduate students in their final exam. Then Schachter went out to the last NFL game he would ever referee.

No Super Bowl ever went as crisply. He moved it along, halted flareups immediately, separated the players, and signaled "ready for play" without a moment's hesitation. The fired-up teams in an exciting game full of pressure were given no chance to do anything except play football. Schachter and his staff flawlessly moved through their "mechanics" and the game went off without a hitch. Then, a little maudlin and a little misty-eyed, Norm Schachter walked from the Orange Bowl and 22 years. . .

He was years from mandatory retirement, but he had completed his feat of working a Super Bowl every five years and he was ready to call it quits. He didn't feel old; mile after mile on the exercycle in his basement had kept him trim. But a lot of time had passed and he had seen the game change a lot.

He still had his cherished anonymity, for if no one knew him it meant he had worked a good game. He recalled one time in Baltimore when he had honored the request of two youngsters for an autograph. As they walked away, one said to the other, "Who was that old buzzard, anyway?"

Free Substitution and Specialization

Chuck Bednarik, two-way player.

One of the most disputed pieces of football legislation ever can be found in rule three of the college and high school books, "Periods, Time Factors, and Substitutions," and in rule five of the professional book, "The Players, Substitutes, and Their Equipment." Those rules permit free substitution in football. In the history of the sport, that subject may have been debated more than any other by the decision-makers of amateur football. In the pro game, free substitution ranks as one of the most vital rules ever passed.

"Platoonery," the derisive term given it by its opponents, was actually practiced in the twenties by Knute Rockne of Notre Dame. His "shock troops" started a game and then gave way to the regulars. Rockne explained that he did not "start that gang to wear down the opposition. I start them so my regulars—and particularly my quarterback—can have a chance to study the formations of the opponents and spot their strengths and especially their weaknesses."

It was a mixed blessing to be a shock troop, because football was going through a period of rules changes at the time. At first a sub-stitute could not return to the game at all, then could return in the second half if he had gone out in the first. Finally, another change was passed providing that a player leaving the game had to stay out for the rest of the quarter.

World War II decimated rosters and it became necessary to use every able body. Free substitution was adopted by the colleges in 1941 and the pros in 1943. Strangely, coaches often ignored the rule, even though it was available to use. The first to take advantage of it was Fritz Crisler of Michigan in 1945. He threw two platoons at the great Army team led by Doc Blanchard and Glenn Davis and held the high-scoring Cadets to a respectable 28-7 victory. Michigan went on to win the Rose Bowl championship in 1947. Army, with Red Blaik as coach and Sid Gillman his assistant, adopted two-platoon football.

A rules change stopping the clock when the ball changed hands assisted "platoonery." The switch to it continued among all colleges that could afford to recruit 22, not 11, good players. Edwin Pope of the *Miami Herald* wrote that Fritz Crisler's first step in 1945 "grew into a monster that bankrupted athletic associations and disgusted aficionados of solid old-time football."

One-way football was restored in 1953. A player leaving the game had to stay out the rest of the quarter. That was modified in 1955 to allow him to return once in the quarter. Other easements followed but in general there was one-way football in the colleges for 10 years until two-platooning was restored in 1965. During the same period, coaches found themselves forbidden to "coach from the sideline" by sending substitutes in and out with plays, so they developed elaborate hand signals that made them appear to be magicians performing their best tricks on Ted Mack's Original Amateur Hour.

The professionals' debate over free substitutions was of far shorter duration. The wartime rule was limited in 1946 to only three men at a time, but in 1950 free substitution became standard in pro football.

This was the time of the Eagle and "umbrella" defenses. While the colleges were in the throes of debate, the pros developed the four-three defense and its great specialists such as linemen Gino Marchetti, Art Donovan, and Leo Nomellini; linebackers Bill George, Les Richter, and Joe Schmidt; and backs Jack Christiansen, Dick (Night Train) Lane, and Emlen Tunnell.

Coach Paul Brown's system of messenger guards evolved and he controlled every play called in the huddle by Cleveland quarterback Otto Graham. This outraged all who believed that a quarterback's mandate included calling plays himself. But other coaches soon adopted the system and sent guards, ends, or running backs on and off the field with new plays.

In 1960, when the Philadelphia Eagles were driving for a championship and were hard hit by injuries, center Chuck Bednarik played five games in which he centered on offense and then stayed in the game to play linebacker. He went 58 minutes in the championship game as the Eagles defeated Green Bay 17-13. One-way football by a player for many games had its last hurrah in the unforgettable picture of 10 members of the Eagles' offensive team walking off the field while Bednarik remained there alone, soiled and sweaty, waiting for 10 men from the Eagles' and 11 from the Packers' bench to join him and get on with it.

bounds lines and relocation of the goal posts on the goal line. These worked so well they became the rules for all NFL games.

In the same playoff, fullback Bronko Nagurski of the Bears took a handoff, moved toward the line, and then suddenly raised up and threw a pass to Red Grange, who scored. Potsy Clark, the Portsmouth coach, went into a rage. But the play counted and during the 1933 NFL meetings it led to the most important rules change of all. Passes could be thrown from anywhere behind the line of scrimmage; previously, the passer had to be five yards back.

In 1945, the Washington Redskins lost the championship game on a controversial play in which a pass by the Redskins' Sammy Baugh out of his own end zone hit the goal posts. By the rules of the day, it was a safety. With those two points, the Cleveland Rams won 15-14. The rule was changed to make it an incomplete pass before the next season.

Preparing to play the Chicago Cardinals on an icy field for the 1947 title, the Philadelphia Eagles lathed their cleats, grinding them to fine points they thought would hold on the ice. But a Cardinals' equipment boy spotted this operation in progress. The Eagles had to abandon their lathe, and donned tennis shoes instead. These did not prove as magical as they had for the 1934 New York Giants, because the Cardinals won the game 28-21. A rule was later added requiring all cleats to be at least three-eights of an inch at the point.

It wasn't enough for the great Rams teams of the early fifties to have the great passing firepower they had. They also gave the league a "hideout play," in which a given number of players ran on the field as substitutes and the same number—plus one—ran to the sideline. That final player lingered at the sideline and then motored downfield at the snap for a long pass. The rule book was changed to prevent such plays, and also the tackle-eligible passes by Los Angeles to Dick Huffman, one of the most fearsome tackles in the league at the time.

The NFL's dead ball rule, sometimes problematical, is nevertheless the salvation of runners—and maybe the game, too. It came out of the alleged "dirty-play" era of the mid-fifties. Runners were then allowed to keep moving ahead until they were stopped by tacklers completely. Flare-ups, pileups, and late hits abounded. Commissioner Bert Bell sold the dead ball rule to the owners to stop the savagery. Now the ball became dead and the play over when (a) the runner was contacted by a defender, and (b) he touched the turf with anything other than his hands or feet. This rule was one of the greatest of Bell's achievements.

In recent years, crackback blocks below the waist and frequent shifting before the snap have become the targets for rules changes of various degree. And changes were made after the 1974 season to prevent the oversized huddles that sprouted that year to conceal defensive substitution —an extra back, for example, or an extra lineman. Once pro players had stayed in the game for 60 minutes and refused substitution; now they were going in and out between every play by the half-dozen. It was an excess that led to compromise. That is one of the ways the style of professional football has grown.

TWELVE

CALLED "COACH"

The twelve coaches named by a Hall of Fame selection
committee as having had the greatest
influence on pro football and, in particular, its strategy.

At 81, he puttered about his office, answering mail and talking on the phone. George Halas was still active in the operation of his football team, the Chicago Bears; he also was president of the National Football Conference.

"I'm very pleased with the way it has all turned out," Halas said. "We have a great league and a fine commissioner in Pete Rozelle. But there is so, so much more to be done . . ."

It was such an attitude—a parental feeling for the league even though he was then a young man of 25—that made him a major figure in the 1920 organizational meeting. It sustained him as he grew to become patriarch of the league and saw it through all the years of its existence. That is a feat no other living person can claim.

As for strategy-making, he has filled thousands of books and ready lists with it. But there would have been none of that for coaches to busy themselves with over the years if Halas and his fellow founders had not created what became the National Football League at Ralph Hay's garage in Canton.

GEORGE HALAS

This is the Halas coaching record for his four eras (1920-29, 1933-1942, 1946-1955, 1958-1967): 321 victories, 142 defeats, 31 ties. He won more games than any other professional or college coach, including Amos Alonzo Stagg and Glenn (Pop) Warner.

In 40 years of coaching, Halas was an immense influence on the style of play in the NFL, on the rules that govern it, on the mechanics of the officials enforcing the rules, and on the equipment worn by the players on the field. In other words, literally no aspect of an NFL game has not been affected in some way by Halas.

Working with associates such as Ralph Jones, Clark Shaughnessy, Luke Johnsos, and Paddy Driscoll, he popularized the T formation with man-in-motion, restoring the position of quarterback under the center, and laying the groundwork for the eminent pro quarterbacks who followed. Halas also influenced the professional style of play by introducing players such as Red Grange, Bronko Nagurski, and Sid Luckman.

Along with his league meeting alter ego, George Preston Marshall of Washington, Halas sponsored the important rules changes of 1933. These established inbound lines on the field that moved the game away from the sidelines, and allowed passes from anywhere behind the line of scrimmage that opened up the game's offense. In 1926, Halas sponsored a rule that allowed coexistence with college football, ruling that any NFL team with a player in its lineup whose college class had not graduated would be compelled to surrender its guaranteed fee for the game.

Halas has said that the twenties were the most fun for him because he still coached and played, too. The thirties have been called his most "significant" decade; in those years he bought out his partner, Dutch Sternaman, hired Ralph Jones as coach, came through financial trials, and was in the first Chicago All-Star Game. But he is probably best identified with the forties—the 73-0 victory of 1940 and the awesome teams led by Luckman and others. Yet a younger generation may know Halas best as the coach who in 1963, his thirty-sixth season, won a record sixth NFL championship. Halas belongs to every era. He once pushed a calliope through the streets to advertise the Bears. When they at last had a big payoff in New York in 1925, he slept on the money bags all the way home.

The NFL commissioner traditionally appears in the locker room of the winning team after championship games. Bert Bell kept that tradition at Cleveland Stadium in 1950 after the Cleveland Browns, transplants that season from the All-America Football Conference, had narrowly defeated Los Angeles 30-28. "Los Angeles probably has the finest personnel of any team ever," Bell said, "but Cleveland is probably *the most intensely coached* team in history."

To intensely coach . . . this is what Paul Brown taught. To carefully organize every function of the team. If it moves, diagram it first, then film it, watch it a couple dozen times, grade it, go over it with players, store it in a film library, and use the small slice of advantage it has yielded to gain a victory someday. Get inside players' heads, test their intelligence, commit plays to their memory by requiring note-taking, and convince them they're chosen men on a messianic campaign. Win cerebrally; make the opposition think instead of play. Work unremittingly to better the other coach and team. Paul Brown is responsible for all these standard operating procedures in football today.

PAUL BROWN

It is safe to say he was the most feared coach in history. His fellow coaches in the Ohio high school association went to bat for him with a massive lobbying campaign to get him the head coaching job at Ohio State—so they would no longer have to play him. When Brown arrived in Cleveland in 1946 to head the new AAFC team—perhaps it was only coincidence and postwar destiny—the Rams left Cleveland for Los Angeles despite the fact they had just been NFL champions. Brown's team arrived in the NFL in 1950 after he had destroyed the AAFC by winning all its championships. He immediately added the 1950 NFL championship.

The retirement of his quarterback, Otto Graham, and the adoption of his methods by others eventually caught up with him at Cleveland, but he returned in Cincinnati with an expansion team in 1968. Two years later he had a division championship, unprecedented for a new team. But "Old Paul," as he called himself, was getting on in years. He retired in 1975 after 351 coaching victories in high school, college, the military service, AAFC, and NFL games—a football record.

The affection of the Cleveland owner, Mickey McBride, for boxer Joe Louis, "the Brown Bomber," led to the choice of the nickname for the new team in 1946. But McBride also had a certain awe for his new coach. The nickname, then, was an obvious, if unusual choice —the Browns.

Half the winning coaches in the first 10 Super Bowls learned their fundamentals from him—Weeb Ewbank of the New York Jets (game III), Don Shula of the Miami Dolphins (VII and VIII), and Chuck Noll of the Pittsburgh Steelers (IX and X).

Brown still receives residuals from a helmet manufacturing company for his invention of the facemask during the fifties. And he has lived to see the passing of the fury over his play messengers. Many teams use them now in a game in which "coaching from the sideline" was once expressly forbidden.

He grew up in Massillon, Ohio, one of the early cradles of interest in football. Eventually, Brown made a national name for himself coaching Massillon High School teams. A full-color feature about them appeared in LIFE magazine. Then his horizons expanded and he went on to conquer new worlds. He became the head football coach against whom all others are measured.

Steve Owen was a kindly dinosaur, a football fossil. He was born in *territorial* Oklahoma. He became a football gypsy, a 240-pound tackle for the touring Kansas City Cowboys in the twenties. He was sold to the New York Giants for $500. "The price was staggering for that time," he later said, "but I had seen fat hogs bring more in Kansas City." He worked at a coalyard on the Harlem River during the off-season. He was named the Giants' head coach in 1931 and led them 23 years, third longest tenure in NFL history after George Halas and Curly Lambeau. He coached the Giants through 1953, and in 1950 he sprang the umbrella defense on the Cleveland Browns and shut them out 6-0. Owen opened a window on football's past and helped mold its future.

STEVE OWEN

He had been a tackle of legendary strength and tenacity, and his playing experience helped him mold a philosophy of stout defense and fundamental football. It would bring him some big upsets but it would also one day help bring him down.

His personal circumference grew until he weighed 285 pounds. As Owen roamed the sideline, his corpulent form frequently blocked entirely the view of the game for Giants' bench warmers. However, Jimmy Cannon wrote, "No one thought of him as obese. He wore his fat like a suit cut by a good tailor. It was the width of him that impressed people, and the bulkiness suggested strength. He squinted through steel-circled glasses and the lower lip was swollen with a lump of snuff which he seldom chewed."

For all those who looked askance on the changing game, Owen served up such football homilies as these: "This is essentially a game played by two men down in the dirt. The fellow who hits first and harder will usually be the winner."

"The best offense can be built around ten basic plays, the best defense on two. All the rest is razzle-dazzle, egomania, and box office."

On rushing passers: "They can't throw a pass when they're flat on their backs."

And on employing few assistant coaches: "A coach's job is to blow up the footballs and keep order, and that doesn't take much help."

After becoming coach in 1931, Owen led his team into 8 of the first 14 NFL championship games, winning in 1934 in the Giants' famous "Sneakers Game" victory over the Chicago Bears. He won again in 1938 over the Green Bay Packers with the new A formation, actually a primeval formation he was still toying with in the fifties.

A scandal in 1946, when two players involved themselves with gamblers before the playoff that New York lost to Chicago, ended Owen's run at the championship. But his greatest year in football still lay ahead.

Owen and Philadelphia coach Greasy Neale were great friends. During the off-season they enjoyed bull sessions at Toots Shor's restaurant in New York, went to the races or baseball games, and traveled to Miami for the Orange Bowl or New Orleans for the Sugar Bowl. It is virtually indisputable that Owen's umbrella emerged from Neale's Eagle defense, that they huddled together to discuss mutual tactics against Cleveland in 1950, and that the four-three defense of later years evolved from the strategy of both men.

The same Browns he had tormented in 1950 drove Owen from the NFL three years later with a crushing 62-14 defeat at Cleveland. Owen resigned. He later coached in Canada and in minor leagues and was a scout. He died at the age of 66 in 1964.

100

Vince Lombardi headed off the march to complexity. He reversed the trend to more and more complicated football and took the Green Bay Packers and the entire game back to the basics. His teams lined up and ran the same plays—strongside sweeps and weakside slants—over and over. Or they drew the defenders up close to the line of scrimmage and then quarterback Bart Starr dropped play-action passes over their heads. No team ever blocked or executed its plays better than the Packers.

Lombardi was far from the first coach to go back to fundamental football but he did make it the theme of the sport in his time. Teams throughout pro football copied his ball control offense, sweeps, systems of option blocking and running, "bend but don't break" defensive philosophy, and four-three defense techniques in which the tackles clogged up things inside to keep blockers off middle linebacker Ray Nitschke, who made 60 percent or more of his team's tackles.

Lombardi won NFL championships in Green Bay in 1961, 1962, 1965, 1966, and 1967. The latter two teams won the first two Super Bowls against the American Football League. Lombardi coached the Washington Redskins in 1969 but cancer took his life the next year. The trophy given annually to the winner of the Super Bowl was named for him.

It is difficult to name any strategy actually invented by Lombardi. He learned the fundamentals of the sweep while he was a player at Fordham for Jim Crowley and Frank Leahy, who had played for Knute Rockne. Lombardi learned rule blocking while he was a line coach at West Point, from his tutor and fellow Army assistant Sid Gillman. His simple concept of "run to daylight" actually had been part of football for decades and needed only

to become the title of a popular and superbly written book to grow into a part of the language.

Lombardi's play-calling system of colors for offensive formations was borrowed from Tom Landry when the two of them were New York Giants' assistant coaches. And John Wayne said, "Winning isn't everything, it's the only thing," while playing a football coach in a 1953 film called "Trouble Along the Way." That was about 10 years before the quote became attached to Lombardi.

VINCE LOMBARDI

He set in motion a simpler age but also one of reaction and caution. The next step after "bend but don't break" was to drop back in zones, give up the short passes, and stop everything deep. And Lombardi spawned the "error-free" coaches. They followed his precept that, "All your effort in football or in business should be directed toward taking the risk out of it." Accordingly, the Packers, having decided on some minute change in the blocking for a play, would run it two dozen times in practice —or until it became rote for them. In the same manner, today's Lombardi disciples will drill a ball carrier at length on the fundamentals of passing the football from his left hand across his body to the right hand, and stage a run-through with assistant coaches before training camp starts on where each of them will stand during limbering-up exercises.

Lombardi was as much symbol as football coach. As the sport's "man of the sixties," he was a sentinel of authority in a turbulent time, a stern disciplinarian who kept alive the simple verities of an earlier time. Acquiring this special place in American life, he accented the shift to pro football as the new national diversion. It is hard to believe he was an NFL head coach for only 10 seasons.

He was, like George Halas, born of native European stock—a French mother and a Belgian father. His given name was Earl but the red curly locks with which he was crowned assured he would go through life as "Curly." He founded the franchise in pro football's smallest city, Green Bay, and with it won three straight championships in the late twenties. Once a renowned passer himself, he became the first NFL coach to throw the ball on any down, anywhere. He brought Don Hutson into the league and together they won three more championships. And well past the close of World War II, Lambeau was still fighting Halas, his Chicago contemporary, in the annual Packers-Bears rivalry, the oldest and most stirring in pro football annals.

History can turn on small things, such as Curly Lambeau's tonsils in 1919. He had just completed what was, in retrospect, a year among American sports legends. He had been the starting fullback as a freshman on a Notre Dame team coached by Knute Rockne; George Gipp was in the same backfield. A tonsillectomy laid Lambeau low, however, and during the period of recovery and questioning about his future he accepted a job with a meat packing plant in his hometown of Green Bay. He eventually disdained college.

But, like the young Halas, he longed to play more football. He started a team, the "Packers," with a loan from his employer. It became an awesome outfit that beat others from surrounding towns by outrageous scores. Lambeau floated another loan in 1921, this one from a friend for $50, and bought a franchise in the new National Football League.

With a skill in trading that would have impressed a Buddy Parker or a George Allen of a later time, Lambeau acquired three supposed malcontents in

CURLY LAMBEAU

1928 who became Packers' mainstays—Johnny Blood, Cal Hubbard, and Mike Michalske. They were the nucleus of the championship teams of 1929, 1930, and 1931. Then, with Don Hutson in the lineup, Green Bay won again in 1936, 1939, and 1944.

But while Halas had hung on gamely during the lean years and at last emerged his own man, Lambeau had surrendered control, for survival's sake, to a corporation. It weathered many storms and the greatest was Hutson's retirement in 1945. Without Hutson, the Packers lacked a drawing card and therefore the funds to combat the All-America Football Conference for the good college players. The team lost seven straight games in 1948 and built a deficit of $30,000. Green Bay fans responded to the financial crisis by paying $42,000 to view an intrasquad game.

Some people felt Lambeau's insurance interests—the walls of his coaching office were covered with diplomas naming him a top salesman—and his California real estate holdings were consuming too much of his time. The lodge outside the city he acquired to house the Packers became a negative symbol; previously, the players had lived in town. A week before Lambeau resigned in 1950 in a clash of wills with the executive committee, Rockwood Lodge burned. The committee moved quickly to name a new coach, Gene Ronzani, and at that moment Lambeau was riding the train out of Green Bay after 30 years as its only coach.

He later briefly coached the Chicago Cardinals, Washington Redskins, and the College All-Stars. He built a home near Green Bay, where he lived to see the Vince Lombardi era begin. After his death in 1962, City Stadium became Lambeau Field.

He was one of the most urbane men ever to coach, yet to all who knew him he was "Greasy." His only previous experience as a pro coach was with the Ironton Tanks in Ironton, Ohio, yet he came to lead the mightiest team in the NFL in the late forties. The Philadelphia Eagles played like marines assaulting a Pacific Island and Greasy drove them like a company commander, yet they frequently talked back to him—without reprisals on his part. Few men were as colorful and interesting, or a greater paradox, than Alfred Earle Neale.

He played pro football with Jim Thorpe on the 1917 Canton Bulldogs. At the same time, Neale was the starting left fielder for the Cincinnati Reds; he batted .357 in the 1919 World Series. Then a football coaching career eventually led him to seven colleges, one of which—Washington & Jefferson—he took to the 1922 Rose Bowl and played a scoreless tie with California.

He once tried major league third base coaching with the St. Louis Cardinals, but he and

GREASY NEALE

the manager, Billy Southworth, were fired after six weeks. Neale went back to college football.

He was working as an assistant coach at Yale when the Eagles found him. He got the job after a strong recommendation from his lifelong friend, Steve Owen of the New York Giants, and because the Eagles' new owner, Alexis Thompson, was a Yale man to the core. He and Neale met at Morey's, the famous all-male club in New Haven, and Neale was hired there.

Two events followed that transformed him into a genuinely great coach. First, he went to Washington, D. C. and watched the Chicago Bears defeat the Redskins 73-0 in the 1940 championship game. Second, he made a great personal discovery. Sitting in a

New York restaurant, he began a conversation with a man who was associated with Fox Movietone News, makers of motion picture newsreels.

"I marvel at the way you fellows seem to catch the outstanding plays of every game," Neale said.

"Oh, we film the entire game and then select the important plays," the man replied.

As calmly as he could, Neale asked, "Would you by chance have the entire footage of the Bears-Redskins game?"

The man did in fact have it and sold the film to Neale for $156. The coach watched it for three to five hours a day for three months before going to Philadelphia to take over the Eagles. He became the second coach to adopt the new T formation and with it built the Eagles into a powerhouse, eventually winning the 1948 and 1949 NFL championships.

On defense, Philadelphia played the "Eagle." With its strong pass rush, variety in use of linebackers, and four-deep secondary, the Eagle was one of the forerunners of the four-three defense.

Thompson, the owner Neale loved, lost millions financing the Eagles' rise to greatness. He sold them at their peak, before the 1949 season when they won their second championship. A year later they lost the opening-game showdown with the paragon of the former All-America Football Conference, the Cleveland Browns. It was the beginning of Greasy's last season. The new owners released him before the 1951 season began. Years later, as the team waned again, majority owner Jim Clark would say, "Let's get hold of Greasy, I made an awful mistake firing him." But Neale never coached again. A frugal man, he lived well in retirement. He died at 81 in 1973.

Following the building of the tower of Babel, and its subsequent destruction by the Creator, mankind ran in all directions babbling in strange new tongues. The same thing took place in professional football with the arrival of Clark Shaughnessy.

Teams today set up in formations such as split switch or duce right twin or trips right change. Their wide receivers run arrows, corners, flags, lookies, stars, sticks, streaks, and straights. Linemen ace, Ben, bim, Bob, do-dad, or Ed block. Defensive linemen make bex, lex, Rex, and Tex and Tillie and Willie charges. Deep backs work sky and cloud forces and linebackers thunder and lightning blitzes. Coach and player communicate day-to-day in this manner: "We can go Yale here but if we have to we can buzz the coverage, or we may sloop it."

The terms Shaughnessy did not invent, he inspired. He overwhelmingly influenced pro football by giving it its proclivity for language and committing it to the modern period in which the new terminology was central to everything done in the game. He hung out at Chicago Bears' practices in the thirties, learned the T formation, improved on it, borrowed it and took it to college football at Stanford. He pioneered the organization of playbooks by back action—counter, dive, flow, full, tear, toss, slant, or veer. The "Shaughnessy System" simplified teaching, made play-calling scientific, reduced practice time, and made film-grading and scouting systematic. He taught five of the first great T formation quarterbacks—Sid Luckman, Frankie Albert, Sammy Baugh, Bob Waterfield, and Norm Van Brocklin. He coined "Nickle defense."

But he was aloof and superior. With sarcasm, he disparaged the elementary coaching points of others. More than once, they responded by locking him out of the room.

Driven by failure as University of Chicago coach, Shaughnessy seized on the Bears' new system and, as its Einstein, became obsessed with it. He often worked all night at home, taking 15-minute cat naps, then getting up again to study more game film and draw more plays. "Our living room was full of film and notebooks and screens," his son, Clark, Jr., recalled.

CLARK SHAUGHNESSY

Shaughnessy never practiced moderation in the making of football strategy. At Los Angeles in 1948, he overwhelmed his players with new formations. They won the division championship but he was fired.

Shaughnessy coached between 1915 and 1962 at Tulane, Loyola of New Orleans, Chicago, Stanford, Maryland, and Pittsburgh; was an unofficial advisor to the Chicago Bears in the thirties, a consultant to the Redskins in 1944-46, Rams' head coach in 1948-49, and a Bears' assistant from 1951 until 1962. He died in 1970 at the age of 75.

As the 20-year-old coach of Tulane in 1915, he answered a newspaper ad placed by a shoe salesman. Yes, he would share the apartment while the salesman was away. The salesman was Huey P. Long, later the colorful governor of Louisiana.

To supplement his Tulane salary, Shaughnessy took a job in the off-season as athletic instructor at Morro Castle, the Cuban West Point in Havana. He took a ferry over from Key West. The castle overlooked the Havana harbor, grandest on the Spanish Main. One can imagine Shaughnessy sitting there looking out over the bay and daydreaming of his teams making dramatic off-tackle runs, laterals, and passes . . . and winning the big bowl game.

What others intend to try someday, Tom Landry is trying now. What others say can't be done without frequent error—shifting often before the ball is snapped—Landry is doing every play. Those who don't have him on their schedule call what he does Mickey Mouse. Those who do play him want rules passed to stop him. He is a little of the old and a little of the new; he has a genuine love for both Jesus Christ and the computer. He is a very complex coach but also a very successful one; he put the Cowboys in the playoffs eight straight years from 1966 through 1973, won Super Bowl VI, and reached Super Bowls V and X.

Landry will be seeking new ways to foul the theory of the defensive flop until the day he retires. This has been going on since the Cowboys first took the field in 1960.

An expansion team, the undermanned Cowboys had to entertain to attract fans. And Landry had spent a decade as a New York Giants' player and assistant coach studying and shaping the four-three defense. He concluded, rightly or wrongly, that automatic response by this defense was uniform everywhere. If a defense saw a split backs formation, for example, it knew immediately how to react. Landry decided the only answer was to show many formations, shift often from one to another, send men in motion to set up new formations, and avoid the easy revelations of the routine offensive sets. Even in their lean years, the Cowboys were a multiple-formation team. "We were never stopped," Landry recalls. "We were outscored sometimes, but we were never stopped."

"Flip-flop . . ." Ninety percent of pro football's teams do it with their safeties to get the strong safety —the better tackler of the two—on the side of the tight end. A half-dozen teams also flop outside line-backers. The new three-four teams may exchange the positions of safeties, outside linebackers, and inside linebackers to the side of the "strength" of the formation—as many as six of the eleven players. Landry can, therefore, hold up the deployment of more than half a team with his shifts, motion, and other pre-snap gadgetry.

His defense was "Doomsday" when tackle Bob Lilly was at his peak, but it was never an all-out assault force as the name might imply. Rather, the Cowboys disdained the hit-and-react style of Green Bay or the blitz madness of Chicago or St. Louis. They carefully filled every gap, each player fighting the natural reaction to go to the ball and holding his place instead; the runner had to come to one of them sooner or later.

Cowboys' cornerbacks were in constant peril. To force second-and-long yardage situations, the Cowboys brought their linebackers up close on first down, forcing man-to-man coverage behind them. A former cornerback, Landry wrote harsh rules for those who played the position for him.

The antithesis of Lombardi, he once said, "If the whole emphasis is on repetition and execution and cutting out mistakes, the game comes down to one thing only—personnel. Well, I reject that as the idea of football. To me it's a great deal more than just trying to out-personnel the other team."

He is a package of contradictions, a deeply committed Christian with a coaching style that places him on the radical fringe of pro football. He is a modest man who never refuses a writer's request and is so soft-spoken that when he addressed the New York Giants' defense during film sessions in a darkened room, cornerback Dick Lynch kept falling asleep.

TOM LANDRY

The times clouded Don Shula's achievement in 1972.

Football was in flux. There had been a merger, and the conferences were groping for new identities. Teams were working overtime to get a "book" on all their new opponents. This coincided with the arrival of the age of zones and the accompanying dismay about whether the game could overcome them. As a result, some may have felt that when the Dolphins went through an entire 17-game schedule without a defeat and won Super Bowl VII, they somehow had merely exploited the confusion of the times.

History's perspective proves that was hardly the case. When Shula coached Miami to a perfect record and a Super Bowl championship, and followed that with another Super Bowl title and an overall two-year record of 26 victories and 2 losses, he had done just what George Halas or Paul Brown or Vince Lombardi had done before him—outcoached everyone in the game.

Shula was the winningest coach in the five years after realignment. He became the first ever to win 100 games in his first 10 years. And he moved into fifth place in history in most victories, behind Halas, Curly Lambeau, Steve Owen, and Brown.

Already an addict for zones, he adopted the three-four defense (the Dolphins called it their "53 defense" because that was the jersey number of fourth linebacker Bob Matheson) and this gave Shula even more effective zones, arraying a blizzard of linebackers and deep backs across the field.

Shula converted Larry Csonka from just another big fullback into one of the greatest ever and built a trapping, misdirection, and influence attack around him, guards Bob Kuechenberg and Larry Little, and center Jim Langer. It was at its best when the Dolphins systematically took Minnesota apart

DON SHULA

to win Super Bowl VIII, their second in a row.

He watched every minute detail of his team's planning, and sent assistants on to become head coaches, most notably his former Baltimore assistant Chuck Noll to the Pittsburgh Steelers.

Shula has said, "I'm no miracle worker and don't make me out to be one. I don't have a magic formula that I'm going to give to the world as soon as I can write a book. I'm not a person with a great deal of finesse. I'm about as subtle as a punch in the mouth."

Indeed, he had been only an average NFL player, a cornerback for Cleveland, Baltimore, and Washington. He had then scrambled for a coaching job, and after a year each at the universities of Virginia and Kentucky as an assistant, he landed back in pro football on the staff of the Detroit Lions.

He became head coach of the Baltimore Colts in 1963. They were playing the old Cleveland system, but he wanted to put in the Lions' system, which was really the old Chicago Bears' system. He decided to leave well enough alone. He jousted with quarterback John Unitas for the right to call Colts' plays and he frequently berated his team in practice field and locker room outbursts. The Colts were consistent winners but in January, 1969 became the first NFL team to lose a Super Bowl game to an AFL representative, the New York Jets quarterbacked by Joe Namath.

Shula emerged his own man in Miami in 1970, tanned and temperate, and introduced his methods to the Dolphins in four daily practices during part of training camp that year. He found a dutiful and gifted quarterback in Bob Griese. Then a team only four years old, the Dolphins made the playoffs immediately and a year later reached Super Bowl VI, losing to Dallas. Their perfect season followed.

In the early years of the American Football League opponents of the San Diego Chargers often took the field undermanned but earnest, forlorn but determined. The Chargers were not on the field to greet their opponents for the warmup. Suddenly, when it seemed the rivals were in their most compromising stretching exercises, the Chargers appeared. Ernie Ladd, Earl Faison, Ron Mix, Ernie Wright, and other mastodons trundled onto the field in a direct path through the opponents. Mouths fell open as the awesome size of these men was dramatized up close. Sid Gillman had won the first round before a down had been played.

"With Sid it is eat or be eaten," said the late Jack Horrigan of the Buffalo Bills. Gillman taught the new league how to organize, scout, draft, and work methodically for the coaching edge. He ensured that the competition in the AFL was tenacious from the start; others were whipped into line simply by attempting to stay even with Gillman.

The best training aid in the early years of the league was a Chargers' game film. Gillman put together a professional style offense with quarterback John Hadl, wide receiver Lance Alworth, and running backs Keith Lincoln and Paul Lowe. Gillman had coached the greats Norm Van Brocklin, Tom Fears, and Elroy Hirsch in Los Angeles. He brought to the Chargers an expertise unmatched anywhere else in the league in the intricacies of throwing and covering forward passes. With Alworth and, later, Gary Garrison, he refined the delicate pass routes. The Chargers' receivers played games with the minds of defensive backs. They gave "feelings"— an Up "feeling," or a Corner "feeling," and each pattern had a "breaking point,"—which was when the defender broke up in grief, provided the moves

SID GILLMAN

by an Alworth or a Garrison had fooled him.

On defense, Gillman defined everything that could be done with five receivers—two wide receivers, a tight end, and two running backs—on a field 100 by 53 yards. If there were three out for passes and two kept in to block, was it, for example, two out on the left side of the defense and one on the right? Such matters consumed Gillman and those around him.

In Los Angeles, he gave George Allen his first pro coaching job. With the Chargers he hired Al Davis, Don Klosterman, and Chuck Noll. All became important pro football coaches or executives.

He had an Ohio period, a California period, and a Texas period. He played end at Ohio State and then coached at Miami of Ohio, winning 31 and losing 6, and at the University of Cincinnati, winning 50, losing 13, and tying 1. Between Miami and Cincinnati, he spent a year on the staff at West Point.

Moving to Los Angeles as head coach in 1955, he immediately won a divisional championship, but four frequently trying years followed and he joined the new Chargers in 1960. He won five divisional titles and one AFL championship with the Chargers. Poor health forced his resignation in 1969. He returned to coach one more year, 1971, with little success.

The Texas period followed. He joined the Dallas staff. But he longed to lead his own parade again and became general manager, then head coach as well, of the Houston Oilers. They had lost 18 of 19 games but were 7-7 under Gillman in 1974. Then after he and owner Bud Adams disagreed about the correct rate of speed for spending Adams's money, Gillman resigned.

Raymond (Buddy) Parker used to defeat Paul Brown almost as regularly as he got out of bed and went to work each morning. His Detroit Lions of 1952-53 won consecutive NFL championships, something only two other teams—the 1940-41 Bears and 1948-49 Eagles—had done since the NFL was divided into two divisions in 1933. The Lions were loaded with tough, proven veterans at virtually every position, players such as Bobby Layne, Doak Walker, Pat Harder, Dick Stanfel, Les Bingaman, and Jack Christiansen. Parker gave them a model playing system that was fundamental and that worked. He had been in the NFL since 1935; he knew it inside and out. He could analyze what an opponent was doing and make a sideline decision to counter it quickly and wisely. Parker was a pro football titan in the fifties.

BUDDY PARKER

Long before George Allen, Parker was a master trader who found the older player who could make the difference for his team—a Pat Harder to play fullback, a Jim Martin to play defensive end. A half-decade before Lombardi, he was a coach who won by going back to the basics and battering away with them.

Parker used the simple play-calling system the Bears had pioneered in the early forties. He shaped his attack to his personnel—in 1951 power plays for Harder were the offense, in 1952 Layne option plays, in 1953 halfback plays for Bob Hoernschemeyer and Gene Gedman, in 1954 the new slot offense with Walker flanked wide.

Parker and Layne, the Lions' quarterback, shared a camaraderie approaching blood-brotherhood, and Layne could audible his way through an entire game. No other team could work the clock and stretch as much action out of the last two minutes;

the term "two-minute offense" began with Parker, Layne, and the Lions. And they made play-action passes an NFL staple.

The Parker defense—until middle linebacker Joe Schmidt arrived—was the Eagle, another creation of the forties. The 300-pound Bingaman was stationed at middle guard like a Maginot Line pillbox; Bingaman's primary mission in life was to stop the Marion Motley trap plays of arch-rival Cleveland.

The players in the NFL's biggest chess game of the early fifties belonged to Parker of Detroit and Brown of Cleveland. One season after becoming the Lions' head coach, Parker won the NFL championship in 1952 and he did it beating Cleveland during the regular season and in the championship game. He won his second straight championship from the Browns in 1953. Brown gained revenge the next season in a decisive manner, winning the title game over Detroit 56-10. Parker went home and used a pocket knife to slash holes in a portrait of himself. A disastrous 3-9 season in 1955 followed, and Layne missed the next with a broken leg. Parker then shocked all pro football by resigning just before the 1957 season.

Two weeks later he turned up as the head coach of the Pittsburgh Steelers. They now display consecutive Super Bowl trophies but in those days they were a coaching Siberia. Parker traded for Layne and struggled vainly to build a championship team. He resigned after the 1964 season.

Any person who thinks of quitting his job should study Parker's life first. He told off everyone he ever worked for—the Chicago Cardinals, Lions, and Steelers. He retired to his home in Texas, there to brood about one of the strangest careers a pro coach ever had.

Hank Stram created the first of his American Football League gadgets in 1962 with the Dallas Texans. It was the two tight end offense, and he devised it to deal with the wild blitzers of Boston. Another blocker inside gave the Texans extra protection against the charging Patriots' linebackers who terrorized the early AFL.

That same year Stram played a three-four defense, stacking three linebackers behind linemen, and used zone coverage on almost every down. In the season's climactic game, the Texans defeated Houston in an epic six-quarter struggle for the AFL championship. But slim attendance in the face of the crosstown Cowboys drove the Texans to Kansas City, where they became the Chiefs.

Otis Taylor arrived to add a deep threat to the offense and the two tight end system gave way to one of the most dramatic innovations of the decade—the tight end in the I formation. Fred Arbanas lined up there and then shifted to one side or the other, delaying the tipoff of the strength of the formation—essential information needed by the defense before it could adjust.

HANK STRAM

Buck Buchanan arrived to play defensive tackle and the three-man front gave way to a four. The Chiefs, however, altered it by playing over and under shifts, placing one tackle head on the center. Behind that fearsome front they stacked three unusually good linebackers—Bobby Bell, Willie Lanier, and Jim Lynch.

Quarterback Len Dawson, who was resurrected from NFL waiver lists in 1962, became one of the greatest ever, handing off in the Chiefs' I to halfback Mike Garrett or throwing play-action passes.

The Chiefs went down disappointingly in Super Bowl I, losing to the mighty Packers 35-10. The next preseason, however, they faced an NFL team for the second time, the Chicago Bears. The Bears relied on knowing the strength of an offensive formation. They shifted their safeties, outside linebackers, and tackles to the side of the tight end. Kansas City kept Arbanas moving left and right, added other shifts and man-in-motion, and won 66-24.

The merger of NFL and AFL was followed by the New York Jets' surprising victory three years later in Super Bowl III. Then it was 1969 and the Chiefs, second in the Western Division to their rivals, the Oakland Raiders, won a playoff and then defeated Oakland to become the last champion of the original AFL. Their opponent in Super Bowl IV was the Minnesota Vikings.

There is a moment in the movie of that game in which a Vikings' linebacker stands up from the huddle, looks to the sideline, and shrugs his shoulders as if to say, "How do I know what they're doing?" Minnesota couldn't stop the Chiefs' I and multiple offense gadgetry or penetrate their odd defense and stacked linebackers. Kansas City won 23-7. A wistful Stram clutched the Super Bowl trophy. It had been some decade.

The Chiefs grew old and little new blood came in. They played another six-quarter game and lost it, 27-24 to the Miami Dolphins in a playoff Christmas day, 1971. The Dolphins were on the way up, the Chiefs on the way down. Stram had spoken of his "moving pocket" with Dawson becoming the "offense of the seventies," and when his team faltered he saw this statement flung in his face. He and the Chiefs parted after the 1974 season. He was a television analyst one season and then accepted a generous contract to rebuild the New Orleans Saints.

CONFRONTATION

The point-and-counterpoint process in which pro teams
"mess with each other's minds" and
play a physical guessing game of confrontation.

Running Off-Tackle

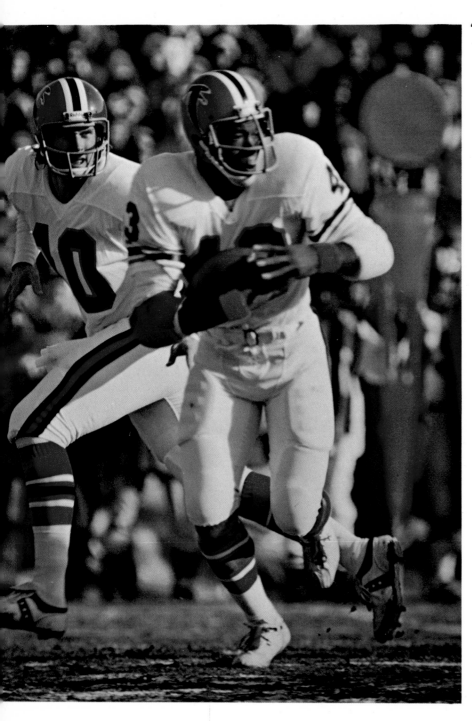

Dave Hampton of the Atlanta Falcons looks for an opening off-tackle.

"If I were allowed to run one play, it would be the fullback slant to the weakside. In my opinion it is the one great play in football."

Chuck Knox, *head coach, Los Angeles Rams*

Steve Owen once observed, "No matter which one a coach prefers, he has to make his off-tackle play work, or he might as well give up. It sets up all other plays, and when a club can't make it, it can't make anything."

Owen won 150 games as head coach of the New York Giants, so he must have known what he was talking about.

The off-tackle play is the most basic running play in the game and with it begins a point-and-counterpoint presentation of the thought processes in professional football today. This is how the teams of the National Football League confront each other at the line of scrimmage, present problems and roadblocks for each other, and reach solutions.

Off-tackle is where everybody wants to run—and will if the defense has not set up half-a-dozen measures to stop it.

It's the old bread-and-butter play of the single wing formation that Pop Warner invented a half-century ago. The defense is weakest at its corner, and that's where the off-tackle play attacks. If it succeeds, the defense then has to weaken either its center or its flank to compensate.

The most fundamental off-tackle play today—and indeed the number one play in the NFL—is the weakside slant. It is remarkably simple. The fullback slants to the weakside—the side without the tight end—and,

depending on the blocks that are made, may run straight ahead or cut inside or outside.

This is the play that Jim Taylor of the Green Bay Packers and Jim Brown of the Cleveland Browns ran to gain big yardage for their teams in the sixties. It was later the play that Matt Snell ran to gain most of the 121 yards he gained while leading the New York Jets to their shocking Super Bowl III upset of the Baltimore Colts.

Chuck Knox, who was then Jets' line coach and who is now head coach of the Los Angeles Rams, took a runner named Lawrence McCutcheon and, using the weakside slant as the foremost play in his attack, turned McCutcheon into a 1,000-yard runner.

The same thing happened to Jim Otis, who had been a journeyman player until he joined the St. Louis Cardinals and they began to rely on the slant.

"It is a very big play for me," Otis says. "I like its versatility; depending on the block the tackle makes, I may run the play in any one of three places. The halfback's block on the linebacker is important, too. If he makes that it's going to be a great play."

The slant is run to the strongside as well as the weakside, and there are, of course, off-tackle plays for halfbacks, too.

The Jim Otis Off-Tackle Express
The St. Louis Cardinals run the most fundamental play in professional football, the weakside slant by the fullback. Jim Otis's backfield partner, Terry Metcalf, makes an acceptable block on Dallas Cowboys' linebacker Dave Edwards and Otis blasts through for a 12-yard gain.

113

Sweep

It is an awesome sight when it is successful. It is the second basic running play, the sweep.

There are many types: the power sweep, with both of the offensive guards leading the halfback around end; the fullback sweep, in which the halfback himself becomes the lead blocker; and the option sweep, in which the halfback may run or pass.

Even the casual football fan might be able to sketch the blocking pattern of the classic power sweep. However, the play is run today in many ways varying from the classic pattern.

Running back Altie Taylor of Detroit says, "I've played for three coaches and each has had his own way of running the sweep. For example, Bill McPeak [backfield coach of the Lions in 1967-73] taught us to dip deeper in the backfield before making our cut. He said, 'You have to lose yardage to make yardage.' It sounds crazy, but it worked!

"The way we run it now, it's a speed play and we get outside before the pursuit can get over. The guard and I turn upfield as soon as we see daylight."

The sweep is aimed at the defensive end, outside linebacker, and the defensive back coming up to force the play. These players may be moved around by the defense in many ways to fool the blocking. A sweep can wind up not being very effective.

Chuck Knox of Los Angeles says, "It looks impressive for a guard to come out of there really running hard. But does he know where he's going? If he can't pick out the man he is going to block he can't carry it out.

"There are just too many variables involved in trying to run the sweep.

Mercury Morris follows his Miami Dolphins' escort, led by guard Larry Little, on a power sweep.

1

2

3

4

5

What if your tackle misses his block? You could end up with a four- or five-yard loss. The sweep was a good play against the four-three defense but we face so many different defenses today that the sweep can seldom be run the way it once was."

Defenses actually caught up with the sweep while Lombardi coached the Packers. He developed varieties of the play and continued using it. It remained his favorite play. "I've diagrammed it so many times I think I see it in my sleep," he once said.

The fast little backs in professional football today such as Otis Armstrong of Denver, Mercury Morris of Miami, and Greg Pruitt of Cleveland bring to their teams the speed necessary to turn the corner and get into the open. They are in sharp contrast to the "big backs" concept Lombardi followed when he set up the sweep for Paul Hornung and Jim Taylor, and later for Donny Anderson and Jim Grabowski.

All professional coaches have worked to develop an offensive unit such as the one Lombardi built and teach it the sweep fundamentals as well as he did with the Packers. Mostly they have worked in vain.

The Swift-Striking Raiders
Charlie Smith of the Oakland Raiders runs a sweep for a touchdown against the Detroit Lions. George Buehler, one of the guards leading the way, crunches a cornerback for the final block as Smith breaks free with clear sailing ahead.

115

Up the Middle

Trapping an All-Pro

Even an all-pro defensive tackle such as Joe Greene of the Pittsburgh Steelers occasionally becomes the victim of the trap play. Guard Ed Budde of Kansas City moves behind center Jack Rudnay to trap Greene (75). This allows runner Woody Green to get through for a good gain.

"The best running play in football is one straight ahead. The next best running play is one which is almost straight ahead."

Paul Brown, *Cincinnati Bengals*

Intently watching the defender ahead, O. J. Simpson follows guard Reggie McKenzie on the Buffalo Bills' "46" trap play. Below, Miami center Jim Langer blocks Manny Sistrunk of Washington in Super Bowl VII.

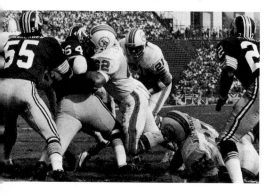

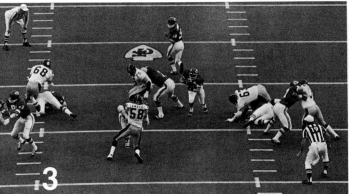

Slants and sweeps send the offense running at the corner of the defense or around it. The third basic strategy is to run up the middle.

That takes courage. This is a relatively small but very crowded bit of terrain extending from tackle to tackle. It is a place into which none but the sturdy should venture, because it is populated by men of immense size and strength.

Yet it is an area into which the offense must go to prove it can attack its center, and thereby keep the giant defensive tackles and mobile linebackers at home.

A game begins with the offense saying to the defense, in effect, "We're going to run wide on you until you stop us." Usually, they're taken up on the offer. So they start faking and opting for the trap play up the middle.

There are "short traps," against a defensive tackle, and "long traps," against a defensive end or linebacker. Buffalo's "46" play—in which guard Reggie McKenzie leads running superstar O. J. Simpson—is a long trap.

The subtleties that are at work on such plays, along with raw power, are apparent as McKenzie describes how he watches the eyes of the defensive player to aid him in blocking for Simpson.

"I can read O. J. by the moves or the reactions of the defensive man," McKenzie says. "If the defender's eyes are going outside, well, nine times out of ten so is 'the Juice.'"

Ordinary head-to-head blocking is called "man" blocking. There also is double-team and cross-blocking.

Blocks in the NFL aren't necessarily aesthetic. Any block that successfully gives the ball carrier running room gets a high grade.

Defensive linemen who appear as motionless figures on play diagrams turn into raging tigers on game day. When a team encounters an Otis Sistrunk of Oakland and learns it cannot "man" block him, cross-block him, trap him, or double-team him, there is only one alternative left— run plays to the other side of the line.

Below, the ubiquitous Simpson tumbles up and over, demonstrating the frequent results of running up the middle.

Formations

Overshifted defensive lines move a big lineman into a position where he is head on the center. This makes life more complicated for centers, as Jim Otto of Oakland finds out. At right, the three elements of any defensive formation—deep back (top), lineman, and linebacker.

"I don't like those big defensive tackles hovering right over me. But if they want to fight me instead of going for the ball, that's what I'm there for."

John Fitzgerald, *center, Dallas Cowboys*

the expected point of attack, the over and under defenses emerged. In them one tackle moved over to become head on the center. Such a shift to the strongside, the side with the tight end, was an over. A shift to the weakside was an under.

This placed big men near the probable path of the runner. In addition, the tackle head on the center had an advantage, because the center was occupied with snapping the ball before starting his block. Overs and unders made the trap play more difficult for the offense. Finally, the "odd" lines (as opposed to an "even" four-three alignment) presented new problems for the offense in its preparation simply because they were different.

Linemen also can shift into the gaps between offensive linemen, and this is standard procedure for all teams on short yardage plays.

All this is hardly new. While at Illinois, Red Grange saw his opponents overshift when Illinois played an unbalanced line. The Detroit Lions shifted their linemen against the Chicago Bears in the forties. And the New York Giants used overs and unders frequently in the fifties.

They became widespread in pro football when they were used successfully in the American Football League in the sixties. The even, man-to-man conditions in the four-three became more demanding as the number of pro teams multiplied. Teams were unable to find, draft, and play 11 exceptional men on defense. The over and under defenses were better suited to the times.

Ermal Allen, Dallas Cowboys' assis-

Variety of formations is the defense's reply to the offensive basics.

The four-three was the standard defense in the NFL for perhaps 15 years after its emergence during the fifties. It presented four linemen and three linebackers, hence its name, the four-three. It was a balanced alignment, symmetrical in respect to the football, with its defensive tackles head on the offensive guards and its ends head on the offensive tackles.

The middle linebacker was well back so he could move from side to side, and the linemen protected him, keeping offensive blockers off him so he could make the tackle.

In order to move linemen nearer

tant coach, says, "In 1962 pro teams played seventy-five percent even and twenty-five percent odd. Today, it's sixty-five percent odd and thirty-five percent even."

The four-three's status declined further with the Miami Dolphins' "53" defense of 1972. It was given that name because Bob Matheson, formerly a substitute, became a key player in the defense and his jersey number was 53.

In reality, it was a three-four with three linemen and four linebackers. Matheson was the fourth linebacker in the defense.

New England, Houston, Oakland, Denver, and Buffalo are other teams that have played the three-four.

"The fourth linebacker can support the linemen on running plays, or become another defender against the pass," former coach Sid Gillman says. "The defense has tremendous flexibility."

It appears that the overs and unders and the three-fours have led to the decline of two of the most romantic symbols of NFL defenses—the front fours who lined up evenly and charged after the runner or passer, and the famous middle linebackers whose names became bywords. In the three-four there are two "inside linebackers," talented but submerged functionaries in a striking new defensive formation in the NFL.

"Every team playing four linemen ends up in an overshift or an undershift. Hardly anyone plays just a straight four-three anymore."

Bum Phillips, *Houston Oilers*

Here are four overhead views of offensive and defensive formations photographed in the Astrodome. From top to bottom, they are: far vs. four-three, Houston Oilers vs. St. Louis Cardinals; I vs. over, Oilers vs. Cincinnati Bengals; split backs vs. under stack, Oilers vs. Cardinals; and far vs. three-four, Cardinals vs. Oilers.

119

Bubble

There is a vulnerable spot in the over and under defenses. It is called the "bubble."

It is the area of the middle linebacker who has changed places with the defensive tackle who shifted. The linebacker now is opposite a guard and well off the line of scrimmage. The linebacker must take the position off the line in order to be ready to pursue to the left or right in case the play goes elsewhere, and to enable him to drop back fast on pass coverage.

He is, therefore, a weak link, in comparison to the linemen who are bigger than he and nearer the line. That is why running into the bubble is a strategy that is followed often by teams challenging over and under defenses.

The way the bubble is attacked varies from team to team, according to coach Tommy Prothro of the San Diego Chargers. "For example," says

Dave Osborn of the Minnesota Vikings takes a handoff from Fran Tarkenton as his teammates cross-block, one of the effective measures used against over and under defenses. The cross-blocks are being made by tackle Ron Yary (73) and guard Steve Lawson. At left, running back Jim Bertelsen on the move for the Los Angeles Rams.

Prothro, "they want to first determine, how close in is the linebacker? What are the two linemen nearest him going to do? Are they going to pinch in and protect him? All these things affect the way teams block against the bubble."

There are other ways of challenging overs and unders in addition to running into the bubble. One is to avoid being "typed." For example,

the Buffalo Bills are known as a right-handed team; they run more plays to their right side than to their left. It is common for opponents to shift in that direction against Buffalo.

Cross-blocking is another tactic used against odd lines. And counter plays and crossbucks have been used against shifts since the time of Knute Rockne.

Probing the Vikings' Defense

The Dallas Cowboys run into the bubble against Minnesota. Their target is the area of middle linebacker Jeff Siemon (50). A lead block by halfback Walt Garrison clears the way for running back Calvin Hill to make a first down.

"A lot of teams base their offense against odd lines on running into the bubble."

Jeff Siemon, *Minnesota Vikings*

Stacks, Stunts, Slants

A Successful Stunt

The Pittsburgh Steelers carry out a stunt so successfully that it puts linebacker Andy Russell in perfect position to make the tackle. The action occurs in the left side of the photographs. Defensive end Dwight White charges to the outside against the Kansas City Chiefs and Russell comes inside, arriving in time to meet ball carrier Willie Ellison head-on. Below, the Baltimore Colts with linebackers Mike Curtis (32) and Ray May (56) stacked during their Super Bowl V victory over the Dallas Cowboys.

The game begins to grow interesting as the offenses and the odd defenses try to out-think each other.

"Let's say you're in a far formation," explains Tommy Prothro of San Diego, "and the defense is in an under. You want your fullback in better position to block the strongside so you audible and change to split backs. But when you do that they change their defense and shift to an over."

The incessant shifting is marshalled by a shouting quarterback and middle linebacker. At the same time, other players on defense may be calling out adjustments to each other. And all 22 players are racing to get into position and be set for the required full second. That's why defensive end Jack Youngblood of Los Angeles says, "It can be sheer madness at the snap."

The madness increases if the defense has decided to stack, stunt, or slant. A stack is a linebacker directly behind a lineman. A stunt is an unusual charge by linebackers and linemen or linemen alone, in which they loop around each other instead of charging straight ahead. A slant is a planned charge by a lineman to the left or right instead of straight ahead. Fullbacks run weakside slants and defensive linemen slant (pro football strategy can be very imaginative but its language is often redundant).

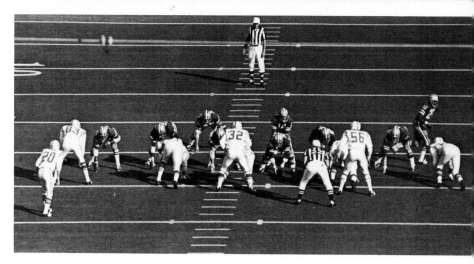

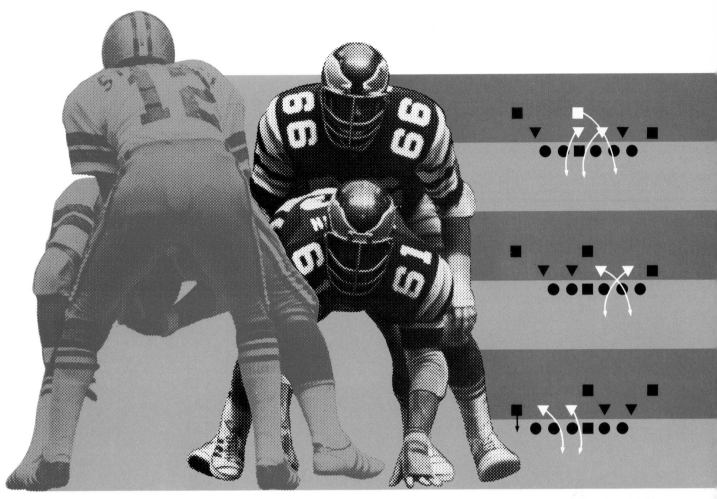

Because of their personnel, American Football League teams adopted the stack defense in the sixties the same way they did overs and unders. Kansas City and its coach, Hank Stram, were the stack's main exponents and gave a display of its variety while defeating Minnesota in Super Bowl IV. That was the last Super Bowl game between the original AFL and the NFL.

The very next year, Baltimore, a longtime NFL team, moved into the American Football Conference and went all the way to Super Bowl V, where it played the stack extensively and defeated the Dallas Cowboys.

"The advantage of the stack is that the offense doesn't know whether the linebacker will peel off to the right or left, or barge in straight ahead," says Stram, now coach of the New Orleans Saints.

Stunting is commonplace and there may have never been a better example in modern times than Detroit's 26-14 victory over the vaunted Green Bay Packers on Thanksgiving day, 1962. The Detroit line threw Green Bay quarterback Bart Starr for 110 yards in losses that day.

"They came out stunting," Green Bay tackle Forrest Gregg said later. "Most of the time their line comes straight in. But they traded routes in this game. We couldn't find them. It took us a half to pick up the stunts."

"If the situation is right, we'll say, 'Hey, let's mess with their heads.' We run about twenty stunts a game, and the other club never knows how many of us are coming or from where."

Joe Ehrmann, *Baltimore Colts*

Linebacker Bill Bergey of the Philadelphia Eagles stacks ominously behind a lineman as he confronts Dallas quarterback Roger Staubach across the line of scrimmage. At right from top to bottom, a stack, a stunt, and a slant.

Pinch

The Pittsburgh Steelers happened by accident on a strategy that they used while winning Super Bowls IX and X, and that became the best recent example of another measure that may be taken by the defense.

In addition to shifting, stacking, stunting, or slanting, the defense may position its linemen in the gaps between offensive blockers and "pinch."

This is a charge against one offensive player, rendering him helpless, fouling up blocking plans, and freeing other defenders to make the tackle.

The Steelers had exceptional personnel for such a strategy in defensive tackles Joe Greene and Ernie Holmes. The players themselves began experimenting with it during 1974 as a means to shorten pass rushing routes for the Steelers' defensive ends.

Moving the big tackles nearer the center forced the offensive line to constrict, allowing the ends to rush outside them.

"As we fooled around with the defense, we found it worked against running plays, too," says George Perles, Pittsburgh's defensive line coach.

"It makes them think and that leads to doubt and confusion and a lot of trouble," says Greene. "They know its coming but they still don't know what to do with it."

One center, Bill Lenkaitis of New England, said after playing against Greene, "It was the most miserable

Giant Jethro Pugh of the Cowboys does battle with Doug Van Horn of the New York Giants. At right, a cadre of angry Cleveland Browns swarm running back Franco Harris of Pittsburgh.

A Pinch by All-Pros
The Steelers use their defensive tackles, Joe Greene and Ernie Holmes, to stop a Minnesota Vikings' play during Super Bowl IX. While Greene (75) smashes over Vikings' center Mick Tingelhoff, Holmes loops around Greene to tackle runner Dave Osborn for no gain. In the inset, a smiling Greene.

spot I've ever been in."

Defenses can pinch in the middle as in the classic use of the four-three defense as played by the teams of Vince Lombardi, which jammed up the middle to keep blockers off middle linebacker Ray Nitschke. Or, as mentioned earlier, they can pinch to give support to the linebacker in the bubble. Or they may pinch to the inside because that is the favorite running territory for the offense.

"How do you stop Greene when he's that close to you and so damn strong? There are no rules for that. Our blocking patterns were completely destroyed."
Bill Lenkaitis, *center, New England Patriots*

"Scrape"

"Scrape" is a term used by linebackers almost interchangeably with "stunt." It means virtually the same thing. From out of their stacked position behind linemen, the linebackers "scrape" off the linemen as each charge in different gaps in the line.

A common scrape in the NFL is by the middle linebacker around the weakside defensive end in an over defense. The big defensive end fills the bubble area and the linebacker moves to the outside.

Stunting and scraping is a way of life for the inside linebackers in the three-four defenses of New England, Houston, and other teams. With only three linemen, these teams give ground in important gaps in the line and must stunt linebackers into them quickly to fill them.

"I've got to split the gap between two offensive linemen before the play develops and hold the hole until one of the linebackers comes up and makes the tackle," says middle guard Curley Culp of Houston. "If I don't, I'll be out of the play and probably sitting in one of the linebacker's laps."

Plugging up the holes and making their scrapes in the three-four defense is another challenge facing Sam, Mac, Mike, and Will, or Sara, Meg, and Wanda, or whatever they are called from team to team in the NFL's defensive jargon.

They are key performers and their positions are demanding. "It takes great physical gifts to play linebacker these days," says coach Bud Grant of Minnesota.

Their positions in stacks and the deployment out of them is adding new variety to the way they play. Outside linebackers are no longer always on the outside and the middle linebacker often moves away from the middle in over and under defenses.

Defense is the job of all 11 performers, but the linebackers play key roles in holding the offense to "three and out," three downs and a punt.

Jim Lynch of Kansas City (51) and Phil Villapiano of Oakland form a composite of NFL linebackers. Behind them, a diagram of the traditional four-three defense in which modern linebacking techniques have emerged.

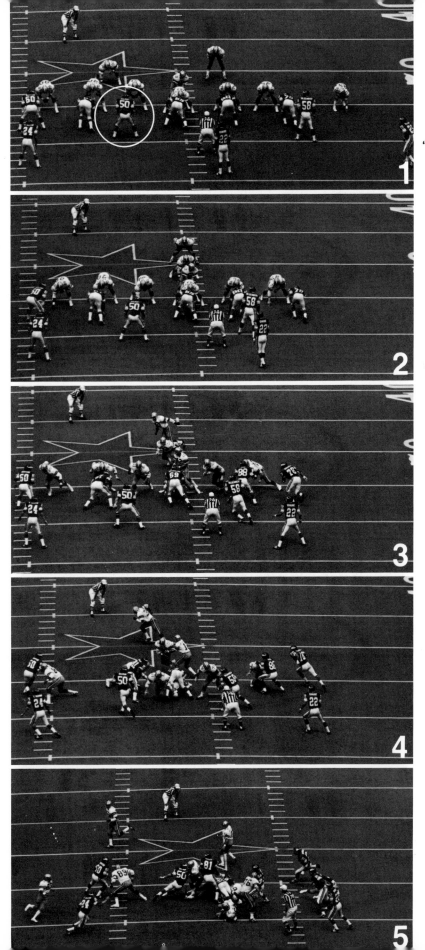

A Well-Executed Scrape

Scrape, the act of a linebacker stunting around a lineman and arriving at his destination in good position to stop the runner, is carried out flawlessly by Jeff Siemon of Minnesota. He works a stunt with defensive end Carl Eller against Dallas that ends with Siemon in the right place to tackle Cowboys' running back Walt Garrison. Above, Siemon comes up to meet another Dallas runner, Robert Newhouse.

Dangers of the Scrape

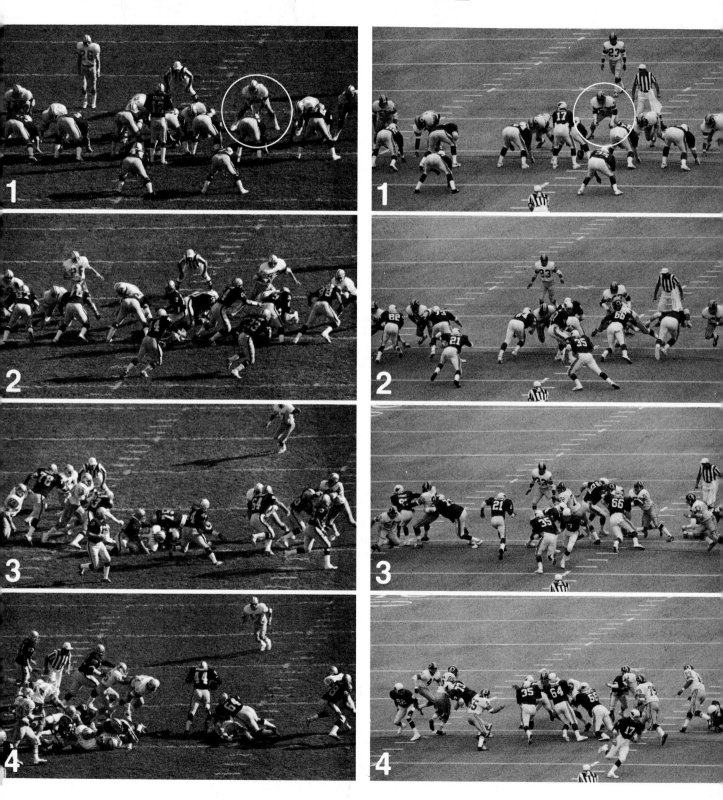

There is danger in the scrape.

It is a precise and demanding technique that inexperienced linebackers may have trouble learning and, as a result, may find themselves missing tackles.

An NFL coach, explaining why he had traded a linebacker of great promise, said, "He simply couldn't handle our scrape defense with all its offset alignments. He had trouble particularly working our stunts. We kept hoping he would pick it up but he never did."

If the scrape is not performed correctly it may end in disaster for the defense. If a linebacker scrapes too wide he leaves a big hole for the offense to run through. Or the linebacker may not square-up to the line of scrimmage or "maintain leverage inside-out," staying in position to make a quick adjustment once he has moved into the gap.

Teams that favor odd lines often stunt their linebackers back in the direction away from the shift. For example, a team in an over may attempt to fool the offense by slanting or stunting back to the weakside. The offense's answer, once it has picked up this tendency on the part of the defense, is to use counter plays. The ball carrier will start in the direction of the weakside and then come back strongside.

The Perils of Linebacking

At far left, a stunting Detroit linebacker (52) scrapes too wide around his defensive end and is out of position to tackle Marv Hubbard of Oakland. Hubbard gets past the linebacker with plenty of room in front of him. At near left, Washington's defensive tackles pinch and the middle linebacker moves to fill a gap behind a tackle. The St. Louis Cardinals run in the other direction, however, as Jim Otis takes a handoff from quarterback Jim Hart. At right is Walter Payton of the Chicago Bears, one of the quick running backs with which NFL linebackers have to contend.

Reading and Pursuit

"The secret of pursuit is just to get up and run."

Walt Michaels, *assistant coach, N.Y. Jets*

Since the dawn of football, defenses have been trying to see and identify formations and advance movements that tip off the play. They also must "read" the offense to narrow the margin of error as they guess which way to shift their line, whether to stack, stunt, or slant. When they guess wrong they must pursue with great hustle and desire to cover up the mistake.

These two elements, reading and pursuit, are paramount in professional defense.

Defensive teams in the NFL are given very specific rules for the way they pursue ball carriers. As assistant coach Ermal Allen of Dallas says,

defenders don't run after the man with the ball "like field mice."

Marion Campbell of the Atlanta Falcons adds, "People think pursuit is just hell-bent-for-leather. It's not.

"If the ball ends up on the sideline you want ten men on defense to end up there, too. The eleventh has reverse responsibility. That's a pursuit technique, too, and it's awfully important."

In any NFL game, only half a team's coaching staff is with the team on the sideline. The other half is seated in the press box far above the field where they see things develop and report to the head coach by telephone. One of the little-known secrets these coaches watch for is whether the opponent is taking proper lanes of pursuit on defense.

"You must be proper in pursuit or

A Cavalry of Redskins

The Washington Redskins' superior pursuit is evident as four players race to the rescue of safety Ken Houston and help bring down Terry Metcalf of St. Louis. At left, five Detroit Lions stop Buffalo's O. J. Simpson. At right, Don Woods of San Diego gets the same treatment from Jack Lambert (58) and other members of the Pittsburgh Steelers' defense.

the guys up there in the boxes will spot it and the next time they'll do something to take advantage of it," Campbell says.

Cautious defenses wary of this aspect, such as the defense of the Minnesota Vikings, put restrictions on the pursuit range of their middle linebacker. This is in sharp contrast to the onetime Chicago Bears' defense in which Dick Butkus made tackles from sideline to sideline.

Points of Attack

"Reading" an offense starts when it leaves the huddle and sets up in its formation. Whatever the formation may be, there are inbred, common-sense principles that guide the offense's points of attack.

Four of the most popular offensive formations in the NFL are diagrammed on this page. They are split backs, far, near, and I. "Far" means the halfback is on the far side, away from the tight end, and "near" means the halfback is on the side near the tight end.

The sweep is run most often from split backs formation. The best blocker of the two backs, the fullback, is on the same side as the tight end. That's strongside power.

Far is good for weakside running because the fullback is in position behind the quarterback and can get to the weakside faster than in split backs.

Near is a common goal-line or short-yardage formation and defenses can expect a lot of inside plays from it.

The halfback starts from a very deep position in I and can watch the blocking develop, and pick his way through if the defense does not pursue properly.

Those are the general principles. In the diagrams, the likely points of attack or paths taken by each running back from the four formations are shown.

The defense has other information, too. From its film scouting and computerization of much data, it knows which back the offense preferred to give the ball to on a given down and distance and in a given area of the field.

The relatively simple principles shown here are what Tom Landry of the Dallas Cowboys saw in 1960, when he went to an offense that constantly shifted from one formation to another until just before it snapped the ball to start the play. Other coaches who have not followed his lead believe such shifting is too complicated and breeds too many mistakes.

Landry also has used two tight ends in the game—and not just on

Split Backs

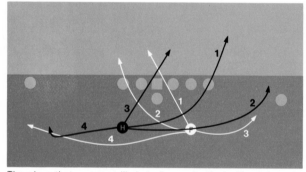

The plays that are most likely to be run by the halfback from the split backs formation are, in order, an off-tackle run, a sweep, a trap, and a pitchout. The likely plays for the fullback are the trap, weakside trap, pitchout, and weakside sweep.

Far

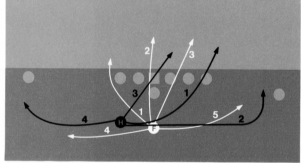

Likely points of attack for the halfback from far formation are the power off-tackle run, sweep, trap, and weakside pitchout. For the fullback: the weakside slant, trap, misdirection play, pitchout, and strongside pitchout.

Near

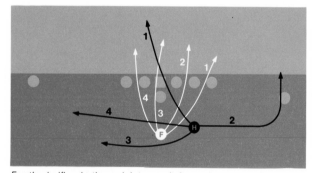

For the halfback: the quick trap, pitchout, reverse, and weakside sweep. For the fullback: the power off-tackle play, lead the halfback inside tackle, trap, and misdirection play. The near formation is best suited for runs by the fullback.

I

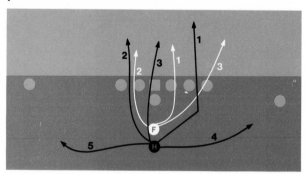

For the halfback: the off-tackle run, weakside run, delay or trap, pitchout, and weakside pitchout. For the fullback: the delay, weakside delay, and off-tackle trap. In all his carries from I formation, the halfback runs to daylight.

The Cleveland Browns in split backs formation against the three-four defense of the Houston Oilers. At right, defensive end Vern Den Herder and linebacker Nick Buoniconti, two members of the Miami Dolphins' defense who have the experience to read an offensive formation and know what to expect.

the goal line where extra blocking is needed. The defense must quickly identify the formation based on where the tight end is; if there are two, it makes decision-making more complicated.

Once the play begins, each defensive player watches for patterns of blocking that will tip off what play it is. This has grown more complex in recent years. Two pulling guards, which once automatically meant a sweep was starting, may not mean that today.

Run to Daylight

The offense's reply to a defense that is reading and pursuing well is to run to daylight.

Just as they are fundamental principles in defense, so run to daylight is in offense. As an act of common sense, it must have been part of the game from the moment the first ball was inflated. It gained definition through Vince Lombardi, however, and now permeates all pro football.

Every play has a strict design and is aimed at a particular place in the line. But the linemen, however big and strong they may be, may not be able to make their blocks well enough to pry that place open for the ball carrier. It may work out that the blocker nearest the point of attack has carried his man in the opposite direction. New running room is opened up, the back adjusts, and "runs to daylight."

Against defenses set in overs and unders, working unexpected stunts and slants, and expertly reading and pursuing, running to daylight is a necessity.

O. J. Simpson of Buffalo and Franco Harris of Pittsburgh are two

outstanding runners who have *carte blanche* from their coaches to free-lance their way when they see blocking break down or defensive pursuit filling the point of attack.

"I stutter-step up at the line, slow up and look around instead of blasting into the hole," Simpson says. "I'm an optimistic type. I always believe there's a hole there someplace if I can just find it.

"I know if I went charging into my assigned hole all the time, there'd be a lot of blockers with cleat marks all up their back. Why should I do that?"

Ermal Allen, assistant coach for the Dallas Cowboys, analyzed the running game of the Pittsburgh Steelers before the two teams met in Super Bowl X. Allen said, "Pittsburgh is a team that doesn't do anything fancy. What they think is fancy is to give the ball to Harris and let him run all over the field with it. They can have a play called to one hole but that doesn't make any difference to Harris. He can go anywhere, and he can wind up cutting outside and out-running everyone."

> **"The Steelers can have a play called to one hole but that doesn't make any difference to Franco Harris. He can go anywhere."**
> Ermal Allen, *assistant coach, Dallas Cowboys*

Practical Power
Above, Franco Harris of Pittsburgh picks up speed as he runs through a big hole in the Cincinnati defense. In the sequence below, John Fuqua of Pittsburgh begins a play that is a veer to the inside, but, seeing daylight, promptly changes his course. At left, the Steelers have the run to daylight philosophy turned against them by the best runner in the game, O. J. Simpson of Buffalo.

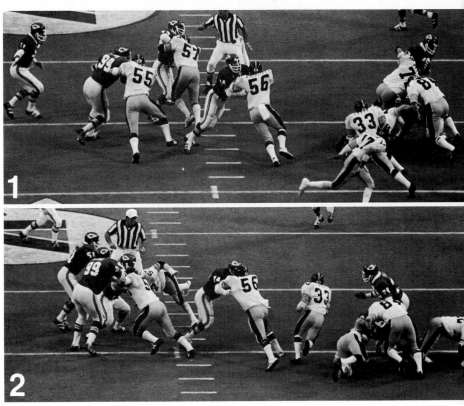

Misdirection

Misdirection is another answer by the offense to reading and pursuit.

A misdirection play is one that goes in the wrong direction—wrong according to the running back action that it shows. The flow of the backs appears to be starting toward one point of attack and suddenly hits an altogether different one.

Misdirection gained widespread use in football through the success of the Miami Dolphins' Super Bowl champion teams. Coach Don Shula explained it this way: "What we want to do is make those defensive linemen hesitate. If they know what you are doing, they are so big and quick they are going to destroy you. But if we can get them to wait and look—where they are not sure what they are doing—we have the advantage."

At the time, Shula had a back of great power who used the small edge gained through misdirection to maximum advantage. "If the defense took one small step to chase the play (i.e., were fooled by the misdirection), Csonka would break a tackle and get by them," says Walt Michaels of the New York Jets. "You couldn't arm-tackle him."

Others tried to imitate Miami with mixed results. A losing coach said after a game, "Instead of doing what we can do best, we tried to finesse it too much in the first half and run things like misdirection plays."

A High Water Mark
The Miami Dolphins put misdirection on display like never before in Super Bowl VIII against Minnesota. Halfback Mercury Morris starts from right to left as if the play is a sweep, but fullback Larry Csonka instead takes the ball up the middle for a big gain. At left, Cleveland's Greg Pruitt, a fast and deceptive runner.

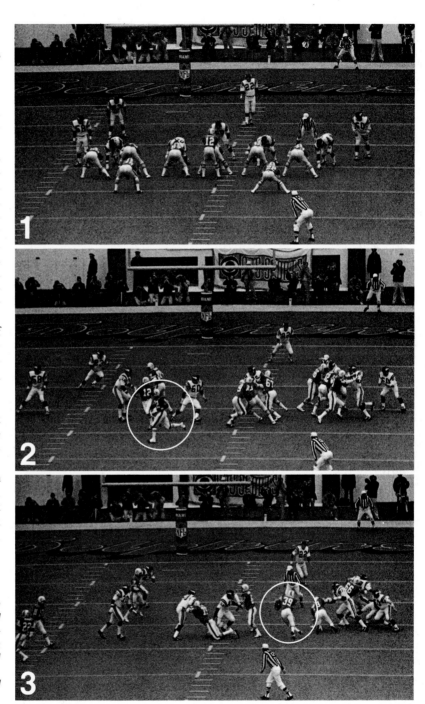

Influence

Influence is a third reply by the offense to the defense's reading and pursuit.

It is a term that is much older than "misdirection" but they both mean trickery and deception.

Misdirection is deceptive movement by backs; influence is deceptive movement by linemen. Miami put both into its attack and the total package was an exasperating puzzle for a defense to solve. Once the threat of a sweep by Mercury Morris had been established, misdirection could be used to cause hesitation in the defense. And it was compounded when the Dolphins began to employ false movement by guards Larry Little and Bob Kuechenberg, or run companion plays which looked alike at the start but became different plays as they developed.

Influence has meant many things in college and pro football—blocking a man and when he fights the pressure having the ball carrier run behind him; luring him across the line—for example, by setting up as if to pass block so he can be trapped by someone else; and, in the most widely used meaning, pulling a blocker as if on a sweep or trap, thus causing the defensive lineman to read the play wrong, follow the blocker, and leave his position vacant to be run through by the ball carrier.

Using Their Influence

The St. Louis Cardinals use deception to turn the Washington Redskins' pursuit to good advantage. When two St. Louis linemen and a running back move toward the left side of the picture, they are followed by the hotly pursuing Redskins. The play, however, goes in the opposite direction. Most of the Redskins are out of position as a result of the Cardinals' "influence."

The latter ploy is a "sucker trap"; "false trap" is a kinder term meaning the same thing.

The false trap was used against Henry Jordan, the aggressive tackle of the Green Bay Packers, in the mid-sixties, and the late assistant coach Chuck Drulis of St. Louis said he recalled seeing false traps in one of the Cleveland-Detroit title games in the fifties.

Many strategies are born of mistakes and false traps probably started when a guard pulled by mistake, thinking the play was a sweep, and his coach was surprised to see that it fooled the rival defensive tackle. Consequently, it became part of the playbook.

Influence blocking is now one of the major themes of NFL line play. It forces defenders to stay alert.

"If a guy is sitting in there on the snap not paying attention he may go running with that first look," says Marion Campbell of Atlanta. "The next time, he'll get the same look but it'll be a false trap."

A team successful with deceptions such as misdirection and influence can then make its normal blocks better. The defense has begun to hesitate and read and is a prime target for ordinary straight-ahead blocks.

Pulled Out of Position

A San Diego defensive tackle, in the middle of the photo above, is pulled out of position following the offensive guard in front of him, who pulled as if on a sweep. The Oakland Raiders run the ball into the area vacated by the influenced defender.

Force, Gap, Coordinate

To be fooled is to fail. After a defense is burned by trickery it must force, gap, and coordinate in order to prevent it from happening again.

The defense must combine the movement of the cornerback, safety, or linebacker to force the running play inside with the remainder of the coordinated defense filling every possible gap in the line, waiting for the runner if he chooses to go there.

Every stunt and slant must be covered up so that a vacated place is filled by someone else.

That sort of coordination is essential against a runner such as O. J. Simpson of Buffalo. "The thing you've got to do against Simpson," says linebacker Mark Arneson of St. Louis, "is stop yourself from trying to be the hero. Everyone has to stay in position and keep all lanes filled."

Coach Bill Arnsparger of the New York Giants says, "Against O. J., who is probably the greatest ever, you've got to play position. The temptation is to rush up and fill a hole. Then, whoosh, he changes direction and heads for the place you just came from. If everybody holds their ground you make out a lot better."

Arnsparger formerly molded Miami's defense and is one of the coaches who is changing defensive thinking with his emphasis on coordination.

Giants' defensive end Jack Gregory reached this rationalization: "Defenses are more demanding now. A player has to make more sacrifices. It's the no-name, no-star era. The Arnsparger defense is set up so that if you do your job everything else will fall in place.

"You can't freelance, and you can't individualize. I do my job, the guy next to me does his, the guy next to him does his, and so forth down the line.

"But the winning of a game today is not due to one person. It's all men working together. I'm reconciled to it and I see it working.

"If you've got pride, if you want to be somebody, lead in tackles and sacks and win, you try harder."

The deceptive tactics of offenses today have modified the thinking of many coaches, even "gapping" innovator Tom Landry of Dallas. "The theory is good, that if they're going to run to daylight then you stick a head in every gap," he says. "But it doesn't work that way because of the influence blocking and other things the offense is doing now."

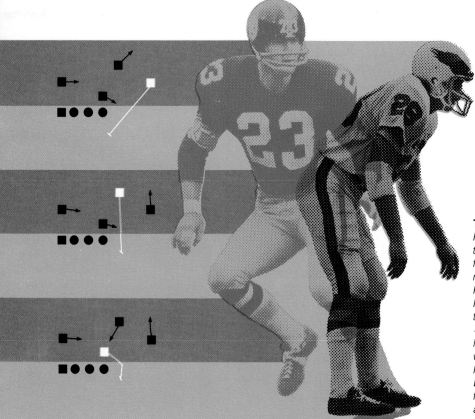

The Cowboys' Coordination
Here are two superb examples of the way the Dallas Cowboys coordinate their defense. In the first sequence of photos, cornerback Mel Renfro comes up to force a Pittsburgh Steelers' play and stops Franco Harris in his tracks. In the second sequence, the Cowboys move evenly into eight gaps —shown clearly in the second photo —and leave St. Louis ball carrier Donny Anderson with no place to go. At left, defensive backs Mike Wagner of Pittsburgh (23) and Bill Bradley of Philadelphia, and at far left, from top to bottom, three types of forces against running plays —by the cornerback, safety, and outside linebacker.

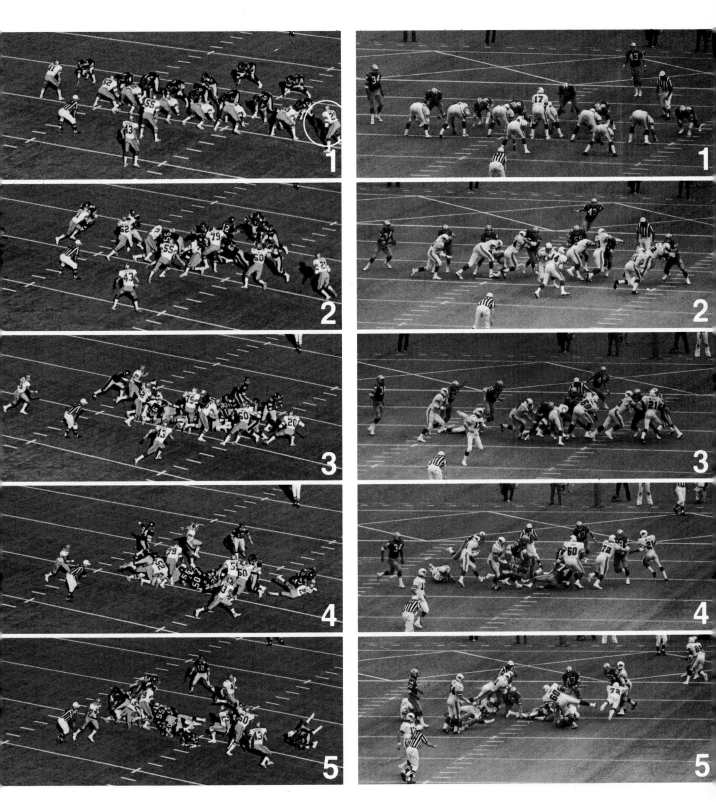

Play Without Keys

The burden of proof returns to the offense. Facing a defense that has read what it is doing and has filled every gap, it may decide the best recourse is to run a play without keys.

This is the ironic conclusion a coach may reach in a sometimes upside-down world of NFL strategy. The Green Bay Packers once pulled guards and ran unstoppable sweeps, yet 15 years later a defensive coach may say of a rival team, "If they pull their guards they're dead, because they'll lead us right to the play."

Once it seemed essential to pull the big guards and tackles to gain yardage. Now the opposite may be true; they must be kept "home" or they'll tip off the play.

The result is the "keybreaker" play, without any of the sure giveaways— pulling linemen, flow to the same side by the back without the ball, and crackback action toward the line by a wide receiver. They are thrown out and the play is run "solid," without keys.

When a game reaches a moment such as that, the sport of football has just gone full circle. It has progressed from the simple to the elaborate and back to being simple again. Coaches who have labored for decades to devise better ways to move bodies into position as blockers, in order to run the ball more effectively, now find they can do so by not moving those bodies at all and using "keybreakers."

But such plays are far from standard practice. "I don't think anyone would use them as a game plan," says Marion Campbell of Atlanta. "It's just something teams have in their offenses as a gimmick, to see if the

Mike Thomas, a young member of the Redskins' running cast.

defense is awake."

The mental give-and-take—action and reaction in the controlled meleé that is the running game—goes on. Offenses run off-tackle, sweep, and trap. Defenses shift into overs and unders, stack, stunt, pinch, and scrape. Offenses read, pursue, run to daylight, and work misdirection and influence trickery. Defenses coordinate. It goes on NFL weekend after NFL weekend, year after year. What develops out of the violent chemistry of the meeting of two teams may not occur in the same pattern when they play other teams a week later. They will have to use new strategy and counter-strategy against new rivals. It is a demanding business and they can be thankful that an alternative method for gaining yardage exists and has been around since its invention in 1906. It is called the forward pass.

A Solid Sweep

The Washington Redskins run a "solid sweep," one totally devoid of keys such as pulling guards, against St. Louis. The Cardinals are denied any tipoffs to the direction of the play and Redskins' runner Larry Brown (43) has a moment's advan- as he moves around left end.

143

Pass Rush

"The defensive linemen are paid to rush the passer and if they can't, they're stealing."

George Allen, *Washington Redskins*

The passing game is a series of contrarieties. It begins with the furor of the rush as the biggest men on the field charge after the passer with dangerous intent. After that comes the ballet delicacy of the throw and catch. For a moment time seems suspended. But the delicate interlude ends, and violence is rudely restored as a deep back or linebacker crashes into the pass receiver and brings him down.

Second and 10 and third and 7 or more . . . these are the downs on which the offense is most likely to pass.

The pass rush applies the pressure that compels the development of NFL quarterbacks and the growth of new passing strategy.

The young quarterbacks who last are those who can stand up to the rush, find receivers, and throw passes to them. NFL teams scout hundreds of college teams each year at great expense to find receivers who can either outrun or deceive the new coverages and get free to catch those passes before the quarterback is overcome by the rush.

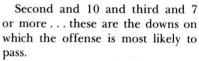

An awesome and frightening sight, Bill Gregory of Dallas bears down on passer Fran Tarkenton of Minnesota at left. Above, two players on the same team who rank as two of the best pass rushers ever, the Vikings' Alan Page and Carl Eller.

Bob Lilly's Epic Sack
Bob Lilly of Dallas makes the most memorable sack of his career in the Cowboys' victory over Miami in Super Bowl VI. Lilly (74) puts tremendous pressure on Dolphins' quarterback Bob Griese and eventually brings him down for a 29-yard loss.

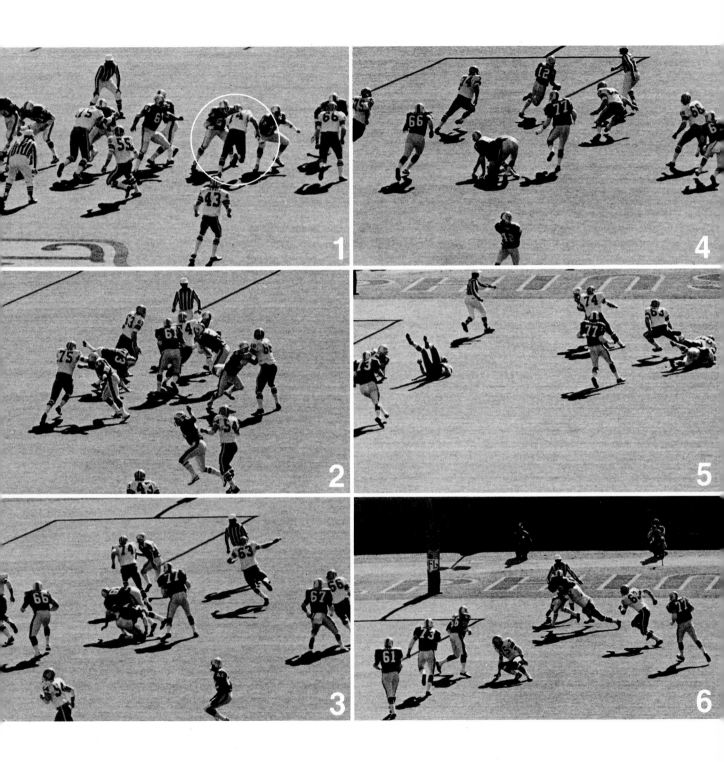

Pass Protection

Five men of immense size and unusual temperament bear the major responsibility of pass protection. They are the offensive tackles, guards, and center. Against an even rush, the tackles block the defensive ends, the guards block the defensive tackles, and the center—if he is not facing an over or an under—is free to drop back and look for weakened spots in which his help is needed. The center also may have double-teaming assignments if one of the rushmen is regularly succeeding in getting through to the quarterback.

Pass blocking is a "retreating war" so it is a part of the game that requires extraordinary unselfishness on the part of the offensive linemen. Backing up while taking punishment and resisting the instinct to attack, offensive linemen must be content to know they are keeping their man off the quarterback for the few precious seconds he needs to throw the pass.

The blockers must cope with strong defensive linemen, and in addition must face stunting moves in which the defensive ends take an inside rush and the tackle loops around, or the tackles exchange their lanes of rush.

The spread of three-four defenses gave pass protectors a new problem they never expected to have. There are only three rushmen in a three-four defense and it would appear that such a defense would offer a weaker rush. But teams using the three-four supplement their rush with

In the Pocket

The Houston Oilers form an efficient passing pocket to hold out the onrushing front four of the Dallas Cowboys. Quarterback Dan Pastorini has called a pass in which both running backs stay in to block, so he has maximum protection. The Dallas defensive ends are held off on the outside and the tackles are bottled up in front of the pocket. At left, an end zone view of San Diego's Dan Fouts dropping back to pass against the Cincinnati Bengals. Right, pass protection by Philadelphia's Mark Nordquist and Jerry Sisemore (76) against Council Rudolph of St. Louis.

still may face a second in the form of a running back.

The backs may stay in to block and then, seeing the situation is well in hand, will flare to the sideline or over the middle for passes. This system is a team's "flare control" and forms the

basis for the calling of pass plays. In a typical team's playbook, for example, "50 passes" are passes in which the backs may release but only after checking for blitzes; "60 passes" are passes in which the backs release and flood to one side or the other.

frequent blitzing by linebackers, and this leads to the unexpected problem: Each offensive guard must check to see whether the inside linebacker in front of him is blitzing. While he is doing this, a defensive end who has stunted or taken an inside rush may go right by the distracted guard.

The harried pass blocker's best friend is the running back who stays in the backfield to block instead of releasing for a pass. If a big defensive lineman gets by his first blocker, he

Stretching Coverage

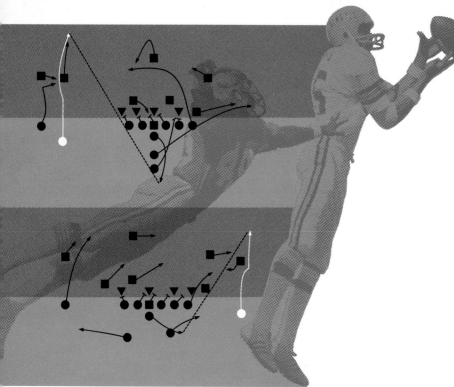

Players adept at stretching coverage are Cincinnati passer Ken Anderson, wide receiver Cliff Branch of Oakland, and Anderson's target Isaac Curtis of Cincinnati. A banner over Branch's head as he scores a touchdown emphasizes the importance of speed in passing. Diagrams at left depict offensive plays good for stetching coverage deep and wide.

These are the factors taken into account by the offense: Where will the defenders line up? How will they check the receivers at the line of scrimmage? What coverage will they play and how well can they disguise it? Which defenders backpeddle well and which do not? Which play aggressively and which play conservatively?

A consideration that has taken on even larger importance with the abundance of zone defenses is "stretching" coverage. In zones, deep backs and linebackers retreat and "fill up the field" rapidly as the play develops. Exceptionally fast receivers are needed against zones to get behind the zones or to involve defenders deep and free other receivers "underneath" the zones.

The passing combination of Ken Anderson to Isaac Curtis for the Cincinnati Bengals has succeeded in this strategy because of Curtis's great speed. Cliff Branch of Oakland, Mel Gray of St. Louis, and Harold Jackson of Los Angeles are other sprinters who typify the model receiver for the zone age.

A second requirement is a quarterback with the arm to reach the extremities of zones, not only with arching passes dropped over a defender's head against man-for-man coverage, but also with accurate passes thrown into the zones' weakened areas.

Zones may be stretched both vertically and horizontally, if the arm of the passer is strong enough for it. It is generally accepted that the test of a quarterback's arm is whether he can throw the bomb, but it is equally difficult to pass, for example, from the right hashmark and reach a wide receiver with an accurate pass 18 yards downfield on the left sideline.

The Limits of Pass Defense

Zones can be stretched vertically and horizontally. The Minnesota Vikings test the horizontal limits of Pittsburgh's zone in Super Bowl IX. Fran Tarkenton lays the pass over the head of the cornerback into John Gilliam's hands before the safety can race all the way to the sideline.

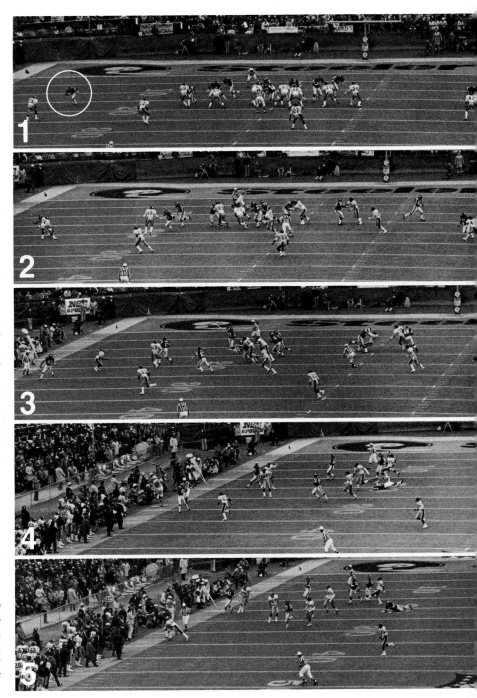

Linebacker Control

1

2

Opening Up the Middle

The flow of Pittsburgh backs Preston Pearson (26) and Rocky Bleier to the defense's right takes Kansas City's middle and right linebackers in that direction. It opens up the middle of the Chiefs' defense and Pearson turns into that area to take a pass from Joe Gilliam. Below, Dallas linebackers "take their drop," forming a perfect picket line along the 46-yard line. The photo illustrates well the problem the offense faces in coping with the front line of linebackers and a cornerback in zone defenses. Right, Andy Russell (34) of Pittsburgh and Mike Kolen of Miami, and a diagram of how linebackers drop.

Linebackers are the commandos of the defense. They have expert training and their skills set them apart as gifted men. They know their own job and at times they also must do the job of linemen and deep backs.

They range all over the field,

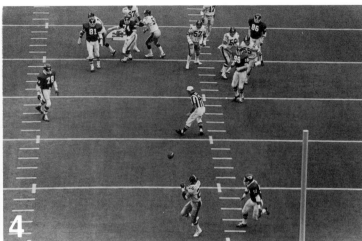

sometimes terrorizing the quarterback by joining the pass rush, or backing off uniformly and setting up an unbroken human barrier to his passes.

The inexperienced quarterback may find that not only does he have giant linemen rushing him, their arms high in the air, but downfield at eye level there also is a line of short zones, with a "rotated-up" cornerback and the linebackers blocking a clear view of his receivers and waiting to intercept any pass he tries to throw through them.

Linebackers must be "controlled" or the offense hasn't a chance. Ways must be found to prevent them from moving forward to blitz and moving backward to cover passes. No offense ever succeeds doing that for four quarters but measures exist for getting it done often enough to win.

Flare patterns send running backs to the flats, where quarterbacks can dump passes off to them if a heavy rush is on. If the offense is successful with such passes, linebackers grow wary of blitzing. Screen passes and draw plays further control blitzing. Finally, the safety-valve flare patterns can draw linebackers out of the middle of the defense and open it up for passing.

But the primary method of linebacker control, and one that has been refined in pro football for decades, is the nemesis of the second line of defense, the play-action pass.

"When a defense has a Terry Metcalf to worry about, the linebackers aren't so quick to fly out of there and get into their coverage. They're the key, really; if you can control the linebackers, you can do many more things."

Jim Hart, *St. Louis Cardinals*

Play-Action

Play-action is the tried, proven, and most widely used method of linebacker control. It is also a strategy rivaling influence and misdirection as the best modern example of trickery and deception in pro football.

A play-action pass is one that looks exactly like a running play at the start. It is intended explicitly to fool the linebackers. They come up fast to stop a run and they drop back to defend against passes. Deep backs behind them read the line; if it sets up in pass blocking, the secondary reads pass. But the linebackers also must read the backfield action, and that is why "play passes" work against linebackers and have for decades.

The essence of a play-action pass is the same as in a sandlot game when the quarterback says in the huddle, "I'm going to fake to you and throw a pass." It is a lot more advanced than that in pro football, to say the least.

Linemen cannot leave the line of scrimmage during a pass. Within that legal framework, an offense carries out all the elaborate run-blocking actions it normally uses in an ordinary weakside slant or trap play or pitchout. Linemen actually pull and trap, or if the design of the running play being acted out calls for them simply to "man" block straight ahead, they fire out hard as if on a running play and then quickly fall back to meet the rules governing them on passes.

Each lineman works hard to give the impression he is making the best run-block he has made the entire game. Each play-action pass is designed with as much of this sort of

make-believe as possible. "If the formation is to the right, for example, the only player who can't do much is the left tackle," says assistant coach Jack Faulkner of the Los Angeles Rams. "So he has to make his act look good in play-action."

In a typical play-action pass, the quarterback fakes a handoff to the halfback off-tackle and the onside guard pulls to make it look like a long trap. The flanker fakes a crack-back block on the safety. If everything works correctly, the safety may be up too close and the flanker can get behind him for a pass.

Play-action passes often are seen on first down and also inside the 20-yard line, where the offense expects to see zone defense abandoned in favor of man-for-man.

It is interesting to trace the evolution of the term "play passes." It is an abbreviation of "play number passes," which is what pro teams called play-action passes in the fifties. The reason is that in their system for calling passes, a play-action pass was called by using the number of the running play out of which it developed. For example, a pass that began with the offense running 36, a weak-side slant, was called "36 pass." Hence, it was a "play number" or a "play pass."

James Harris of Los Angeles fakes the football into the arms of running back John Cappelletti to start a play-action pass for the Los Angeles Rams. Right, Dan Fouts of San Diego reaches to simulate a handoff to a back out of the picture as middle linebacker Jim Carter of Green Bay reads the backfield action.

Quarterback Joe Ferguson of the Buffalo Bills fakes to O.J. Simpson, a running back all linebackers and linemen and deep backs must respect. Ferguson then withdraws the football and looks downfield for a pass receiver, confident that his fake to Simpson has gained him a precious few seconds of indecision by the defense.

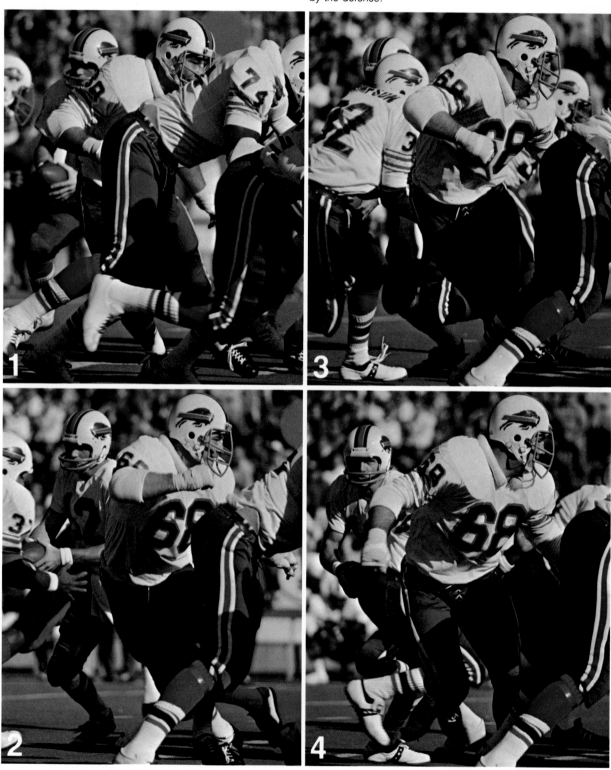

Play-Action Masters

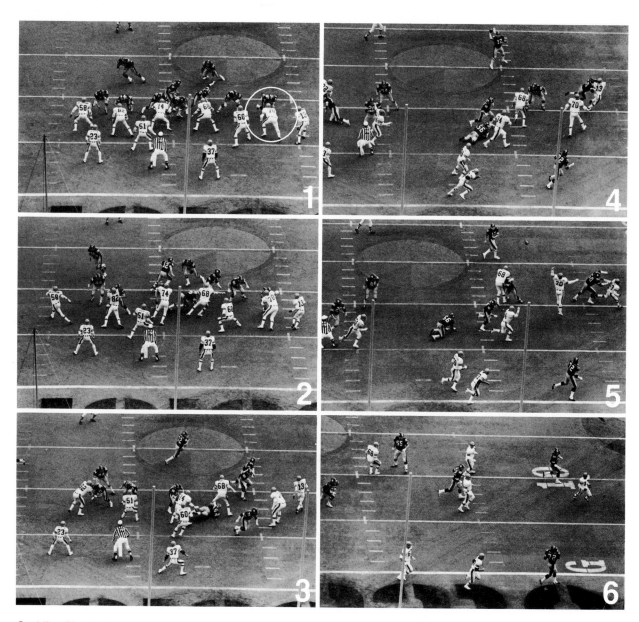

1

2

3

4

5

6

Goal-line Play-Action

Terry Bradshaw of Pittsburgh fakes to Rocky Bleier and throws a touchdown pass to guard-tight end Gerry Mullins.

"Bill Kilmer is the best play-action passer in football today. That's Washington's great strength. You've got to be able to control their play-action passes to do any good against them."

Tom Landry, *Dallas Cowboys*

Few strategies in the so-called modern era of pro football have had the sheer staying power of play-action.

It was responsible for one of the few times the Cleveland Browns of Paul Brown were surprised in a game in the All-America Football Conference. The New York Yankees saw that Browns' middle guard Weldon Humble was leaving the line too quickly the moment he read that it

was a pass play. Using play fakes, the Yankees piled up four touchdowns by Spec Sanders and Buddy Young and Cleveland had to fight back to gain a 28-28 tie.

No quarterback ever used play-action more effectively than Bobby Layne of Detroit. And another fifties quarterback, Y. A. Tittle of San Francisco, used it to throw passes to running stars Hugh McElhenny and

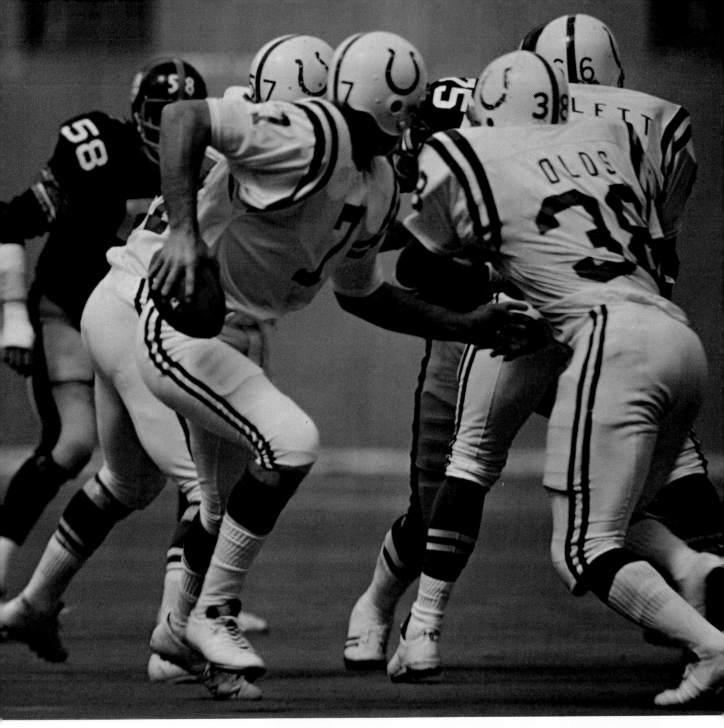

Joe Perry. Tittle also had a play in which his halfback faked into the line and then fell down. As rushing linemen lost track of him, he jumped up and ran into the clear for a pass.

Bert Jones of Baltimore, above, is a rising play-action master. His predecessors have included, from left to right, Bobby Layne of Detroit, Bart Starr of Green Bay, and Bill Kilmer of Washington.

Coverages

The word itself is an accomodation; they are "coverages" only when they succeed. It is a fact, however, that they have been succeeding frequently recently and that is why this is the most talked-about area of pro football in the seventies.

It has changed quite a bit since the "I've got one," "I've got two" system of the forties. That meant as the end came off the line, a defensive halfback shouted, "I've got one." Then if a back came out of the backfield, the linebacker shouted, "I've got two." And so it went.

Coverage today is light years from that in sophistication. Tom Landry of Dallas, who is identified closely with "multiple offense," has coined the term "multiple defense" to describe what is going on now in coverage. It is the fastest-growing area of the game.

Breaking Up a Pass

Wide receiver Mel Gray of St. Louis has the pass in his hands but loses it when it is stripped away by cornerback Nate Wright of Minnesota. Above, Paul Warfield of Miami is tackled so hard by Tom Casanova of Cincinnati that he flies out of his left shoe.

Today the man-for-man and combinations of the past are mixed with zones in dizzying varieties and craftily disguised by the secondaries. The movement of all 11 defensive players is coordinated.

"You watch the four linemen get off at the snap of the ball, the linebackers go to their zones, and the backs cover their guys . . . well, it's a painting," says defensive end Fred Dryer of Los Angeles. "If you had paint on your feet, you'd have a great picture."

1 Man-for-Man

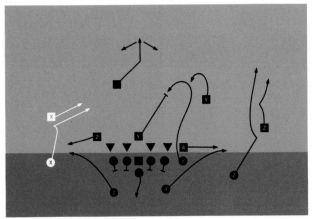

This is an example of man-for-man coverage. The primeval defense relies on speed and reaction because each defender covers one man alone until the whistle blows. The numerals 2 and 4 are the offensive backs and the coaching symbols X, Y, and Z stand for the wide receivers and tight end. Corresponding symbols on defensive players name who is responsible for each. There has been no wholesale abandonment of man-for-man because it is needed for variety.

2 Zone

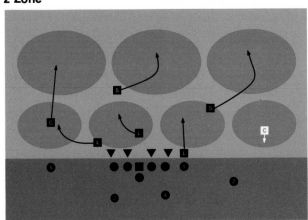

This is zone coverage that is "rotated," or "rolled up," or "revolved" to the side of the tight end, the strongside. The cornerback and the linebackers on that side fill the short zones and the other cornerback and the safeties fill deep zones. Zones revolve to the strongside or weakside, depending on which wide receiver they fear the most. They are far from fail-safe, because man-for-man is the predicament each defender faces if the ball is passed to a receiver in his area of responsibility.

3 "Safety Zone"

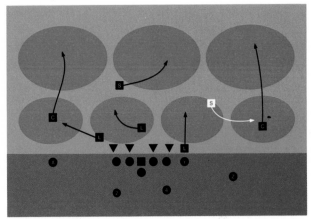

The first variation in rotation is what is called, for lack of a better name, "safety zone." In it the safety, not the cornerback, on the side of the rotation takes the short zone. Defenses are coordinated, and the assignment of the responsibility for forcing a possible running play to the inside, and zoning, are related. Strongside safeties force often and, if it is a pass instead, stay up close to play the short zone. That accounts for the frequent use of "safety zone" by all zoning teams.

4 "Linebacker Zone"

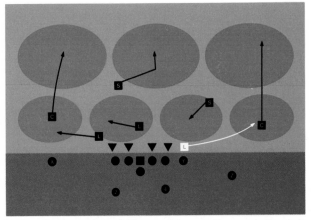

Variety is the spice of life on defense. No quarterback is given the luxury of seeing the same "look" in the defense twice in a row. The second variation in rotation is "linebacker zone." The linebacker, not the cornerback, on the side of the rotation takes the short zone. It is a demanding zone assignment for the linebacker because he must sprint to his area at top speed once the ball is snapped; he may have to run with a fast back all the way.

Eight Men Deep

5 Five Short, Two Deep

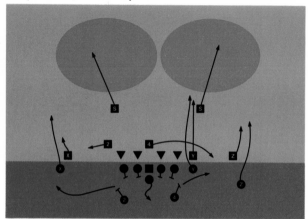

It is rather cumbersome to speak its name—"five short man-for-man, two-deep zone"—but it is one of the fastest-growing, most widely adopted strategies in pro football. The Pittsburgh Steelers played it while winning consecutive Super Bowl championships. The corresponding symbols in the diagram name the offensive players taken man-for-man by the cornerbacks and linebackers. The safeties, meanwhile, zone. A linebacker must deny the tight end the inviting deep middle.

6 Combination

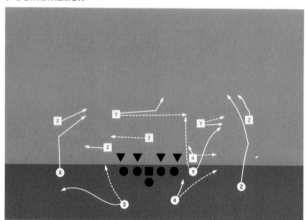

In this example of so-called combination coverage, the linebackers and safeties work together to cover the backs and tight end. Reading the diagram from left to right, the 2 back is covered by the outside linebacker if he goes to the flat or by the middle linebacker if he releases over the middle. The tight end, Y, is covered by one safety if he releases to the inside and by the other if he does not. Finally, the 4 back is covered by the outside linebacker on his side.

7 Zone Strong, Man Weak

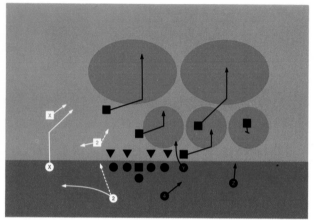

A weakness of the rotation zone shown in diagram 2 on page 159 is the unusually large area left on the weakside. One answer to the problem is to zone on the strongside and play man-for-man on the weakside. In this diagram, five-sevenths of the secondary is the same as in diagram 2. The cornerback and linebacker on the weakside, however, do not run to zones but instead pick up the split end and weakside running back immediately and cover them wherever they go.

8 Three-Four Zone

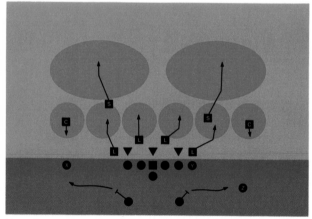

Here is an example of the way the linebackers and deep backs in the three-four (or Oklahoma, or "53" defense) can set up in six short and two deep zones. Six short zones can be a formidable barrier for both passers and receivers. This and all other coverages diagrammed here are only representative samples. Refinements and adjustments are made constantly in defenses based on a team's next opponent. And one small adjustment creates, in effect, a new pass defense.

With the three-four defense, the team without the ball can now have as many as eight men deep to cover passes. It is the latest development in coverages that led a frustrated coach Tom Fears of New Orleans to comment that defenses have filled up the field. Quarterback Joe Namath of the New York Jets complained, "They should outlaw the three-four. Now you're throwing into eight different-colored jerseys downfield, and they're using them in twenty different kinds of zones. It's hurting offensive football more than anything."

When simple rotation zone was played more than any other coverage, a rival quarterback had a clue to its rotation. He watched the middle linebacker, who dropped off away from the direction of the rotation.

The quarterback is robbed of that key by the three-four, however, as linebacker Gregg Bingham of Houston explains. "With our three-man front and four linebackers," he says,

"it's easier to disguise what we're doing. We've usually got eight men back on pass coverage instead of seven. Against us, a quarterback is almost forced to read the safeties since there's not just one middle linebacker to read."

Cornerback Herb Adderley of the Green Bay Packers comes up on Bobby Joe Conrad of the St. Louis Cardinals, and safety Ken Houston of Washington watches the action in front of him intently. Below, deep backs at work. They are, from left to right, Tom Casanova, Roger Wehrli, Willie Brown, and Dick LeBeau.

Man-for-Man

In the mid-seventies, the team that still plays a lot of man-for-man pass defense is also the team that is known as the most scientific in the game. It is the Dallas Cowboys, and they continue to play man-for-man on first down. The reason is coach Tom Landry's overwhelming desire to commit linebackers up close to play the run, stop it cold, and force the offense into a situation it hates—second down and 10 yards to go.

Charley Waters of the Cowboys described the feeling a Cowboys' cornerback can have in Pat Toomay's *The Crunch.* "All that space . . . all that green," Waters said. "It's like a long shot in pool. Since I'm so damned slow, my only chance is to hit the receiver hard before he gets into his route, then recover and try to stay with him for awhile."

Waters has since shifted to safety.

Like man-for-man defense, the bump-and-run strategy described by Waters has not vanished from football, either. Instead, it is one of many tactics a team may decide to use, depending on its opponent.

The Oakland Raiders were the main proponents of bump-and-run until they gave it up as their prime pass defense strategy in 1971.

"Man-for-man was all I'd ever played until last year," cornerback Willie Brown said in the *Oakland Tribune* in 1972. "But you can't use it that much in these days . . .

"If you show a little zone and show a little 'man,' you can slide off of one and into the other smoothly, you can throw the quarterback off a little."

Man-for-man coverage is responsible for confusion in the names of

How Timing Beats It
The Dallas Cowboys demonstrate how timing can defeat man-for-man coverage as Roger Staubach releases the ball even before Drew Pearson (88) has turned to the outside. The ball and Pearson come together before the coverage arrives.

the positions of safeties and the way they play. In basic man-for-man, linebackers cover running backs, cornerbacks cover wide receivers, one safety covers the tight end, and the other is free to roam. He is a "free safety," and the other is the "strong safety," always lining up on the strongside.

The "free safety" is not always free, however. The design of the defense may have him definitely committed to one side or the other to double-team or work in a combination with another player. Furthermore, his team may not flip-flop its safeties, so which of them is "strong" and which is "free" varies from play to play depending on whether the offensive's strength is left or right.

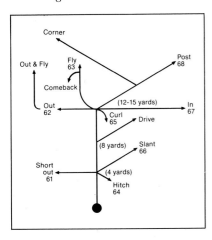

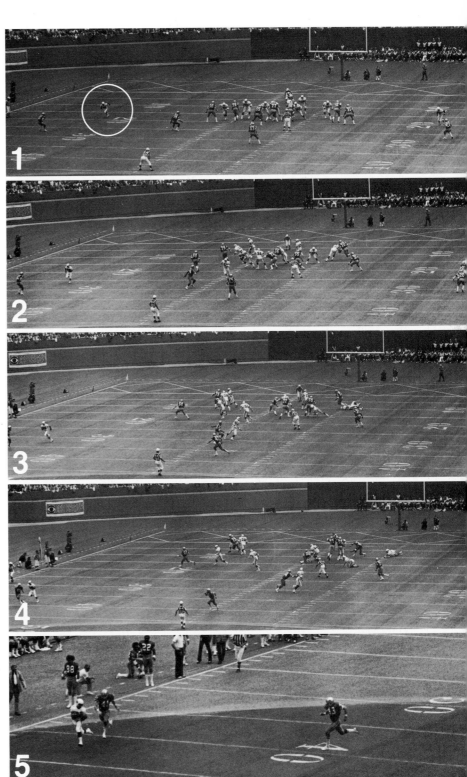

How Speed Beats It

In the same game, St. Louis turns the tables on Dallas and makes the Cowboys themselves have second thoughts about playing man-for-man. Wide receiver Mel Gray, on the left side of the sequence of photos, turns on the speed and gets past the Cowboys' cornerback for a catch he turned into a sensational 80-yard touchdown. Above, a typical team's "tree" of pass routes for a wide receiver.

163

Zones

"There are hardly any 'pure zones' anymore. In the last two years we have seen a great deal of multiple defense on sure passing downs."

Tom Landry, *Dallas Cowboys*

Paul Krause, patrolman of the far reaches of Minnesota's defenses, retreats to a deep zone at left. Below, the three-deep zones of Pittsburgh and St. Louis are seen in frontal and rear views. In each, there are four short zones filled by linebackers and a cornerback, and three deep zones taken by the safeties and a cornerback.

Zones—the ominous, stultifying and, some say, unfair, collective coverages—have been the talk of pro football in the seventies.

Wide receivers could be heard complaining vigorously as zones slowly became a way of life for the defense during the past decades.

"Will I ever see man-to-man coverage again?" Lance Alworth of San Diego asked in 1967. "Maybe, when I'm old and lose my speed."

Paul Warfield of Miami said of zone defense, "I don't see any need for it. We're all professionals. Whether you're a cornerback, strong safety, or weak safety, you should be able

A diagram of a typical team's conception of the possible passing zones on the football field, and Cleveland's Oscar Roan and Baltimore's Bruce Laird fighting for the ball in mid-air.

corner post corner

fan fan

flat slot hook hole hook slot flat

to cover a receiver without resorting to zone defense."

Zones exist as the natural recourse for a defense that was burned too often for its own good in pro football's bomb era. They also exist because of a rules disparity that has existed since the time of Walter Camp. He headed the rules committee at the turn of the century that compelled the offense to station at least seven players on the line of scrimmage at the time of the snap. But no such rule applies to the defense; it can have no men—or all 11—on the line at the snap if it wishes.

In zones, defenders get "as deep as the deepest and as wide as the widest man" in their assigned zone and back off to cover areas not individuals.

Any strategy is played better and better as it is used more and more. Zone defense and its growth have

been marked by rapid improvement in the speed and agility of linebackers as they cover zones the way deep backs do. Linebacker Andy Russell of Pittsburgh was expressing this trend when he said, "I think Bud Carson (the Steelers' defensive coordinator) would really like to have seven defensive backs out there."

The "front line" of a zone makes it effective. The linebackers in the short zones chuck receivers and slow their progress into the second line of zones. If the receivers make it through, the quarterback's view of them is blocked by the tall, wide, and quick linebackers.

Zones multiply to stop runs as well as passes, and to confuse quarterbacks. A cornerback will come up to force a possible run, and play the short zone. If the receiver on that side has taken a wide split, however, and might crackback on the cornerback, then force will be reas-

signed to the safety. Typical calls just before the ball is snapped might be, "Cloud" for cornerback force and "Sky" for safety force.

Confusing the quarterback, a middle linebacker who normally drops in the direction opposite the rotation might change and go the other way, making it harder for the quarterback to "read." The "hook" or "hole" areas vacated by the middle linebacker would be filled by someone else.

"It's frustrating sometimes. A wide receiver might run a mile in thirty-yard bursts, play after play, before the ball is thrown to him once."
Cliff Branch, *Oakland Raiders*

Beating Zones

Offenses beat zone defenses by stretching them vertically and horizontally, using speed to force man-for-man situations or taking zones deep and opening up areas for other receivers.

The Dallas Cowboys use formations such as double wing and triple wing that put a back on the periphery of the formation where he can become a fourth fast receiver and drive the defense out of its zone into man-for-man.

Other ways used for beating zones are passing into the seams or dead areas of the zones, flooding a zone with two receivers, using play-action to bring the linebackers up close, isolating a back on a linebacker, and passing to the weakside away from the rotation.

It is also beneficial for quarterbacks with the arm and the will for it to fearlessly throw into the rotation, says Ermal Allen of the Cowboys. "There is just as good a seam on the strongside as on the weak, provided the receiver can avoid a second chuck," Allen says.

A chuck is a legal bump against a receiver to delay him in his pass pattern. Defenses are allowed an unlimited number of chucks within three yards of the line of scrimmage and the receiver may be chucked once by each defender beyond that point.

Against zones, teams train their receivers to be patient and to catch the ball in a crowd.

Two other steps remain to be taken against zones: They are to throw passes to the tight end, and throw underneath zones.

Working the Weakside

Terry Bradshaw of Pittsburgh beats Cincinnati's zone with this weakside pass to John Stallworth. In this case, the left side is "weak," or away from the tight end, and Stallworth comes into the picture in the second frame. Bradshaw's pass reaches him before the zone can collapse around him.

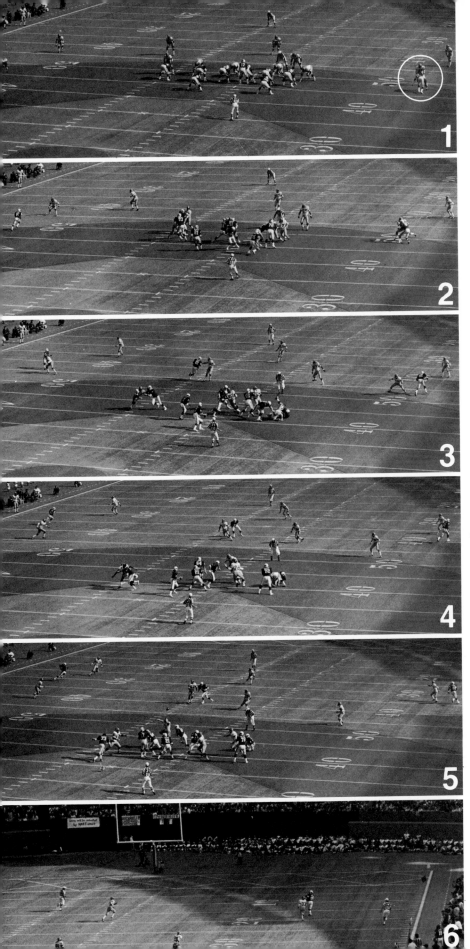

"Nobody can cover me one-on-one. And I don't think the zone has taken that much away from the passing game. I've caught quite a few long ones against zones. You can still get deep if you have the right personnel."

Harold Jackson, *Los Angeles Rams*

"The basic idea is to force the other team out of the zone into man-for-man coverage. We're well-equipped to do that. Fred Biletnikoff specializes in the short stuff and Cliff Branch has such great speed he sometimes runs right past the zone."

Ken Stabler, *Oakland Raiders*

Forcing Man-for-Man

The speed and range of St. Louis's Earl Thomas, on the right side of the sequence of photos, forces Washington's corner-back into a man-for-man confrontation that Thomas wins in the final frame. Above, Miami's Bob Griese, a cool quarterback who can out-think the variety of zones.

Tight End Passes

Faced with challenging zone defenses, coaches discovered a solution right in their own midst. It was the tight end, who was often left relatively untouched as the safeties went deep and the linebackers split up to go to their zones. Or tight ends filled the weakened area in the middle of two-deep zones, or slipped in behind linebackers who were frozen by play-action by the quarterback.

"Initially, everything they were going against was pure zone," says Tom Landry of Dallas. "They were operating inside and getting into seams without too much harassment. When teams started going to the multiple defenses it got harder for the tight ends and the number of passes thrown to them dropped off."

Tight End Theater
Tight end Jerry Smith of Washington fakes falling down, then gets up and makes this catch for the Redskins. Below, Charles Young of Philadelphia turns to look for a pass as he is pursued by two St. Louis Cardinals.

Free in the Middle
In a sequence photographed through the net erected at Texas Stadium to block placekick attempts, tight end Stu Voigt of Minnesota gets free in the middle of the Cowboys' zone and Fran Tarkenton completes a pass to him from out of his own end zone.

Underneath Zones

The demands made on passer and receiver are shown in this completion from Washington's Sonny Jurgensen to Charley Taylor.

The method that most offenses have used for beating zone defenses has been to pass "underneath" them, into the vacant areas between the line of scrimmage and the defenders who have dropped to their zones.

The targets for such passes often have been the crafty receivers such as Fred Biletnikoff of Oakland, men lacking blazing speed but able to pick their way through traffic and hang onto the ball under duress. But an even larger development was the emergence of running backs as more important passing targets.

Just as zones led to more emphasis on running, it also led quarterbacks to throw more passes to their backs. Some became league leaders. In 1973, Fred Willis of Houston became the first back to lead a league or conference in pass catching since 1933. Willis caught 57 passes for Houston to top the AFC. Backs then led the entire league in receiving for the next two seasons, Lydell Mitchell of the Baltimore Colts with 72 in 1974 and Chuck Foreman of the Minnesota

Vikings with 73 in 1975.

In general, backs are covered most often by linebackers who are not as light and as fast as deep backs. So backs can get open underneath zones.

Wide receivers can, too, but it could be said that the challenge to do so has been an emotional as well as a physical one for them. Relegated sometimes to secondary or "decoy" status, they have faced an adjustment problem against zones. They have been forced to give up the quick payoff of the bomb for a game strategy in which they patiently chip away at zones and wait for a human error to capitalize on for a long reception.

"Intermediate passing" is the name of the game as the receivers run the "outs," "hooks," and "turns" to entice cornerbacks and safeties up close until the proper moment comes to sprint around them for a game-winner.

Timing in passing has reached its third stage in pro football. At first

it was the combination between passer and receiver in which the former made the throw just as the latter made his cut and looked back for the ball. John Unitas and Raymond Berry of Baltimore were experts at such passes. Next came the free-lance approach of people such as Don Maynard of the New York Jets who, when a defender committed himself to the left, turned right and took Joe Namath's pass. Against zones, passer and receiver attempt to time the pass as the zones open and close like trap doors. A receiver running a "slant" or "in" senses an open area as he passes the cornerback, is aware that it has closed when he reaches the linebacker, runs into another open area, and so on. The speed and reaction of these cornerbacks and linebackers are studied in game film, enabling the receiver and passer

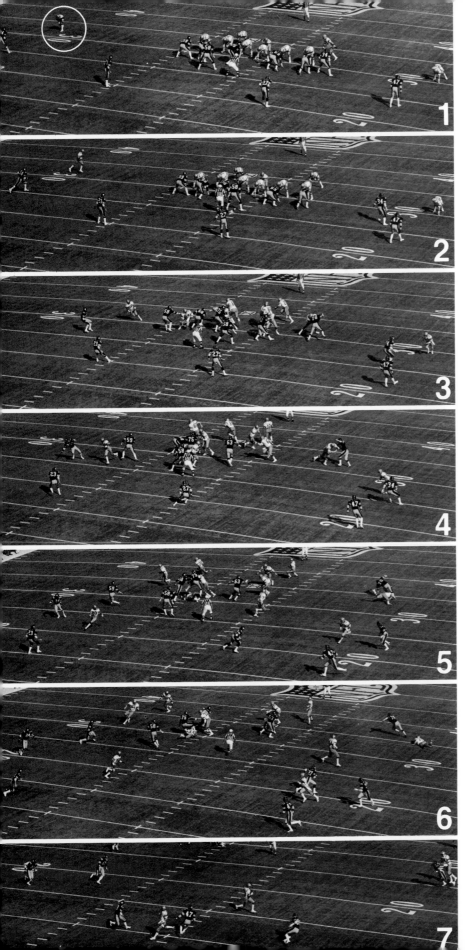

to work out the proper timing for the release.

It can also be seen that zone defenses test a receiver's courage like never before. He may pair one-on-one with a cornerback on a sideline pattern, but when the play calls for him to venture over the middle he enters an area of danger. Despite changes in the "chucking" rule, he may still be bumped once by each defender when he is three yards past the line of scrimmage.

For one man to have to beat several almost seems unfair. The Dallas Cowboys' multiple offense is an attempt to equalize this confrontation. The touchdown by wide receiver Drew Pearson in Super Bowl X was a good example. Dallas set up in double wing and Pittsburgh moved into a defense against it. Dallas shifted to split backs; Pittsburgh adjusted. Dallas put Pearson in motion toward the ball; Pittsburgh made its third adjustment—but too late. Pearson crossed underneath the Steelers' zone, other receivers carried defenders in the opposite direction, and Pearson made the catch and raced into the end zone untouched.

Under the Steelers' Zone
Drew Pearson of Dallas goes in motion toward the quarterback, turns upfield, and crosses under the Pittsburgh Steelers' zone to score a touchdown in Super Bowl X.

171

By the Numbers

In 1972 professional football changed its rules by moving in the inbounds lines or hashmarks of the field. The change was made to decrease the effectiveness of zone defenses, but ironically it may have helped them.

The hashmarks were re-painted on all fields 70 feet 9 inches from each sideline. It is easy to form a mental picture of the new location of the hashmarks because they now line up with the uprights of the goal posts.

The football is centered from these lines, or between them, every play. A scant six yards separate them. It is a coincidence that half an offensive line fits in a space of about six yards. Therefore if the center is over a hashmark and the formation is to the wide side the tight end is roughly over the other hashmark.

It also is a distance of nine yards from the hashmarks out to the large six-feet-high numbers straddling yard lines. And it is 12 yards from the numbers to the sideline.

The symmetry of all that provides very tidy points of reference for zone defenses.

The diagram on this page presents a typical arrangement of pure zone by a team using the hashmarks and numbers. During the hurried moments after the snap when a deep back or linebacker is dropping to his zone, studying the moves of the receivers, checking up on the offensive linemen to see if they are setting up to pass block, and backpedalling all the while, he has the hashmarks or numbers below him to guide him as he moves into place.

The rulesmakers may have un-

knowingly assisted zones with their 1972 move of hashmarks but they aided offenses without a doubt with standardization of numbers in 1975. All teams must now create the numbers in the same way and locate them in the same place on their fields. Previously, coaches worked with groundskeepers to locate the numbers at points that served the needs of their particular plan of pass defense.

Jack Tatum of Oakland demonstrates the consequences in store for receivers when coverage has worked well. At left, a diagram of a typical set of rules for an NFL team governing the use of the field hashmarks and numbers in coverage. Right, the Los Angeles Rams drop back along the hashmarks in a night preseason game against Buffalo.

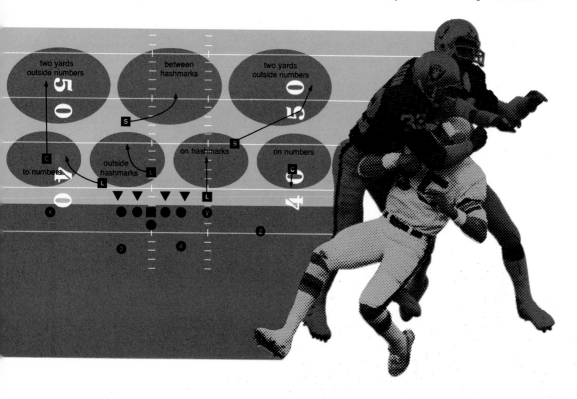

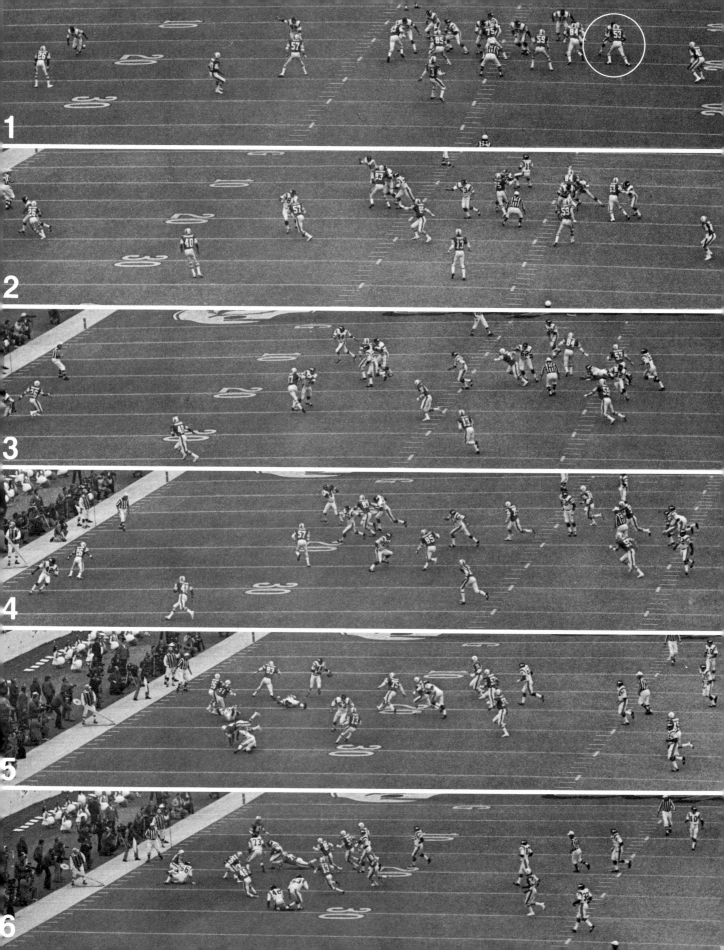

3-4 Defense

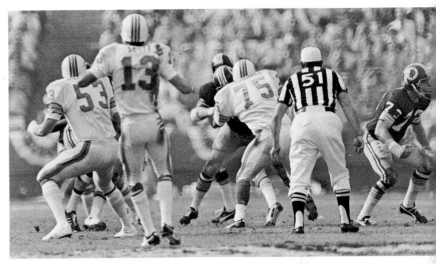

The three-four's advantages are numerous. A team may get away with playing only three linemen because the unpredictable pattern of the fourth linebacker confuses blocking. That player (who in Miami was number 53, Bob Matheson) can rush the passer, play man-for-man, or zone defense. Further, linebackers are the fulcrum of any defense and this one has four of them. They all can hide behind linemen in stacks, or they can set up with a cornerback in five short zones or even six. With such a front line there is no weakened short side as in pure four-three zone. And there are eight men available to drop back and zone the field.

The key to the success of Miami's "53" was the intense preparation of coach Don Shula. He studied game film of opponents and then rushed Matheson to the side where the pass was expected, thus blinding the passer, or dropped extra pass defenders—sometimes including the omnipresent Matheson—to that side.

Miami's use of Matheson as a rusher was, however, rather basic. At first he was the only Dolphins' linebacker who blitzed. Offenses learned to simply "move the slide" of blockers toward him.

Other three-four coaches arranged to work varieties rushing all linebackers . . . and so did Shula.

Linebacker Doug Swift blitzes Pittsburgh's Terry Bradshaw, above, and the "53" is viewed from behind safety Jake Scott during Miami's Super Bowl VII victory over Washington.

Strategy for a Super Bowl

The three-four, or "53" defense of the Miami Dolphins moves its eight pass defenders into position with smooth coordination against Minnesota during Super Bowl VIII. At right, a diagram of the defense and a photo of its key member, linebacker Bob Matheson, at work.

"Nose Man"

"I don't like the word 'sacrificial,' but that's exactly what you have to call it. We sacrifice our bodies so the linebackers can make tackles. I guess we're just garbage collectors."

Curley Culp, *Houston Oilers*

The "nose men" or middle guards of the three-four defenses play pro football's newest position.

There actually have been middle guards since football began, in the six- and five-man lines; in the three-fours of college football; and in the overs and unders of the four-three defense. But there were no middle guards in the game programs of modern pro football until the arrival of the three-four.

The men of the three-man defensive line are outnumbered by five offensive blockers. They must give not an inch of turf and constantly slant and stunt.

Tackle Dan Dierdorf said of New England's three-man front, "They don't ever play their defense straight ahead. If they did they'd be at a tremendous disadvantage. One time they'll slant the nose man. Next time they'll pinch the ends. Their movement is what causes you problems."

The Adaptable 3-4

Two photo sequences demonstrate the variety of line play in the three-four defense. At left, Oakland linebacker Ted Hendricks blitzes and the three-four becomes, in effect, a four-three rush. At right, only three Detroit Lions rush but because of blocking confusion caused by the three-four they still sack the quarterback. At far right, Houston's Curley Culp, one of the "nose men" who are key performers in three-four defenses. On pages 178-179, the three-four of New England piles up the Green Bay Packers.

Situation Defenses

Clark Shaughnessy wrote the glossary of defensive terminology for the Chicago Bears. Some of the words stuck. Others didn't. "Silver" defenses (based on coinage) and "quatro" (for an ordinary four-man line) never caught on as standard defensive terms in the NFL.

But "nickle" did. It meant a defense with five backs. Today it is one of the most common of the so-called situation defenses, which are used at a particular juncture of the game to meet a specific need and to help coaches get the most out of their personnel.

Bud Grant of Minnesota created the "Hack defense" with Dale Hackbart as a fifth back in the late sixties and says such a defense had long been played in the Canadian Football League.

Grant and George Allen of Washington became two of the leading proponents of situation defenses. Washington frustrated a rookie Green Bay quarterback named Scott Hunter with a five-man line in a 1972 playoff game. Grant also adopted the five-man line and played it often. Minnesota and Oakland also used six-back defenses.

In a nickle defense, a big but slower linebacker is removed from the game in favor of a smaller but faster deep back. There are now five backs to cover the three main receivers—the wide men and the tight end.

In a six-back defense, that imbalance is increased but the linebacker-weak secondary must be supported with a strong pass rush.

Stunts by the linemen are common in these defenses.

Tom Landry of Dallas added such defenses in 1974 and 1975. "They're good if they become a pattern for the team," he says, "but at first they hurt the confidence of the guy who is taken out. He thinks he's been removed from the game because he's less of a football player. But once the situation substitution has become a pattern for you, it's an acceptable thing."

It is possible for a sharp quarterback to simply watch the players coming onto the field for the defense and thus determine which situation defense is coming. Defenses tried to shield the quarterback from such an advantage with oversized huddles in which all the possible substitutes went onto the field and the un-needed ones left just before the snap. Such tactics were prohibited by a tightening of the rules after the 1974 season.

Six Backs at Work

The six-back defense that Minnesota frequently plays in passing situations works against the Pittsburgh Steelers in Super Bowl IX. Middle linebacker Jeff Siemon also drops off in pass coverage. Pittsburgh's pass to tight end Larry Brown is incomplete. Above, the five-back or nickle defense of the Washington Redskins. Below, cornerback Ken Ellis is poised to cover a receiver for the Green Bay Packers.

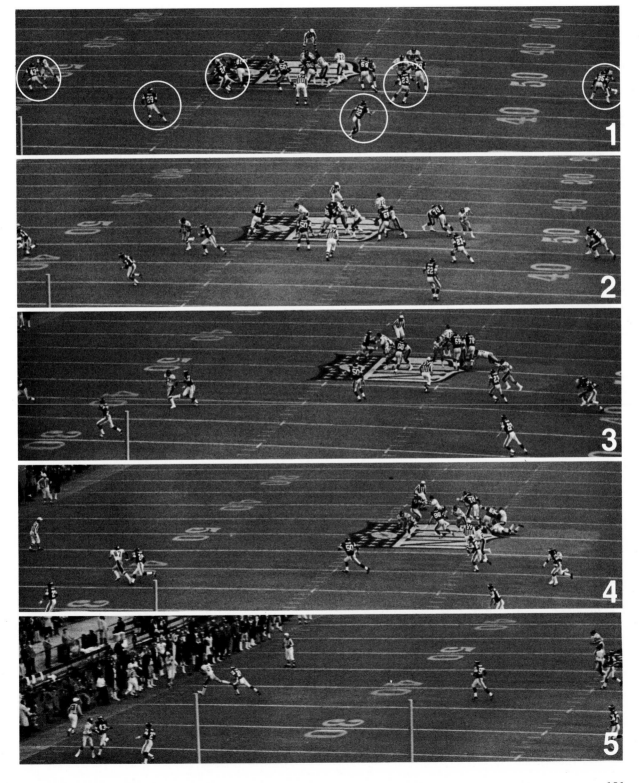

Linebacker Blitz

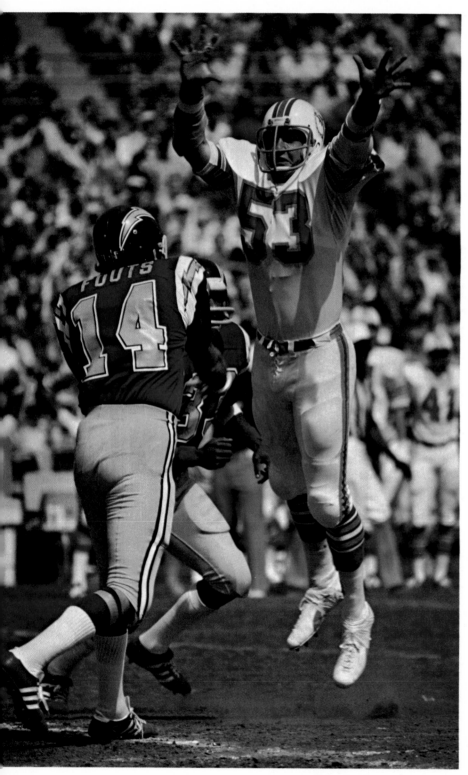

It's halcyon days are long gone but the linebacker blitz is still a terrifying weapon the defense can launch at the quarterback at any time.

Blitzes are often a desperate measure. They are used against runs as well as passes. There are specific rules for their use. They make actors out of linebackers the way play-action passes do offensive linemen. And the terminology for blitzing is one that you can trip over if you are not careful.

Blitzes are desperate when they are used as a last resort, one last try to pressure the passer after the regular four- or three-man rush has grown weak and is being blocked effectively every play. Each time he blitzes to join the rush in this manner, a linebacker deserts pass coverage and leaves a cornerback or safety all alone behind him to play a receiver man-for-man.

In addition, the linebacker is no longer in position to make the deep back's job easier by chucking the receiver as he leaves the line. For these reasons, a blitz call in a defensive huddle may prompt a cornerback to cast a quick glance at his linebacker as if to say, "Okay, pal . . ."

Blitzes are aimed at the side on which a run or pass is expected to go. "You blitz to take away a team's strength," says linebacker

Stopping a Touchdown
A blitz by linebacker Ted Hendricks of Baltimore stops a pass from Craig Morton to Duane Thomas in Super Bowl V. The pass almost certainly would have resulted in a touchdown and the gesture by Dallas tackle Ralph Neely, who had pulled to lead the play, expresses Dallas's frustration. At left, Miami's Bob Matheson blitzes San Diego quarterback Dan Fouts.

Wally Hilgenberg of Minnesota. "If they're running to the strongside, you blitz strong. If they're sending the weak back out in a pass pattern, you blitz weak. The blitz is a great weapon if it's used as a surprise."

Outside linebackers blitz more than middle linebackers. They take the outside route more often than the inside, because there's so much congestion there. And the weakside linebacker goes more often than the strong, because the weak 'backer has the "free" safety behind him to cover the weakside halfback—normally the linebacker's responsibility. The strongside safety doesn't have this luxury because his safety has to stay with the tight end.

The acting awards come when linebackers try to hide the fact that they are about to blitz from quarterbacks. But the wily quarterback may know that the linebacker standing there casually, almost aimlessly, as the signals are called may turn into a screaming, blitzing banshee at the snap.

Blitzing has produced some of football's most colorful language such as that of the Chicago Bears when they had such as "crash buck I" and "double baker burn" and the New York Giants of the early sixties with "raid rhumba," "flame Winnie," and "fry Susie."

Other teams may not have adopted language as colorful but they were very specific about exactly what a "blitz" was. The ordinary weakside linebacker rush was "weak dog." Both linebackers going was "red dog." All three linebackers was "mad dog." And all three linebackers, a safety, and of course the four linemen, was "blitz." It was a portentous term and it was not used lightly.

Safety Blitz

Joe Namath of the New York Jets finds himself safety-blitzed by Autry Beamon, the extra man in Minnesota's five-back defense. Above, in a rare Pittsburgh safety blitz, Glen Edwards (27) moves through a broad avenue in the forward wall of the Kansas City Chiefs.

The very name of the position—safety—seems to preclude the taking of risks. Gamble though it may be, the safety blitz is still another measure defenses may take to press a quarterback and add variety to his game plan.

The safety blitz is a strategy that can be traced directly to one man and one origin, and for which no earlier claims exist. No defense had ever before committed its safety to a mad charge after the quarterback, leaving a glaring weakness in the secondary, until Frank (Pop) Ivy and his free safety, Larry Wilson, unveiled it, probably in 1961.

It was an almost equally radical move when the Boston Patriots of the early sixties at times elected to blitz not only their free but their strong safety. This removed the best tackler of the two safeties from the secondary. It was a dangerous step but it is one that is copied often today. Boston assistant coaches Marion Campbell and Fred Bruney were its innovators and they later became head coach and defensive coordinator of the Atlanta Falcons.

A safety blitz that is successful can dump the passer for a big loss and give the defensive team a great boost in spirit. Or it can end in disaster as it did in Super Bowl X, when Dallas's Cliff Harris blitzed Terry Bradshaw but Bradshaw got off a game-winning 64-yard bomb to Lynn Swann in the deep regions Harris could have helped cover.

Free safeties usually blitz between the tackle-guard or guard-center gap and strong safeties through the tight end-tackle gap. The strong safety can disguise his blitz, and have less ground to cover, because it is common for him to be up close to the line at the snap, whereas the usual location for the free safety is several yards deeper.

Shotgun

"If the other team uses a deliberate pass defense, why shouldn't we use a deliberate pass offense?"

Tom Landry, *Dallas Cowboys*

The life of a shotgun quarterback—Roger Staubach is sacked vigorously by Philadelphia's Bill Dunstan, above; below, he reaches for a low snap, then sets up and gets the pass away successfully.

It was a sensation for the brief time when the San Francisco 49ers tried it in 1960 and 1961. Its appearance resembled football formations 50 years old or more. It put an exciting, scrambling quarterback in a position in which he could use his skills to great advantage. And in 1975 it was being coached by Tom Landry. For all these reasons the shotgun formation of the Dallas Cowboys was of compelling interest.

Dallas used the shotgun or spread (the latter is Landry's term for it) thirty percent of the time while winning the National Football Conference championship and narrowly missing a victory in Super Bowl X.

Landry said he adopted the formation in order to give quarterback Roger Staubach more time to read the eight-deep zones being used in three-four defenses and the five-back nickle defense of the Washington

Redskins and other teams.

Staubach, a two-time NFC passing champion, reacted sharply to questions about whether he had more trouble than other quarterbacks in reading defenses. "If you look at my passing statistics, I must be doing something right," he said.

John Brodie, one of the three quarterbacks or tailbacks San Francisco used in its shotgun of 1960 and 1961, once complained that he had trouble reading coverage from the shotgun because he must be looking down at the ball being centered to him during the important seconds at the start of the play. The quarterback cannot be reading the defense at the same time. That would appear to be a weakness.

But Landry argues, "When you line up in the shotgun you get a pre-read on how the defense is setting. Granted, you lose your initial read with the snap, but you get another one for about a second and a half because you are already back there where you are going to throw the pass, instead of driving back from the center to get there."

The shotgun formation offers new challenges for defenses who are about to play against it. Although it does not appear to be especially good for running, long runs can be broken from it.

Triggering a Touchdown
Staubach works from the shotgun and completes a 34-yard touchdown pass to Percy Howard during Super Bowl X against Pittsburgh.

Screens and Draws

A strategy such as the shotgun formation allows a quarterback to move left or right and escape a hard rush. Screen passes and draw plays, however, are time-honored tactics of football that *encourage* big rushes.

As pass blockers set up on a screen pass, their performance slips a little, hopefully not enough to give away the play and only enough to allow the pass rushers to get by with a minimum of interference. In a typical screen, they are lured further back by a quarterback who pumps once on a fake pass, then retreats further in the pocket. As a back swings into the flat, interior linemen pull from their positions to lead him as the quarterback drops a short pass over the rushers into his hands.

There are outside screens and middle screens. And the screen is one of the rare ones in which centers often pull and lead the play.

Screens get running room for fast backs who may have had trouble getting loose on ordinary scrimmage plays. Screens helped display the talents of such greats as Hugh McElhenny of the San Francisco 49ers and Gale Sayers of the Chicago Bears.

To make screens work, a team must first have established that it can complete long passes and thus force the defense to rush hard. Furthermore, screens are not very effective against teams with outstanding linebacking play.

A Patriots' Screen

The New England Patriots complete a screen pass as fullback John Tarver takes Jim Plunkett's pass and moves upfield behind a screen of three blockers. Above, Atlanta's Pat Sullivan swings a screen pass out to running back Rudy Holmes.

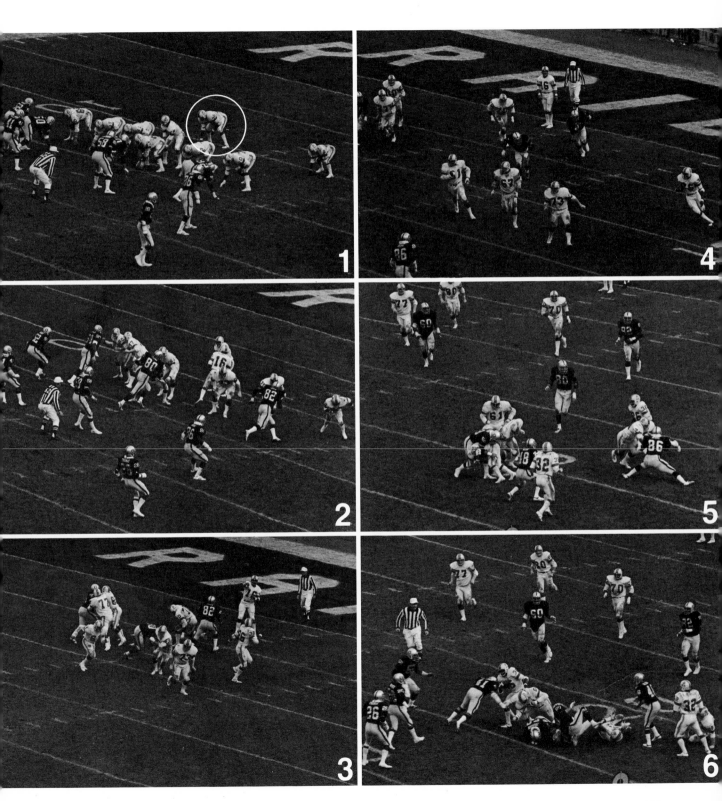

NFL "Spies"

The ball is snapped and the front four begins to battle its way toward the passer. A rusher head-slaps on his first step off the line and a blocker wards it off with a swing of a giant padded hand. Each individual confrontation continues furiously as the rushers claw their way nearer and nearer the expectant passer standing in the pocket. But there is a hidden factor at work here. There is a "spy" on the field.

He is the creation of a defense that has been embarrassed too often by screen passes and draw plays. Each time the defense rushes the passer, all its linemen may appear to be going all-out at first but in reality one of them is "spying," laying back to pick up the draw or delay or move outside to help stop the screen.

Quarterback draw plays, and also scrambling quarterbacks in general, are other subjects of attention for the "spying" lineman. It helps if he is an experienced player who is good at reading an offense.

Merlin Olsen of Los Angeles is a good example of a crafty veteran who has excelled at both all-out rushing and in "playing soft," checking his rush and watching what develops.

If the defense is in an over or under, it is generally the nose man

who spies. During blitzes by linebackers, it is common for one of the linemen to lay back and spy to control the area left vacated by the blitz. When a safety blitzes, one or both defensive ends become spies.

A "controlled rush" has been a growing theme in pro football, at least since the first wild scramble of Fran Tarkenton, and now the concept of "spying" is integrated into the total coordination of a defense on passing downs.

In addition, the other front linemen attempt to keep uniform lanes of rush toward the passer so they also will be in position to stop the draw play if it develops.

Draw Plays and Spies

Dallas's left defensive end takes too wide a charge and gives Terry Metcalf of St. Louis the chance to zip through for a good gain on a draw play. Steve Owens of Detroit, left, is typical of NFL fullbacks who run the draw play well. Above, Merlin Olsen of Los Angeles, one of the defensive linemen who lay in wait to stop draws as other rushmen go all-out for the passer.

Rollouts

Quarterbacks on the Move
Terry Bradshaw of Pittsburgh rolls out and throws a touchdown pass to Larry Brown against Minnesota in Super Bowl IX. Right, Roman Gabriel of Philadelphia lofts a pass to running back Norm Bulaich.

Rollout passes have led quarterbacks to take unusual safety measures.

Away from a pass rush that has begun to dig grooves in the turf with its regularity, quarterbacks can better locate a receiver. They risk injury, however, and as a result Fran Tarkenton developed the dive *under* tacklers and Roger Staubach the slide-into-second-base approach.

But as Pittsburgh coach Chuck Noll says of the scrambling by his quarterback Terry Bradshaw, "Quarterbacks with this ability must not be discouraged. You never win football games allowing fear to take away what you do well."

Man-in-Motion

Man-in-motion was probably invented about the same time as the airplane. Its creator or creators, however, probably never envisioned the uses to which it is put today by NFL teams.

Safeties are frequently the target of the beguilement of man-in-motion. Knowing that a team shifts the responsibilities of its safeties to deal with motion, an offense can force its opponent into using the free safety's tackling ability against a running play or forcing him up and passing deep against the strong safety, who is more suited for stopping runs than passes.

A common man-in-motion is by the flanker, who is the wide receiver on the side of the tight end, toward the ball. If he crosses all the way to the other side of the field, he may force the defense to change its thinking as to which side is the strongside, leading to possible mental errors and personnel mismatches.

Defenses view an offense as two-sided, a left side and a right. If a play purposely starts at a point in which the man-in-motion is directly behind the quarterback, the defense may be unable to agree which side has the responsibility to cover him. Or their indecision about the man-in-motion may cloud their minds about the coverage in general.

Becoming a Pass Target

Terry Metcalf of St. Louis goes in motion to the right, Washington's linebacker and strong safety are up close to the line (second photo), and Metcalf comes open for a swing pass from Jim Hart with only a cornerback left to stop him. At far left, Washington uses the same strategy putting wide receiver Roy Jefferson in motion behind quarterback Bill Kilmer.

Beating Motion

The strategies of NFL teams for playing and defeating man-in-motion vary from one to the other, but they all agree on one point—cover it with deep backs and not linebackers. That was the method tried in the thirties and forties when the early Chicago Bears' T formation with man-in-motion was in its haydey. The results of such a strategy by the Washington Redskins' defense can be seen in the sequence of photos on page 40.

An NFL defense in the seventies would not be so willing to move a linebacker out to the periphery of the formation and out of position to help stop a running play. And no matter how versatile linebackers have become—big enough to support the run and quick enough to support the pass—there are still wide receivers in the league fast enough to preclude any discussion of covering them with linebackers when they go in motion.

"You think about a guy like Isaac Curtis of Cincinnati," says Jim Trimble, director of pro personnel for the New York Giants, "and you forget

One Way to Play It

St. Louis cornerback Roger Wehrli moves all the way across the formation to cover Dallas's man-in-motion, Drew Pearson.

about it right away."

An outside linebacker might move into a stance several yards away from his normal alignment, a "walkaway" stance, to adjust as a back goes in motion. But eventually the back will be turned over to a cornerback while the linebacker warily keeps an eye out for a quick slant pass over the

middle or, worse, a crackback block.

If it is a wide receiver who is going in motion across the offensive formation before the snap, he may be followed all the way by a cornerback or picked up by a safety on the opposite side.

Teams following motion with a cornerback can become the victim of a strategy in which the offense tries to tire the corner who dutifully chases the motion, play after play. But in such a case the defense simplifies its pass coverage rules, gives strict assignments to the other deep backs for covering the remaining receivers, and moves to get the harassed cornerback help.

Zones may be played against man-in-motion. Their variety, in fact, may be increased by it. If a zone has been called, the cornerback who has followed the motion may then stay up close to play the short outside zone.

Covering the man-in-motion with the safety on the opposite side may appear to be the safest strategy. However, the play may begin before the man-in-motion has reached a point at which he is clearly the opposite safety's responsibility.

An Alternative Method

Pittsburgh's cornerbacks stay in place as Isaac Curtis of Cincinnati motions from right to left in the photos. Curtis is picked up by Steelers' safety Glen Edwards and played man-for-man. On pages 198-199, the excitement of the passing game unfolds as quarterback Dan Pastorini of Houston releases a pass to Billy Parks under heavy pressure from the New York Giants' rush.

Variety

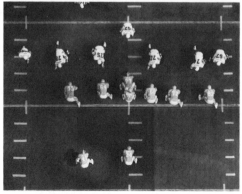

There is a dialogue in *Run to Day-light* in which Vince Lombardi is talking to a retired player who tells him, "You can't fool us old pros."

Lombardi responds, "I hope we can fool a few young pros Sunday."

To "fool a few young pros" is the aim of every NFL team that employs a wide variety of offensive formations.

These creations may be slot, with both wide receivers on the same side; double wing, with the halfback up close to the line and outside his tackle, in a position to release quickly for a pass; or even a formation with three wide receivers and no halfback. Or they may be split backs; near, with the halfback "near" the tight end; or far, with the halfback on the side away from the tight end. The varieties are not infinite but they may seem to be at times.

It is important to remember that in slot formation the "strength" is considered to be the side having the two wide receivers, not the side with the tight end.

Formations are designed especially for opponents from week to week, setting up alignments that hopefully will exploit a weakness.

Seven photographs depict the variety of offensive formations played in the NFL. On page 200 are, from left to right, split backs vs. over stack, Houston vs. St. Louis; far vs. four-three, same teams; and I vs. three-four, St. Louis vs. Houston. On this page, from top to bottom, slot near vs. under, Washington vs. St. Louis; slot double wing vs. under, same teams; the three wide-receiver look vs. nickle, Miami vs. Washington; and near vs. under stack, Dallas vs. Minnesota. Above left, Jim Johnson of San Francisco faces the personal confrontation in which all formations end.

Gadgets

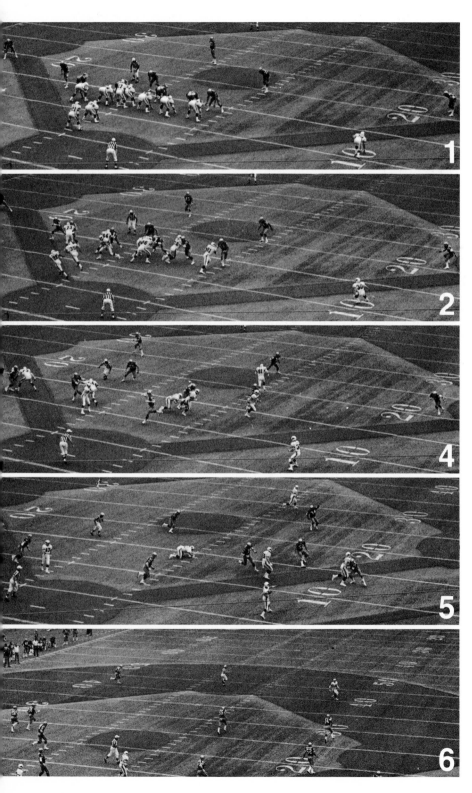

Flea-flickers, double reverses, linemen set as wingbacks and going in motion, and throwback passes to the quarterback are examples of gadget plays, which often occur to coaches at three o'clock in the morning, causing them to sit up in bed and take pencil, paper, and diagram template in hand and give the world an exciting new play.

Gadget plays populate a coach's youth but may hardly appear at all in his older years, when he is wiser, less inclined to take risks, and beginning to turn gray. If questioned on his gray hair, he might attribute it to the failure of some outlandish play that appeared unbeatable on the blackboard but crumbled to pieces the Sunday afternoon of a game. A coach never forgets moments such as that.

Nevertheless, gadgets appear in NFL games, because a coach decides on them against his better judgment or the conditions appear so right for such a play that it demands to be tried at least once.

"Flea-flicker" is one of football's more colorful phrases and, naturally, a term with many meanings applied to a variety of unusual plays. In general, it means a pass to one player followed by a pass or lateral to another.

The Pittsburgh Steelers, considered to be a fundamental team, use another form of gadget play in which they set lineman Gerry Mullins outside the formation as a wingback and then he goes in motion. Mullins is also used at times by Pittsburgh as a tight end.

A third type of gadget that was popular in the fifties was a draw

An NFL Flea-Flicker

Faking a pitchout to the left, St. Louis quarterback Jim Hart then turns right and passes to wide receiver Gary Hammond, who passes far downfield to tight end Jackie Smith. The 81-yard play set up a touchdown.

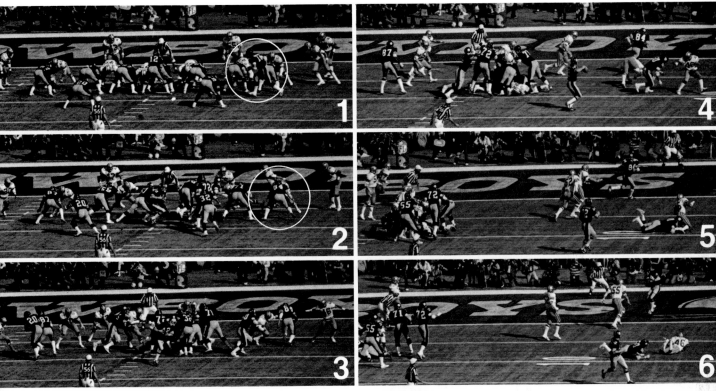

Pittsburgh Razzle-Dazzle
Lineman Gerry Mullins of Pittsburgh takes a position wide to the right and off the line of scrimmage, then moves in motion toward the ball to confuse Dallas's coverage in Super Bowl X. The strategy helps set up the Steelers' seven-yard touchdown pass from Terry Bradshaw to Randy Grossman for Pittsburgh's first touchdown. Right, a ground-level photo of the same play.

play in which the ball carrier suddenly turned and threw the ball back to the quarterback, who then passed. Jim Brown of Cleveland was one of the fullbacks who used this maneuver off the Browns' draw plays.

There are gadget plays and gadget formations. Spreads such as the shotgun and triple wing or trips qualify because they violate the basic principle of protection for the quarterback, usually leaving him in the backfield with only one blocking back.

Goal-Line Plays

The goal line is a white strip eight inches wide. It is twice as wide as any other yard line on the field and it should be for it is the final objective of all the strategy and formations and plays football coaches have conceived since Princeton met Rutgers in 1869. All the A formations, ball control, crackback blocks, moving pockets, veers, wedges, and weakside slants have been designed to send players in possession of a football over or through the goal line for a touchdown. And all the bump-and-run, four-three and three-four defenses, and five-short and two-deep zones in football history have been designed to stop that from happening.

The goal line is not a place for the timid. The hitting is spirited and the

Some Motion, Some Muscle

Houston motions wide receiver Billy Johnson from right to left and he takes a cornerback with him, but it is the line blocking and running back Willie Rodgers's determination that gets a touchdown against Cincinnati. Above, the goal line is a melee of flying helmets and bodies as the Miami Dolphins push over a touchdown against the Pittsburgh Steelers in the 1972 AFC championship game at Pittsburgh.

defense's charges and line blocks are carried out down low, where helmets and pads collide sharply. The submarine tactics of the defense must be met by an offensive line that also gets low and hits with authority.

Near formation, with the fullback in position to run to the strongside, is a common goal line formation and so is the college-style power-I, with a wingback for extra blocking. The use of two tight ends in goal line or short yardage situations has become almost standard in the NFL. A closely bunched formation may not be the choice of a team with a big, strong fullback, however; such a team may set up in a spread in an attempt to draw the defense wide and weaken the middle.

Defenses gap, or fill every hole in the line, to stop the play they expect first, the quarterback sneak. Three deep backs remain off the line to stop surprise passes. And airborne backs who like to leap over the pileup often meet a sturdy extra linebacker, sent into the goal line situation with the specific assignment of drilling the leaping back with a mid-air tackle.

Among teams with mobile quarterbacks, the rollout pass is a goal line favorite. Behind the flow of the backs, the quarterback rolls right. His wide receiver on that side takes the cornerback deep and his fullback flares to the sideline. Provided the tight end is held up at the line of scrimmage, which he usually is, the offense may be able to put the strong safety in an either/or situation in which the quarterback will run if the safety commits or pass if he does not.

APPENDIXES

A history of the game in diagrams; charts tracing the yearly
patterns of offensive statistics in pro football; and
a comparison of rules—professional, college, and high school.

A Diagram History of Football

Football diagrams are little utopias. Any play can appear devastating in a diagram. The following plays and formations and strategies were successful often enough that they have survived where perhaps several hundred thousand others over the last 100 years have not.

1 Wedge

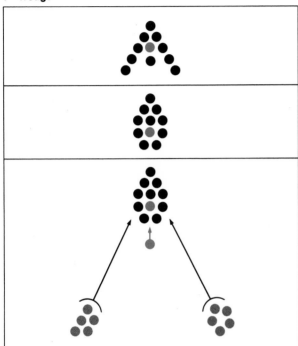

Historian Alexander Weyand wrote that the Princeton wedge of 1884 (top) was "the first great tactical weapon to make its appearance in American football." The ball wasn't kicked off or centered; rather, play began when the wedge moved forward. The person behind the ball carrier pushed him. The wedge was fearsome but Walter (Pudge) Heffelfinger found a solution to it. According to one historian, Heffelfinger "rushed at the mighty engine, leaped high in the air, completely cleared its forward ramparts, and came down on top of the men on the inside of the wedge, whom he flattened to the ground, and among whom was the carrier of the ball." Walter Camp of Yale adopted the wedge for scrimmage play and modified it, making the "shoving wedge" (center). Harvard then contributed the most frightening formation of all in the "mass play" era, the "flying wedge" (below). Two groups of five players each started from 25 yards back, converged around the ball carrier at full speed, and they smashed into the opposition.

2 T Formation

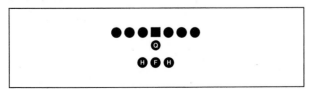

Football players who took the brunt of the wedges actually died on the playing field. "Mass play" led to the reforms requiring seven men on the line of scrimmage when the ball was centered—another innovation. The first T formation resulted.

3 Tackles Back

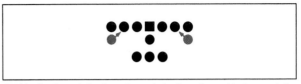

Tackles back, ends back, and guards back conformed to the regulation but tried to restore the momentum of the wedge by shifting linemen up to the line on the snap. This strategy led to the multiple shifts that followed. The tackles back formation shown here was copied from the 1920 book of plays of the Decatur Staleys coached by George Halas.

4 Minnesota Shift

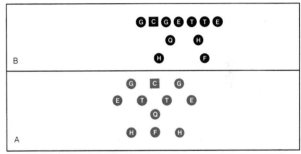

A brilliant coach at the University of Minnesota named Dr. Henry Williams introduced this shift in 1910, according to Alexander Weyand. The original position of the players is shown in diagram A, their eventual position in B.

5 Heisman Shift

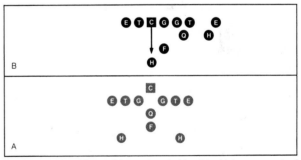

Another popular shift was this one invented by John Heisman, coach of Georgia Tech. He was later the person for whom the Heisman trophy, given each year to the outstanding college player, was named.

6 Single Wing

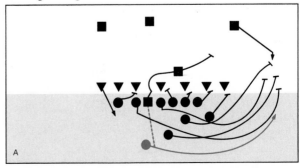

6 continued

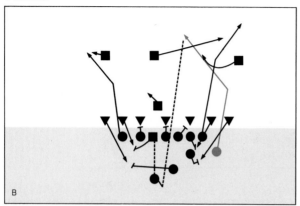

B

Invented by Glenn (Pop) Warner about 1906, it was one of the most successful formations ever and the typical running play (A) was, as Warner himself said, "one of the strongest plays ever developed." It still is today—The Green Bay sweep. A Princeton single wing tailback, Dick Kazmaier, won the Heisman trophy in 1951 and the formation was still being played in 1954 by UCLA, Arkansas, and the Pittsburgh Steelers. A typical single wing pass is shown above.

7 Short Punt

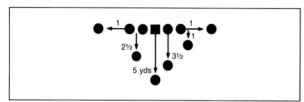

Punting played so large a part in strategy that it was not uncommon for teams to line up in punt formation all the time, hence this popular alignment of the twenties and thirties.

8 Rockne Shift

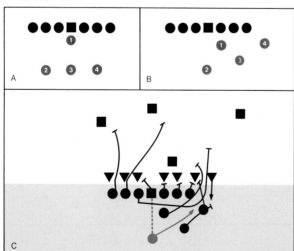

In the Notre Dame system devised by coach Knute Rockne about 1920, the Fighting Irish shifted from the T formation (A) into their "box"

(B) and were then off on a devastating end run, practically all in one motion. The rules were eventually changed to require that all players be still a full second before the snap. Rockne's annual games against Howard Jones of USC displayed the best football to be seen anywhere and coaches flocked to the games, Braven Dyer of the *Los Angeles Times* wrote, "as young doctors would to the Mayo Clinic, to see the masters at work."

9 Double Wing

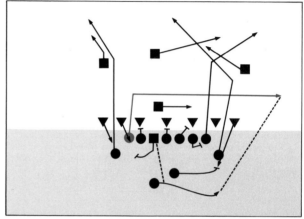

While Rockne was having a poor season in 1928, Glenn (Pop) Warner brought his Stanford University team to New York City to play Army. Warner had had the double wingback formation in his system perhaps as early as 1911, when he was at Carlisle, but did not play it on a regular basis until he moved to Stanford in the twenties. His team beat Army easily and the system was widely adopted while imitation of Rockne waned. Double wing laid the foundation for spread formations such as shotguns that would still be firing in the seventies.

10 Early Man-in-Motion

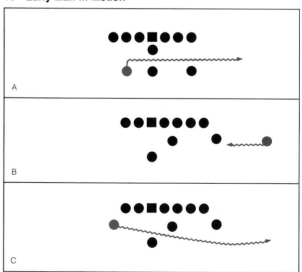

The element that the Chicago Bears would add to the ancient T formation in 1930 had actually been around a long time (A) in the turn-of-the-century T of Amos Alonzo Stagg at the University of Chicago, (B) in the single wing, and (C) in the double wing.

11 Bears' T with Man-in-Motion

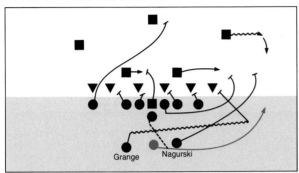

Grange   Nagurski

In 1932, two years after the Bears first used this formation, they played six ties, three of them scoreless, and Ralph Jones, the T-with-motion father, quit as coach. But this formation spread the defense, then light years behind in development; put little, fast men out wide where they could get running room or get downfield for passes; and reinstated a quarterback under the center. The play shown is a lateral to Bronko Nagurski with Red Grange, the man-in-motion, making a crackback block on the defensive end.

12 Invention of Inbounds Lines

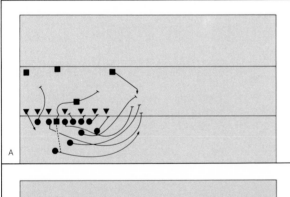

A

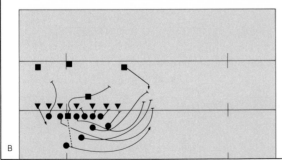

B

The Inbounds lines, or hashmarks, limed onto the dirt floor of the Chicago Stadium in 1932 for the Bears-Spartans playoff, turned coaches into strategists who studied not only power, speed, and deception, but also geography. Plays that ended near the sideline or with the runner going out of bounds had started at the sideline (A); they now began 10 yards in from the sideline (B). Also, the field now had a "short" side and "wide" side of predictable breadth; the side most favored by a team in its running game could be studied by scouts. And hashmarks set up points of reference for players taking their stances or running pass routes, and defenders mapping out the territorial zones they would cover.

13 The Five-Three Defense

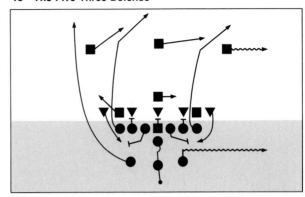

Defenses had previously placed nine, eight, seven, or six men on the line of scrimmage. To reduce that number to five, in order to get more men back in pass protection, was a brazen step. It was probably first taken at Temple in 1930 by a line coach named John (Ox) DaGrosa. The New York Giants copied it in 1934. This became the standard NFL defense for a decade. The five-three had a middle linebacker—30 years before Bill George, Sam Huff, Les Richter, and Joe Schmidt.

14 Don Hutson's First Play in the NFL

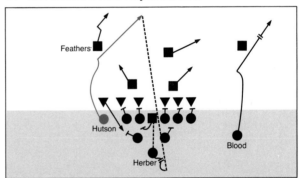

Feathers

Hutson

Herber

Blood

Don Hutson, the Green Bay Packers' great end, scored an 83-yard touchdown on his first play from scrimmage in the NFL. Chicago Bears safety Beattie Feathers stole a look at Arnie Herber's fake to Johnny Blood, and at that moment Hutson, who had been loping along, went into high gear and left Feathers far behind. *True Sport* said, "Herber's pass, counting his retreat, as checked on motion pictures, went 66 yards in the air."

15 Dutch Meyer Spreads

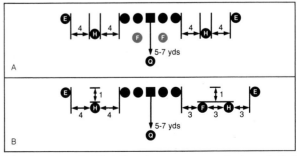

A

B

It is wrong to say that Clark Shaughnessy or anyone else in pro football invented the "three-end offense." Three represented a modest number

15 continued

of ends in the spread formations played by Dutch Meyer at Texas Christian University in the thirties. These were the formations played by TCU quarterbacks, or tailbacks, Sammy Baugh and Davey O'Brien.

16 A Typical Sammy Baugh Pass

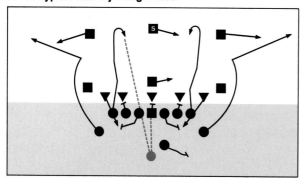

Baugh picked apart the five-three defenses of the NFL as a rookie with the Washington Redskins in 1937. He passed for 335 yards in the championship game against the Bears.

17 Steve Owen's A Formation

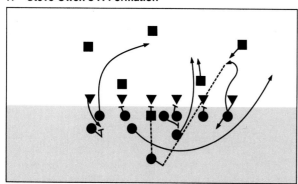

The A formation of coach Steve Owen of the New York Giants had unusual line splits, a line strong to one side and a backfield strong to the other, and a direct snap to the left halfback instead of a T-quarterback. Owen played it and other formations from 1937 to 1952. As a stunt, he once had his team run three plays from three different formations.

18 Oklahoma Defense

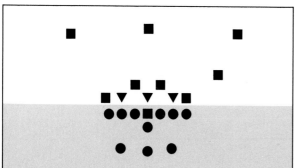

Begun at the University of Oklahoma by coach Bud Wilkinson, probably in 1947, it strongly influenced the new pro defenses that sprouted

immediately afterward. It became the dominant defense in college football for the next 20 years but was scoffed at by the pros until Miami adopted it in 1972 and had a 17-0 season. It is alternately dismissed as weak against the run or weak against the pass. The pros have refined it immensely, and it might become the next standard defense in pro football.

19 Eagle Defense

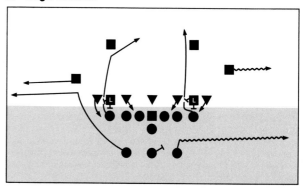

It was first played by the Philadelphia Eagles and coach Greasy Neale about 1948. It evolved out of the five-three and it had the first four-deep secondary, but no middle linebacker. The outside linebackers no longer had to try to cover deep passes but instead harassed and delayed receivers and covered short passes.

20 Steps Taken Against the Eagle

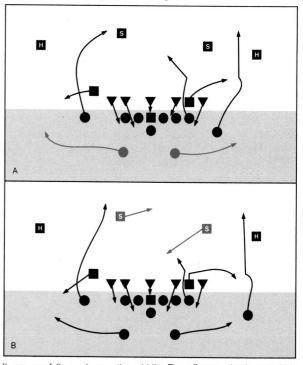

It was woefully weak over the middle. The offenses simply sent their backs to the flat areas to lure the linebackers away, and get an end free in the middle (A). The defense reacted by having one safety fill that area; the other covered behind him if the end went deep, perhaps the start of "combination" pass defense in the NFL (B).

21 Otto Graham Passes

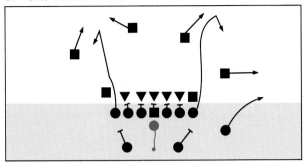

The Eagle was very important as a defense that offenses exploited and out of which much of modern football evolved. Its next challenge was quarterback Otto Graham and the Cleveland Browns, who met Philadelphia for the first time in 1950. Cleveland won 35-10 and its ends, Mac Speedie and Dante Lavelli, were the first to run "comeback" patterns—17 yards downfield, then turning back for the ball at 15 yards. The Eagles had not seen such pass routes before.

22 Umbrella Defense

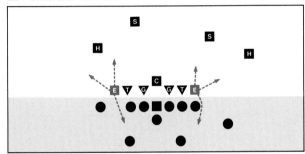

Steve Owen of the New York Giants devised it for the Browns in 1950 and shut them out once and also won a second game. The Giants' deep backs threw a figurative "umbrella" over the passing game, and their ends sometimes rushed and sometimes dropped off to cover passes, in the manner of later outside linebackers.

23 A Rams' Bomb to Hirsch

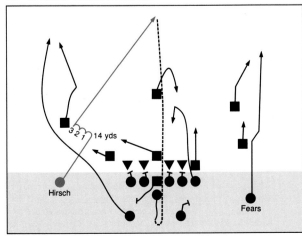

For all its offensive brilliance, Cleveland still played the outdated five-

three defense in the early fifties. Its three-deep secondary was no match for Los Angeles's great end Elroy Hirsch. He scored 17 touchowns during the 1951 season and Los Angeles won the championship from Cleveland. This pass route was Hirsch's favorite during his career.

24 Split T and the Belly Series

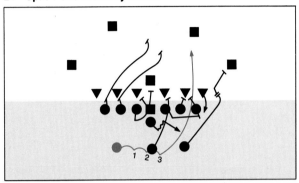

Innovative changes in the T formation had taken place at Missouri, Oklahoma, Maryland, College of the Pacific, and other institutions where football teams were using the split T formation and belly series. The quarterback slid down the line of scrimmage riding the ball in the belly of a back and left it there, kept it, handed off again, pitched, or ran with it. The collegiate triple option, wishbone, and veer systems of later years evolved out of the split T.

25 Continuing Changes in the Eagle

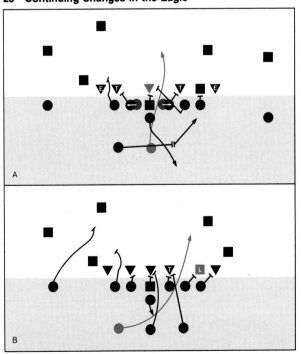

It was put to rest at last by the big line splits that the pros adopted as a result of the popularity of split T. These splits moved the offensive tackles out so far that the defensive middle guard found himself isolated, forced to try to stop the inside running plays alone (A). If his defensive tackles closed in to help, that isolated the outside linebacker (B).

26 Four-Three Defense

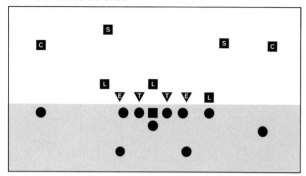

Teams playing the Eagle in the mid-fifties decided to drop their middle guard off and make him a middle linebacker. If their middle guard was unsuited for the new position, they found a player who was. This evolution in the Eagle was as much responsible for the adoption of the modern four-three defense as was the New York umbrella. The distinctive identity of each position in the four-three also crystallized as the result of free substitution, since it was now possible to send an entirely different team into the game to play defense.

27 Slot-T

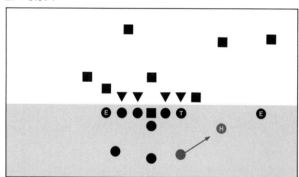

Two decades before, the Chicago Bears had removed one man from the offensive formation by putting him in motion. By the late forties, that player was being permanently stationed out wide, rather than going in motion into that position. He was the "flanker." An alignment placing him in a slot between the spread end and tackle was popular in the NFL throughout the fifties.

28 Three-End Offense

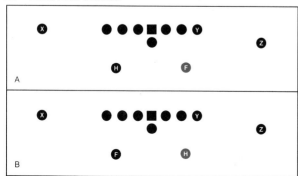

28 continued

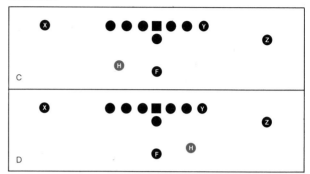

The "flanker" gradually came to be seen not as a halfback removed from the backfield but instead as a third end. Later, the terms "wide receiver" and "tight end" were adopted to name the three ends. Here are four of the most important three-end formations and the names given them in the various systems of language spoken by pro teams: (A) full, split right, or red; (B) half, split left, or green; (C) far, opposite, or brown; and (D) near, wing, or blue.

29 Pass Rush and Linebacker Blitz

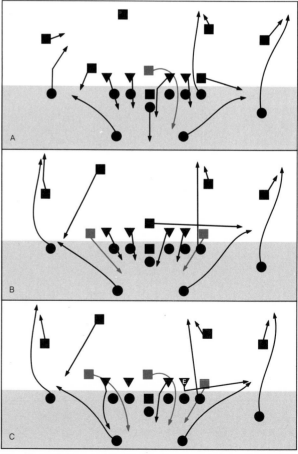

The offense had spread itself wider than ever and was increasingly dependent on the pass. The defense now mounted such methods of rushing the passer as these: (A) the four linemen and the middle linebacker; (B) the line and the outside linebackers; and (C) actual "blitz," the line and all three linebackers.

30   Man-for-Man Coverage

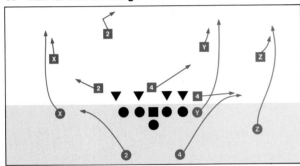

This is man-for-man defense at its simplest and in a form played widely in the fifties in the NFL. The numerals 2 and 4 are the offensive backs and the coaching symbols X, Y, and Z stand for the wide receivers and tight end. Corresponding symbols on defensive players name who is responsible for each.

31   Zone Defense

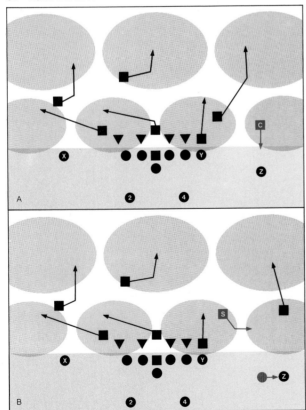

The most basic type of zone defense is "rotation," and was played expertly by the Detroit Lions in the fifties. The defense has "rotated" to the side of the tight end and flanker and there are four zones (oval areas) up

close and three deep. In diagram B, the flanker has taken a position so wide that if it were a running play he could crack back on the cornerback. Seeing this, the defense has changed its zone so the safety not the cornerback is up close. It is this swapping of coverage areas among cornerbacks, safeties, and linebackers that has made zones grow in complexity and produce great problems for young quarterbacks.

32   Green Bay Sweep

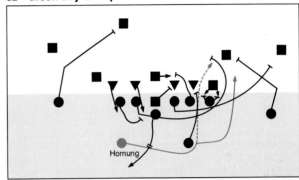

When Vince Lombardi became coach of the Green Bay Packers in 1959, he was convinced that defenses had become so sophisticated that it was time for the offense to go back to the basics—to avoid frills and to carry out fundamentals well. These principles were borne out in his Green Bay sweep, with Paul Hornung carrying the ball. Hornung followed pulling guards Fuzzy Thurston and Jerry Kramer and fullback Jim Taylor in a devastating end run. It is interesting to compare the play with those of Warner and Rockne in diagrams 6A and 8C.

33   Weakside Slant and its Companion Play

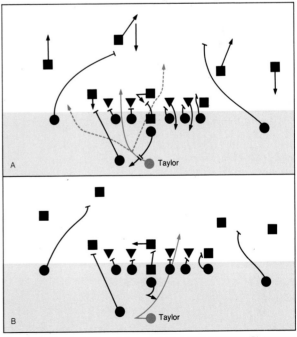

The weakside slant (A) and the companion play it set up (B) became the heart of the Packers' offense after defenses found ways to stop the sweep. Jim Taylor "ran to daylight" where he found it. Jim Brown of Cleve-

33 continued

land, Taylor's contemporary, also ran the weakside slant among other plays, and the play is the most basic one in pro football today.

34 Shotgun

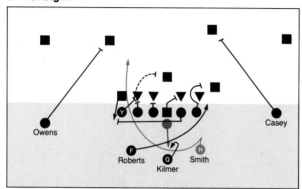

The patterns of play in the four-three defense and three-end offense had grown rather stereotyped by 1960. That was one reason why coach Red Hickey of San Francisco created what he called the shotgun formation. The quarterback stood back from the center as in the formations of old. San Francisco played it with success for part of 1960 and 1961, until it was stopped by Chicago and Pittsburgh and 49ers' players lost confidence in it. Bill Kilmer, John Brodie, and Bobby Waters alternated at quarterback in the system. The play shown here is a shovel pass to halfback J. D. Smith, a play that was also a favorite of the Dallas Cowboys when they revived the shotgun in 1975 and played it part of the time while winning the NFC Championship.

35 Shotgun-inspired Spreads

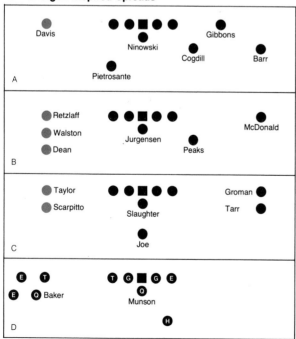

A variety of formations that, like the shotgun, spread receivers and running backs across the field but unlike the shotgun kept the quarterback under

center, sprang up around the league. Examples shown here are (A) Detroit's "Zephyr" formation of 1961, an attempt to exploit the speed of former Olympic sprinter Glenn Davis, "the Zephyr"; (B) Philadelphia's "stacked deck" of the same season, designed for the Eagles' young quarterback Sonny Jurgensen; (C) Denver's "double stack" in the American Football League; and (D) Los Angeles's "outpost and settlement" of 1964. In the latter, the group of players around the ball and quarterback Bill Munson was the "settlement" and the group around a second quarterback, Terry Baker, was the "outpost."

36 Two That Endured—T Double Wing and Triple Wing

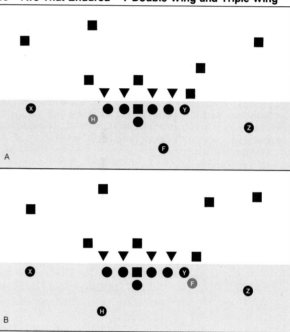

The double wing and triple wing survive today from the era of the original shotgun and its imitations. Triple wing is also called "trips." In double wing (A), the halfback is up close to the line, and in triple wing (B) it is the fullback who is up close to release quickly for a pass. The names for each of them lack real literal meaning, having been plagiarized from the past and Pop Warner.

37 I and its Varieties

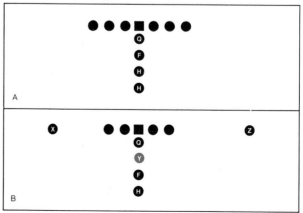

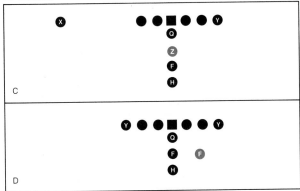

The I formation popular in the NFL today was invented by an obscure college coach named Tom Nugent in the fifties. Hank Stram of the Kansas City Chiefs was the first to place his tight end in the I (B). The Dallas Cowboys frequently have lined up their flanker in the I (C) before shifting. The power I (D) that John McKay perfected at USC is seen in the NFL in short-yardage situations.

38 Wishbone

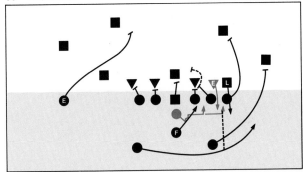

The wishbone reinstated balance in college football and made it more exciting after introduction of the offense by the University of Texas in 1968. But it is a grind-it-out, ball-control offense with only one spread end compared to at least two, and often more, in professional formations.

39 Relocated Hashmarks

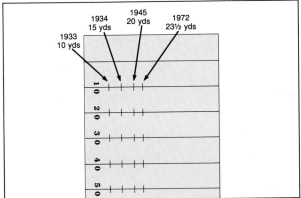

Moving NFL hashmarks in 1972 helped the offense. The defense previously had an advantage on any run or pass to the narrow side of the field.

The 1972 move was actually the third by the NFL since 1933. Hashmarks on college fields remain at a point about 17½ yards from the sideline.

40 Evolution of a Cowboys' Play

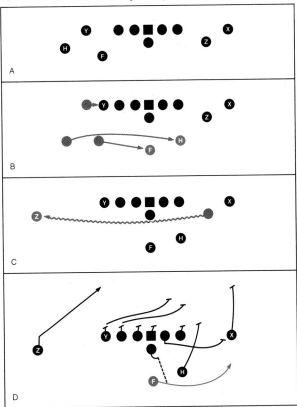

Man-in-motion, which A. A. Stagg used, and shifts, which Dr. Henry Williams popularized, are part of the "preshift" used today by the Dallas Cowboys. It is one of the most unique strategies now being played. Here is an example of how it works: (A) the backs and receivers leave the huddle and line up this way; (B) the backs shift as shown (C) The flanker goes in motion; and (D) the Cowboys are now in their brown left formation, ready to run their play.

NFL Offense: What the Statistics Show

Source in part for first two charts: *The Sports Encyclopedia: Pro Football.* 1974. Grosset & Dunlap, Inc.

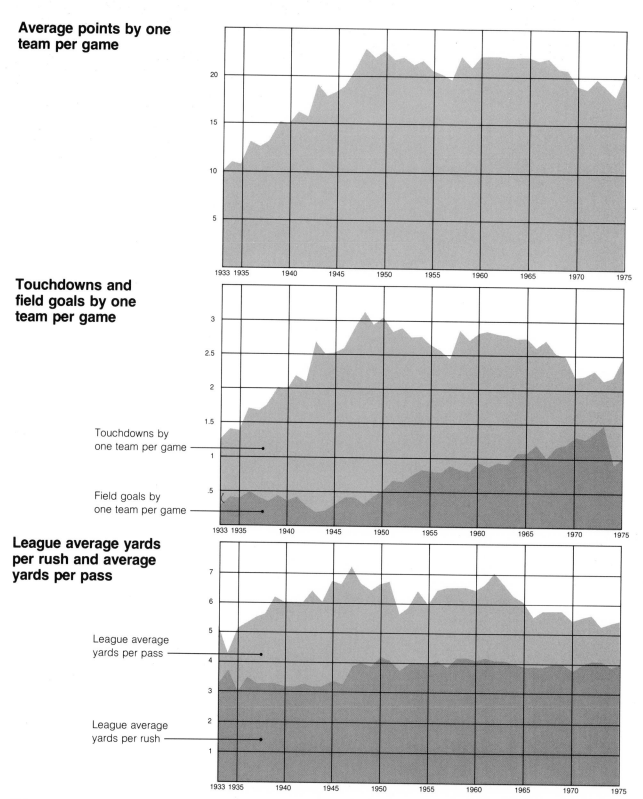

Average points by one team per game

Touchdowns and field goals by one team per game

Touchdowns by one team per game

Field goals by one team per game

League average yards per rush and average yards per pass

League average yards per pass

League average yards per rush

The Rules of Football at Three Levels

A summary of the basic differences in the playing rules of the National Football League, the National Collegiate Athletic Association, and the National Federation of State High School Associations.

PROFESSIONAL	COLLEGE	HIGH SCHOOL
Timing		
Time outs are two minutes in length.	1 minute 30 seconds.	1 minute 30 seconds.
Time outs are called only by a captain.	By any player.	A captain or any authorized player.
Quarters are 15 minutes in length.	15.	12.
There are two minutes between quarters.	One minute.	One minute.
A two-minute warning is given before the end of each half.	No such rule, but a four-minute warning is given if there is no visible clock.	Same as college.
The clock is not stopped after a first down is made and no measurement is necessary.	The clock is stopped, the first down awarded, and play resumes.	Same as college.
Halftime is 20 minutes in length.	15 but can be extended by mutual agreement.	15 minutes plus 3 minutes to warm up.
The offense has 30 seconds to put the ball in play after the referee gives his ready-to-play signal.	25.	25.
The clock is not started immediately after a change of team possession.	Same.	It is started immediately after a change of team possession, except after a fair catch.
When the quarterback is sacked, the clock is stopped to allow the receivers to get back to the huddle.	The clock continues to run.	Continues to run.
If there is a tie there is a 15-minute sudden death overtime and in postseason games there is unlimited sudden death.	Tie-breakers in Division II and III championship games.	Permission for tie-breakers may be given by state associations.
Scrimmage		
The ball is dead when the runner is contacted by a defender and anything other than the hand or foot touches the ground. There must have been defensive contact.	When any part of the runner's body other than his hand or foot touches the ground.	When any part of the runner's body other than his hand or foot touches the ground.
The blocking rule is that during obstruction of opponents by use of that part of the blocker's body above the knees during a legal block, the hand must be cupped or closed and remain inside the frame of the opponent as well as the blocker's body. The arms must be in a flexed position but	The hands shall be in advance of the elbows, inside the frame of the blocker's body and below the shoulders of blocker and opponent. The hands shall be cupped or closed with the palm not facing the opponent. The hands and arms shall not be extended more than one-half of a full	When an offensive player uses a hand or forearm in blocking, the hand must be in contact with the blocker's body and the hand and arm must be kept below the shoulders of the opponent during the entire block.

PROFESSIONAL	COLLEGE	HIGH SCHOOL
not fully extended forward to create a push. By use of up and down action of flexed arms, blockers are permitted to ward off opponents attempting to grasp jerseys or arms and to prevent legal contact to their head. Blockers are not permitted to push, clamp, hang onto, or encircle opponents.	extension and shall not be used to deliver a blow or to grasp, pull, encircle, lift, hook, lock, or clamp an opponent.	
Defensive players may chuck receivers in the three-yard area centered on the line of scrimmage and only once when the receiver is outside that area.	There can be legal defensive contact against receivers until the ball is thrown.	Same as college.
A defensive player may contact opponents with the palm of his hand only on his initial charge and may not repeat it against the same opponent during one contact.	Not allowed anytime.	Not allowed anytime.
The legal clipping zone extends from offensive tackle to offensive tackle three yards on either side of the line of scrimmage.	Four yards laterally and three yards longitudinally in each direction from the middle lineman.	Four yards laterally from the spot of the snap and three yards behind each scrimmage line.
Offensive holding within three yards of the line of scrimmage is a 10-yard penalty, 15 if outside that area.	15 yards.	15 yards.
Offensive players who line up more than two yards outside their offensive tackles may not crackback below the waist when blocking toward the ball.	Offensive players positioned five or more yards outside the legal clipping zone or in motion toward the ball at the snap are prohibited from blocking below the waist toward the ball in the clipping zone (six yards) extended to the sidelines.	No offensive player who is outside the free blocking zone at the snap may block an opponent below the waist while the opponent is in an area three yards behind each scrimmage line (six yards total) extending laterally from sideline to sideline if such block is toward the spot of the snap.
A man legally in motion must be parallel to, obliquely backward, or directly backward from the line at the snap.	Parallel to the line or backwards.	Running clearly backwards.
A fumble may be recovered by the defense and advanced.	It may not.	It may be advanced.
Piling on is prohibited against any player lying on the ground.	Any opponent after the ball is dead.	Any player lying on the ground.
Spearing an opponent is a 15-yard penalty and/or disqualification from the game.	15-yard penalty.	15-yard penalty and disqualification from the game.
Defensive holding is a 5-yard penalty and a first down for the offense.	15 yards.	15 yards.

220

PROFESSIONAL	COLLEGE	HIGH SCHOOL

Passing

PROFESSIONAL	COLLEGE	HIGH SCHOOL
An incomplete fourth down pass inside the 20 is next put in play at the previous spot.	It is put in play at the previous spot.	Same as college.
A pass receiver must have two feet inbounds for a legal catch.	One foot.	One foot.
The penalty for offensive pass interference is 10 yards.	15 yards and loss of down.	Same as college.
Defensive pass interference is prohibited from the time the ball is thrown until it is touched.	From the snap until the ball is touched.	Same as professional.
Pass interference includes waving the arms and interfering with the receiver's vision and opportunity to catch the ball.	Physical contact is required for pass interference.	Same as professional.
The pass interference rules do not apply on passes behind the line of scrimmage.	They do.	Same as professional.
The T-quarterback is not an eligible pass receiver.	He is eligible.	He is eligible.
There can be only one forward pass during each down.	Only one.	Any number so long as all are thrown behind the line.
Only the offense can advance a backward pass after it hits the ground.	Same as professional.	Either team may advance a backward pass after it hits the ground.

Kicks

PROFESSIONAL	COLLEGE	HIGH SCHOOL
Kickoff from the 35.	The 40.	The 40.
Missed field goals attempted from the 20 or beyond are returned to the line of scrimmage.	No such rule.	No such rule.
Only the two end men of the punting team may leave the line of scrimmage until the ball is kicked.	No limit on how many can go downfield before the punt.	Same as college.
A legal fair catch signal is one hand at full length above the head.	One hand above the head waved from side to side.	Same as college.
A receiver who signals for a fair catch cannot block until the ball is touched.	If he signals for a fair catch and does not touch the ball he may not block at all during the down.	A receiver who signals for a fair catch is prohibited from blocking until the down is ended.

PROFESSIONAL	COLLEGE	HIGH SCHOOL
A field goal attempt may be made following a fair catch.	No such rule.	A field goal attempt may be made following a fair catch.
The receiver of a punt may immediately return-kick it.	He may not.	He may not.
Trys for point are made from the 2-yard line.	The 3.	The 3.
Successful trys earn one point.	One if a successful kick, two if a successful run or pass.	Same as college.

The Field

PROFESSIONAL	COLLEGE	HIGH SCHOOL
Hashmarks are 70'9" inbounds from each sideline.	53'4".	53'4".
Single support goal posts.	Single or double.	Single or double.
Goal post uprights extend 30' above the crossbar.	10'.	10'.

Bibliography

Baker, L. H. *Football: Facts and Figures*. New York and Toronto: Farr & Rinehart, 1945.

Betts, John R. *America's Sporting Heritage, 1850–1950*. Reading, Mass.: Addison-Wesley Publishing Co., 1974.

Bierman, B. W. with Frank Mayer. *Winning Football*. New York: Whittlesey House, 1937.

Burness, Tad. *Cars of the Early Twenties*. Philadelphia and New York: Chilton Book Co., 1968.

Caldwell, Charles W. *Modern Single Wing Football*. Philadelphia and New York: J. B. Lippincott, 1951.

Camp, Walter. *American Football*. New York: Harper's, 1891.

Camp, Walter and Deland, Lorin F. *Football*. Boston and New York: Houghton, Mifflin, 1896.

Church, James R., Editor. *University Football*. New York: Charles Scribner's Sons, 1893.

Claassen, Harold. *The History of Professional Football*. Englewood Cliffs, N.J.: Prentice-Hall, 1963.

Clark, Potsy. *Football*. Chicago: Rand-McNally, 1935.

Cohane, Tim. *Great College Football Coaches of the Twenties and Thirties*. New Rochelle, N.Y.: Arlington House, 1973.

College Football Modern Record Book. Shawnee Mission, Kansas: National Collegiate Sports Services, 1975.

College Football U.S.A. 1869–1971. New York: McGraw-Hill, 1972.

Cope, Myron. *The Game That Was*. New York and Cleveland: World Publishing, 1970.

Crisler, Herbert O. *Practical Football*. New York and London: Whittlesey House, 1934.

Curran, Bob. *Pro Football's Rag Days*. Englewood Cliffs, N.J.: Prentice-Hall, 1969.

DaGrosa, John. *Functional Football*. New York: A. S. Barnes, 1946.

Danzig, Allison. *The History of American Football*. Englewood Cliffs, N.J.: Prentice-Hall, 1956.

Danzig, Allison. *Oh, How They Played the Game*. New York: Macmillan, 1971.

Day, A. Grove and Knowlton, Edgar C. *V. Blasco Ibañez*. New York: Twayne Publishers, 1972.

Encyclopedia Britannica. Encyclopedia Britannica, Inc., 1974.

Evashevski, Forest and Nelson, David M. *Scoring Power with the Winged T Offense*. Dubuque, Iowa: Wm C. Brown Co., 1957.

Faurot, Don. *Secrets of the Split T Formation*. Englewood Cliffs, N.J.: Prentice-Hall, 1950.

Flynn, George L., Editor. *Vince Lombardi on Football, Volumes I and II*. New York: New York Graphic Society Ltd. and Wallynn, Inc., 1973.

Georgano, G. N. *Encyclopedia of American Automobiles*. New York: E. P. Dutton, 1971.

Graham, Otto. *Otto Graham, T Quarterback*. Englewood Cliffs, N.J.: Prentice-Hall, 1953.

Hendrickson, Joe, with Maxwell Stiles. *The Tournament of Roses*. Los Angeles: Brooke House, 1971.

Hill Dean. *Football Thru the Years*. New York: Gridiron Publishing, 1940.

Holtzman, Jerome. *No Cheering in the Press Box*. New York: Holt, Rinehart and Winston, 1973.

Huff, Sam, with Don Smith. *Defensive Football*. New York: Ronald Press, 1963.

Layden, Elmer, with Ed Snyder. *It Was a Different Game*. Englewood Cliffs, N.J.: Prentice-Hall, 1969.

Lombardi, Vince, with W. C. Heinz. *Run to Daylight*. Englewood Cliffs, N.J.: Prentice-Hall, 1963.

Liebendorfer, Don E. *The Color of Life is Red*. Department of Athletics, Stanford University, 1972.

Luckman, Sid. *Luckman at Quarterback*. Chicago: Ziff-Davis, 1949.

Lynch, Dick with Jack Zanger. *Witness for the Defense*. New York: Parallax Publishing Co., 1966.

Maule, Tex. *The Game*. New York: Random House, 1963.

Miers, Earl S. *Football*. New York: Grosset & Dunlap, 1967.

Neft, David S., and others. *The Sports Encyclopedia: Pro Football*. New York: Grosset & Dunlap, 1974.

Oates, Jr., Bob. *A Matter of Style*. Boston: Little, Brown, 1973.

Owen, Steve. *My Kind of Football*. New York: David McKay, 1952.

Parker, Raymond K. *We Play to Win*. Englewood Cliffs, N.J.: Prentice-Hall, 1955.

Pool, Hampton, and others. *Fly T Football*. Englewood Cliffs, N.J.: Prentice-Hall, 1957.

Pope, Edwin. *Football's Greatest Coaches*. Atlanta: Tupper and Love, 1955.

PRO!, Official Magazine of the National Football League. New York: National Football League Properties, Inc., 1975.

Riger, Robert, with Tex Maule. *The Pros, A Documentary of Professional Football in America*. New York: Simon and Schuster, 1960.

Roper, William M. *Football, Today and Tomorrow*. New York: Duffield and Company, 1927.

Rote, Kyle, with Jack Winter. *The Language of Pro Football*. New York: Random House, 1966.

Smith, Robert. *Illustrated History of Pro Football*. New York: Madison Square Press, 1970.

Stainback, Berry. *How the Pros Play Football*. New York: Random House, 1970.

Sullivan, George. *Pro Football's All-Time Greats*. New York: G. P. Putnam's Sons, 1968.

Twombly, Wells. *Shake Down The Thunder*. Radnor, Pa.: Chilton Book Co., 1974.

Van Brocklin, Norm, with Hugh Brown. *Norm Van Brocklin's Football Book*. New York: Ronald Press, 1961.

Waldorf, Lynn O. *This Game of Football*. New York: McGraw-Hill, 1952.

Wallace, Bill. *Nelson's Encyclopedia of Pro Football*. New York: Thomas Nelson & Sons, 1964.

Walsh, Christy, Editor. *Intercollegiate Football*. New York and St. Paul: Doubleday, Doran, 1934.

Ward, Arch, *The Green Bay Packers*. New York: G. P. Putnam's Sons, 1946.

Warner, Glenn S. *Football for Coaches and Players*. Stanford University, 1927.

Weyand, Alexander. *The Saga of American Football*. New York: Macmillan, 1955.

Wheeler, Robert W. *Pathway to Glory*. New York: Carlton Press, 1975.

Wilkinson, Bud. *Oklahoma Split T Football*. Englewood Cliffs, N.J.: Prentice-Hall, 1952.

Wilkinson, Bud. *Sports Illustrated Football: Offense*. Philadelphia and New York: J. B. Lippincott, 1973.

Wilkinson, Bud. *Sports Illustrated Football: Defense*. Philadelphia and New York: J. B. Lippincott, 1973.

Zimmerman, Paul. *A Thinking Man's Guide to Pro Football*. New York: E. P. Dutton, 1970.

Index

224